J. (Januarius) De Concilio

Harmony between science and revelation

J. (Januarius) De Concilio

Harmony between science and revelation

ISBN/EAN: 9783741154836

Manufactured in Europe, USA, Canada, Australia, Japa

Cover: Foto ©Andreas Hilbeck / pixelio.de

Manufactured and distributed by brebook publishing software (www.brebook.com)

J. (Januarius) De Concilio

Harmony between science and revelation

HARMONY

BETWEEN

SCIENCE AND REVELATION,

BY

RIGHT REV. J. de CONCILIO, D. D.,

DOMESTIC PRELATE OF HIS HOLINESS,
RECTOR OF ST. MICHAEL'S CHURCH, JERSEY CITY, N. J.

AUTHOR OF "CATHOLICITY AND PANTHEISM;" "THE KNOWLEDGE OF MARY;"
"INTELLECTUAL PHILOSOPHY," ETC., ETC.

FR. PUSTET,
Printer to the Holy See and the S. Congregation of Rites.

FR. PUSTET & CO.,
NEW YORK & CINCINNATI.

CONTENTS.

ARTICLE.	PAGE
First.—Introductory	5
Second.—Herbert Spencer's Theory Concerning Matter—Its Refutation	10
Third.—Modern Science Proves That Matter Must Have Been Created	16
Fourth.—Idea of Self Existence—Did Christians Ever Understand What They Meant by God?—Compliments of Herbert Spencer	21
Fifth.—Formation of the Universe—Beautiful Hypothesis of La Place	28
Sixth.—True Side of the System of Evolution	34
Seventh.—History of the Formation of the Earth	39
Eighth.—Spontaneous Generation or Evolution in its General Sense	44
Ninth.—Evolution In Its General Sense—Verdict of Reason	50
Tenth.—Were All Living Beings Evolved From the Lowest Form of Life, or Was Each Species of the Vegetable and Animal World Effected by a Special Act of the Creator?—Transformism and Darwinism—What is a Species?—Can a Species be Distinguishable From Another?	56
Eleventh.—Evolutionism is Contradicted by History	63
Twelfth.—Evolution in Contradiction With Paleontology	69
Thirteenth.—Does Paleontology Show Any Substantial Change Ever to Have Taken Place in Species?	75
Fourteenth.—Paleontology Demonstrates That Species Have Not Been Progressing Gradually Towards Perfection—It Affords No Traces of Intermediary Species	81
Fifteenth.—Is the Science of Embryology in Favor of Evolution?	88
Sixteenth.—Are Rudimentary Organs Any Help to Evolution	94
Seventeenth.—Are the Reasons Drawn From Classification, Morphology, Anatomy, and Pathology in Favor of Organic Evolution of Any Real Value?	101
Eighteenth.—What is a Scientific Explanation?	109
Nineteenth.—Is the Evolutionists' Explanation of the Facts From Morphology, Anatomy and Pathology Reasonable and Satisfactory?	114
Twentieth.—Origin of Man	122
Twenty-First—Intelligence as the Exclusive Faculty of Man—Faculties Common to Man and Brute Animals—Difference Between the Sense and the Intellect	129
Twenty-Second.—Are Brute Animals Endowed With Any Sort of Intellect?	138

Twenty-Third.—The Exclusive Sign of Intelligence............... 147
Twenty-Fourth.—Is It a Safe Opinion to Hold That Man's Body Was Evolved From the Ape?................... 156
Twenty-Fifth.—Has Mivart's Opinion Any Theological Grounds In Its Support?................... 165
Twenty-Sixth.—Is Mivart's Opinion Scientifically and Philosophically Tenable?................... 173
Twenty-Seventh.—Is Man as Old as a Certain Science Would Make Him Out to Be?................... 180
Twenty-Eighth.—Is There Such a Thing as the Fossil Remains of Man? 187
Twenty-Ninth.—Is Civilized Man the Natural Product of the Savage?... 193
Thirtieth.—Man's Place In the Universe—Are Other Worlds Than Ours Inhabited?................... 201
Thirty-First.—Scientific and Philosophical Reasons for the Plurality of Worlds................... 207
Thirty-Second.—Philosophical Proofs for the Plurality of Worlds......... 214
Thirty-Third.—Philosophical Argument for the Plurality of Worlds..... 220
Thirty Fourth.—The Plurality of Worlds in Harmony With Christian Revelation................... 227
Thirty-Fifth.—What Is a Miracle?................... 233
Thirty-Sixth —Is the Miracle Possible?................... 240
Thirty-Seventh —Can a Miracle be Ascertained?................... 246
Thirty-Eighth.—Has a Miracle Ever Been Ascertained?............... 253

HARMONY BETWEEN SCIENCE AND REVELATION.

FIRST ARTICLE.

INTRODUCTORY.

We will in a few words introduce the persons who are to take part in the dialogue.

The first is B. Armstrong. He is an old doctor of medicine, retired from the practice of his profession, in which he stands very high. A convert to the Catholic Church since his early manhood, he loves her with the ardent zeal of a convert, but much more with the firm and settled conviction of one who has studied her doctrines long and profoundly, and has compared them with the results of modern science, in which he is a very great adept.

The next in rank is George N., a young physician himself, and a son of one of the most intimate friends of the old doctor. He is a frequent visitor at the latter's house, drawn there not only by the evident advantages and improvement he derives from the doctor's conversation, but also by the attractions of the third personage of our dialogue, Adele M.

She is a niece and a ward of the doctor—the very apple of his eye. She is well educated, of a serious turn of mind, which does not interfere with the liveliness and cheerfulness of her disposition.

The three personages are sitting cosily around the table after tea.

Doctor.—"You may go on, George, with the subject. Adele will be pleased with the matter of our conversation."

George.—"Well, Miss Adele, the Doctor and I were discussing before tea the great topic of the relations between religion and science. I need not remind you that the professors of the latter, as a general thing, claim that the results of their science are in direct contradiction, in hopeless conflict with the tenets of revelation; that some day or other Christianity, the best and greatest exponent of revelation, will have to submit to the inevitable, and retire, either gracefully or by force, to make way for the great truths of science. This boast has been made so often and so persistently; it has been repeated over and over again with such appearance of earnestness and conviction; it has been proclaimed with such assurance, that a great number have taken the bait and believe really and truly that modern science has settled religion, and that there is nothing for the latter to do but to give up. Now the doctor was laughing at such unwarrantable pretensions, and, being fully conversant with the true results of science, he is fully convinced that no conflict or opposition exists or can exist between them and revelation. But I was complaining of a real want in this matter when we were interrupted by the tea bell."

Adele.—"Well, out with it; there is nothing to interrupt us now, and we can do full justice to the subject."

George.—"It is very well to say that an educated man, one fully conversant with his religion and very well up in science, can easily find out that there is no opposition between the well ascertained and established results of science, and the *real, not imaginary*, tenets of our holy religion. But how is a poor, unsophisticated man—say a mechanic, a laborer, even a washerwoman—to find that out? The assertion that science has disposed of religion, that the latter is only good for the ignorant and the uneducated crowd, will continue to be made by conceited and unscrupulous scientists, either because they are dupes themselves or because they would dupe others, or because, as a general thing, they know nothing at all of true religious doctrines; I say the assertion will continue to be made; and how are the people to be preserved from and guaranteed against such wholesale lying and deceit? What I would wish is a clear, plain answer to this, couched in such simple language as to be within the reach of every one at least who has had a common school education. Science boasts of having, by its wonderful results, disposed of religion. Well, let every plain man and woman be so instructed as to be enabled to cast that false assertion in the teeth of those who make it."

Adele.—"That is an excellent idea; many a time I have desired such a plain, simple answer to assertions so vague and so sweeping."

Doctor—"The answer exists; it has been given thousands of times by our apologists; perhaps not always in as plain language as one would wish, but it has been given and can be found in hundreds of books. All we have to do is to put it in a plain, simple, forcible language."

George.—"Well, Doctor, why don't you attempt it? I am sure Miss Adele and I will listen to you with the greatest possible attention, and I am sure we shall be greatly benefited by it."

Doctor—"I will try, and, to begin at once, I will remark that there are two ways of meeting the objection that religion and science conflict against each other—that they are antagonistic and opponents— the first is an indirect way; the other is the direct way."

Adele.—"Well, uncle, let us begin by the indirect answer."

Doctor.—"The indirect way is this: to show that science and revelation are two distinct ways, which God Almighty has adopted to teach and instruct man, and to manifest to him His infinite perfection and attributes."

George.—"Must we start from that?"

Doctor.—"Yes, sir; we must start from that. Any other way is worse than useless. If one does not admit the existence of an infinite beneficent Being who, out of the excessive goodness of His nature, determines to manifest Himself to intelligent creatures, whom He has Himself created; that He has chosen two ways of making such manifestation, the first by expressing and imaging Himself in the universe, and letting man discover His perfections by studying and investigating the wonders of creation; the other, by condescending to put Himself in real, true personal communication with man, to reveal to him grander, more sublime, more magnificent things about himself and his nature; I say, if one does not admit these two ways, it were worse than useless to speak of the accord or disaccord between science and religion, because in such supposition the disputants are not agreed upon the terms of the discussion, and necessarily, by the nature of the case, cannot understand each other."

Adele.—"Let me see if I understand it. God is infinite, unutterable beauty and loveliness. He wants to manifest that beauty to intelligent creatures. To attain this object He creates the universe, in which He expresses, as well as could be done, His everlasting fairness and beauty. But He is not satisfied with that. That expression and imaging of His infinite perfections is too faint and feeble. He establishes a personal intercourse with man, and in that intercourse He Himself reveals more and more of those infinite realms of beauty and loveliness which are hid in His nature. Is that what you mean, uncle?"

Doctor.—"Yes; only, with your woman's taste and gracefulness, you have put it in a much better language than I did."

Adele.—"No compliments, uncle."

George.—"But, excuse me, Doctor, if I insist on this point. Your explanation supposes the possibility and existence of a real personal intercourse between God and man, as you maintain that God has revealed Himself in two ways: the first, in creation in all the beautiful world He has made; the second is by revealing the treasures of perfections hid in His nature by a personal intercourse, which He has established with man. Now, scientists are not prepared to grant you this second way, for it assumes the possibility and the existence of the supernatural."

Doctor—"Of course it does; and your scientists must assume that, unless they want to exhibit in the highest degree the lack of that logic in which they are generally so deficient in their works. Our whole discussion turns upon this—is there any conflict between science and revelation? Surely, before saying whether there be any such conflict we should agree upon knowing what is science and what is revelation. We are pretty well satisfied what is meant by science. We should equally as well understand what is revelation, otherwise how could we by any possibility tell whether there can be, or is, any opposition between two things, one of which we know nothing of? Hence, in the beginning of the discussion, we must necessarily assume the idea of the possibility and existence of a supernatural intercourse between God and man, in consequence of which revelation takes place; else the discussion is absurd. The time will come when in the course of our conversations we will ascertain the philosophical foundation for the truth of this supernatural intercourse between God and man. At present we must necessarily take it for granted."

George.—"If I catch your meaning, every time I am attacked upon the disagreement and conflict between reason and revelation, science and religion, I am to keep perfectly cool and say: 'Gentlemen, if you please, we will first try to understand what is meant by religion and science; and afterward, we will at our own leisure ascertain whether there be any conflict or harmony between them, whether they agree or disagree.'"

Doctor.—"Certainly, that is the way; and don't for the world allow any one to carry you away to some other question or issue, which may have nothing to do with the matter. What is science? What is religion? These are the two first important points to be understood and agreed upon by the disputants; and when those terms are understood and their full meaning settled upon, it will be time enough to ascertain whether they agree or disagree."

Adele.—"But, uncle, why do you attach so much importance to that?"

Doctor.—"Because, if the disputants have the right idea of science and religion they can in a moment agree as to the accord or disaccord between them. If they have no such right idea they are throwing away valuable time."

Adele.—"Well, now suppose that the disputants have the right idea of science and religion, will you tell us how they can decide in a moment as to the agreement or conflict between them?"

Doctor.—"Will you please to repeat what is meant by science and what by the Christian revelation?"

Adele.—"By science we understand that knowledge of God which we acquire by the study of His creatures. By such study we arise to the knowledge of the Creator and of that manifestation which He made of Himself in the universe. By the Christian revelation we mean that knowledge of God's nature and perfections which was imparted by God Himself, by a personal communication with man."

Doctor.—"Very good, indeed; then it is as clear as that two and two make four that science and revelation can never conflict with each other."

Adele.—"Why?"

Doctor.—"Because it is evident to the dullest mind that when God, by a personal intercourse which He establishes with man, reveals to the latter more and more of His own perfections, surely such additional and superior information cannot, in any sense, be supposed to be in conflict with the previous information about God, which man had acquired by the study of God's creatures; because in such a supposition the contradiction would fall on God. In nature and the universe God would image and portray Himself in one way, and in the personal intercourse He would reveal things about Himself conflicting and contradictory to the first. Could there be anything more absurd than this? Hence the plainest man has the answer to the question we are discussing, whether there be any conflict between science and revelation. He has to put the following questions to whomsoever may attack him: Do you admit that science means the knowledge of that manifestation which God has made of Himself and of His perfections in the universe, and of all which is contained in it? Do you grant that revelation means that knowledge of Himself and of His perfections which God has made personally to man and which the universe could not impart? If you do, it is evident that these two manifestations, distinct though they be, cannot in any sense conflict with each other; else God Almighty would contradict it Himself."

Adele.—"But suppose, uncle, that some statement of science or some new discovery should appear to contradict a truth or tenet of religion, what is one to do then?"

Doctor.—"Why, do nothing at all. What would you want him to do?"

Adele.—"I mean, how is one to satisfy his mind?"

Doctor.—"You have already given your answer in that word *appear*, for it can be nothing more than appearance. If the universe be really a manifestation of God in His creatures, and if religion be really that manifestation of God which He Himself makes to man in a personal communication, how in the name of common sense can any real discovery of science be in conflict with a truth of religion? God in that case would assert one thing of Himself in the universe, and then He Himself flatly contradict the same thing, when speaking to man personally.

"In the case, then, of an *apparent seeming* discord, of a superficial contradiction, we have to wait, and be absolutely confident that one day it will be found that that statement of science which seemed to contradict some real tenet of religion was either not a real result of science, but a hasty, inaccurate, unwarrantable conclusion from the real datas and facts furnished by observation, or it will be discovered that the fact had been mistaken, and appearances and queries had been taken for facts. Later on a better verification of facts, and more accurate calculations of their value and importance, will correct the apparent contradiction and conflict, and it will be found that the pretended discovery was no discovery at all. On the other hand, the apparent contradiction may arise, not because the statement of science is not true, but from the fact that an opinion of few, or many, on some religious subject, is taken as a real tenet or dogma of faith. When the matter is properly examined it will appear that the scientific result was opposed not to a truth of faith, but to a mere human opinion, respectable, if you will, in consequence of the personal credit of its supporters, but not less human and fallible, and of no importance whatever in the question. In one word, a statement of science seems to contradict a real truth of revelation. You may safely assume that the statement will require amendment, and will receive it some day or other. On the other, a true statement of science seems to oppose a religious tenet. You may take it for granted that that religious tenet is by no means a truth revealed by God and held as such by God's Church, but only a fallible human opinion which must give way to science. We will speak of the direct way in our next conversation."

SECOND ARTICLE.

HERBERT SPENCER'S THEORY CONCERNING MATTER—ITS REFUTATION.

Adele.—"Will you please, uncle, to speak on the direct way of answering the objection that there is conflict between science and revelation ? We proved in our first conversation that there can be no opposition, no real contradiction between science and revelation, because both are two distinct ways which God has adopted of manifesting His infinite perfections, and therefore they cannot contradict each other; one manifesting one thing, the other revealing the very opposite, without throwing the contradiction and inconsistency upon God Himself. This we called the indirect way or method. We are now to enter upon the direct way."

Doctor.—"And I warn you that the direct way is not so easy or so short as the other."

George.—"I suppose not; at the same time I cannot help thinking that it will be more satisfactory to the common run of people; at any rate, more instructive."

Doctor.—"You are right; it will necessarily prove more instructive, as it consists in taking one natural science after the other; in ascertaining what are really and undoubtedly the real result and consequences of such science; in comparing each of these results with the truths of revelation, and in pointing out the fact how no truth of science contradicts, or is opposed to any real principle, statement or fact of revelation."

Adele.—"I have already fallen in love with the direct way, as I presume we shall have to dabble a little in each natural science; and thus I may recall some of my sweet school days."

Doctor.—"We will begin to-day at the very beginning. George, what do you understand by matter?"

George.—"It is very hard to say what matter is, as all scientists freely admit that they know nothing at all about its nature; that all they can know about it is what they infer from the constant observation of its properties. But, at any rate, we may understand by matter all those first substances, whatever they may be, out of which bodies are fashioned."

Doctor.—"Very well, indeed, George. But as there are two kinds of bodies—living, or organic bodies, and not living, inanimate, inorganic bodies—I prefer to speak of the latter first; that is, not living bodies, called otherwise mineral."

Adele.—"So that we agree to limit our discussion at present to mineral bodies."

George.—"In that case I mean by matter those first substances of which mineral or inorganic bodies are composed."

Doctor.—"The first, most important question, then, to be discussed, and in which the apparent antagonism between science and religion may be supposed to originate, is this: Is matter, out of which the mineral world is fashioned, created? The Bible and all Christianity, together with the most colossal intellects of mankind, who have considered it a high honor and privilege to belong to Christianity and to uphold its doctrine, have always maintained that matter was created immediately by God, from no other substance previously existing, but simply by an act of His omnipotent will. Tell us, now, George, what some scientists of our times, and who are so much in vogue, hold about matter."

George.—"Why, they contend that matter is not and could not be created. Here are some words of Herbert Spencer: 'There was once universally current a notion that things could vanish into absolute nothing, or arise out of absolute nothing. The gradual accumulation of experience, however, and still more the organization of experiences has tended slowly to reverse this conviction, until now the doctrine that matter is indestructible has become commonplace.'"

Adele.—"What does Mr. Spencer mean by the organization of experiences?"

Doctor.—"You are to know that our modern scientists never speak like common men if they can help it; they know that man rather likes the mysterious, and is satisfied with high-sounding words, and they take advantage of it to impose upon the simple and the outsiders or profane. By the organization of experiences he means, I suppose, all the different experiences and observations made by scientists, sifted, compared, classified, and brought into a certain order and system."

George.—"Do you clearly understand, Miss Adele, what Herbert Spencer holds about matter?"

Adele.—"I think I do. He maintains that matter cannot have commenced to exist and that it can never cease to exist."

Doctor.—"And what do we call that which can neither have a beginning nor an end?"

Adele.—"I believe we call that self-existing."

Doctor.—"Now, George, please to tell us on what grounds and for what reasons does Mr. Spencer hold matter to be self-existent?"

George.—"As far as I can make out, he rests his opinion principally on two reasons. First, on the impossibility of thinking a thing to have originated in absolute nothingness."

Adele.—"Gently, Mr. George. I cannot say I follow you very well. You must be kind enough to come down from the clouds, to accommodate yourself to my ordinary female brain."

George.—"I have not said anything very hard, but I will try to speak plainer. You will readily grant that a thing cannot exist if it is impossible and contradictory."

Adele.—"To be sure, if the thing is impossible, there is an end of it."

George.—"So you understand that when a thing is impossible it cannot be supposed to exist?"

Adele.—"I grant that much; but how am I to know when the thing is possible or impossible?"

George.—"Very easily. When the parts or elements necessary to make up the idea of the thing clash one against another, contradict, and mutually exclude each other, the thing is unthinkable, cannot be thought of, and is therefore impossible. Try, for instance, to think of a square circle, or a triangle with four angles, and you cannot succeed because the elements which are necessary to make up the idea of a square circle clash with and exclude each other, the square excluding the circle, and the circle repudiating the square; hence the thing cannot be thought, and is impossible. Now it is not thinkable that matter could have originated in absolute nothingness."

Adele.—"Why ? What are the elements in the idea of matter being originated by absolute nothingness, which exclude each other ?"

George.—"Absolute nothingness excludes all existence, does it not ?"

Adele.—"To be sure."

George.—"To originate something supposes something existing and acting ?"

Adele.—"Certainly."

George.—"Then, matter originating in absolute nothingness means absolute non-existence and existence at the same time, which is unthinkable and impossible. 'It is impossible,' says Spencer, 'to think of nothing becoming something.' 'The creation of matter is unthinkable.'"

Adele.—"I see."

Doctor.—"Before we go any further let us dispose of this reason, so much paraded by Spencer and other infidels. You will not be astonished, Adele, to hear that the reason is good, logical, sound, perfectly just and cogent; and yet it proves with the greatest evidence against Spencer the very dogma of Creation which he has feigned to attack. Now pay attention to the following remark. When we speak of the universe being made out of *nothing*, we may take that word *nothing* in two distinct senses. If we said that the world was made out of nothing, taking the word 'nothing' in an absolute sense, it would mean that nothing whatever really existed, and that out of that nothing whatever, something sprang up. Such a proposition is not thinkable; it is absurd and inconceivable.

"On the other hand, if we said the world was made out of nothing, taking the word 'nothing' in a relative sense, it means that the universe was not fashioned out of materials already existing, but was simply the effect of an infinite and almighty energy and power.

"'Nothing,' in an absolute sense, implies the total absence of cause and materials; taken in a relative sense, it supposes the absence of previously existing materials, but implies and imperatively demands an almighty and infinite cause. Now, George, have you remarked in what sense Herbert Spencer maintains that the creation of matter is unthinkable ?"

George.—"Yes, sir, and I must own I am heartily ashamed of him and of his sophism. He takes the word 'nothing' in an absolute sense, meaning that nothing whatever existing, it is inconceivable and unthinkable how anything could come from it. 'There was once universally current a notion that things could vanish into absolute nothing, or arise out of absolute nothing.' Taking the word 'nothing' in an absolute sense, he is right in saying that a creation from nothing in an absolute sense is absurd and inconceivable."

Doctor.—"And so have thought all Christian philosophers, the whole Christian world, and the whole Catholic Church; the absurdity of making anything from universal nothingness, from the total absence of any existence whatever, is laid down, commented upon, and explained in every book of Christian philosophy or theology; in every book of controversy upon this and kindred topics. And when Mr. Spencer very coolly and deliberately asserts 'that there was once universally current a notion that things could arise out of absolute nothing,' and that 'such proposition that cannot be thought of is one which mankind universally professed to think, and which the great majority profess to think even now,' he ought to know that he is *lying*, and calumniating the whole Christian world, or that he is exhibiting his most colossal ignorance and faith in the gullibility of his readers."

Adele.—"So, uncle, if I understand you correctly, the first pitiful reason of Spencer in favor of the self-existence of matter falls to the ground, because, though it be self-evident that nothing can come of absolute nothing, it is evident to the simplest mind that matter can be created from 'nothing,' taken in a relative sense; that is, in respect to materials previously existing. Mr. Spencer and compeers, to prove the impossibility of the creation of matter, ought to take the trouble to demonstrate not by such miserable sophism as he uses, but by true, real, solid reasons, that it is impossible, even for an infinite, omnipotent power to create matter, without previous existing materials. When he has done so, then he may proclaim loudly the self-existence of matter. But so far he has every reason to be ashamed of his so-called proof, which is nothing but a miserable rehash of the saying of the ancients, *From nothing nothing is made*, and which the whole Christian world has understood and explained with a clearness that cannot be mistaken, and which, in a few words, can be expressed thus: From total absence of being nothing can arise; but given the total absence of preëxisting material, omnipotent and infinite power can cause things to exist."

Doctor.—"Very well said, Adele. But George, leaving aside the second reason, which Mr. Spencer has alleged as proving the self-existence of matter, and which we shall have occasion to discuss presently, we will inquire what real science has discovered and proved about matter."

George.—"I think we can easily determine what true science reveals about matter. First, real science has discovered that matter cannot be destroyed by any means whatever within man's power. Matter can be reduced from the solid state into the state of fluid, or gas, and back again. It can be compressed or dilated; it may be divided until our instruments absolutely fail us; it may be reduced to such a state as to escape and place itself beyond our reach and that of our instruments; that is *all* that science has discovered and has *proved;* because so far our observation can go; and as the sciences, which are called experimental, rest upon experience and observation for their proof, it is evident that nothing more can be predicated of matter than what is founded on observation."

Doctor.—"But mark what follows. From the fact that man or his instruments cannot destroy matter, we cannot conclude that it is of its own nature indestructible, permanent or eternal; because otherwise we should draw a conclusion wider and more comprehensive than its premises. All the conclusion we can draw is, that man cannot destroy matter, because we find it to be so on constant observation and experiments. But to say that matter is intrinsically and essentially indestructible, to say that even an infinite power could not annihilate it because man is proved, by constant experience, not to be able to destroy matter either by himself or aided by the most powerful instrument, is to make mockery of logic, and to bid good-by to all common sense and right reasoning."

George.—"But, Doctor, what should we answer to the other reason of Spencer, that it is impossible to conceive matter as non-existent because nothing cannot become an object of consciousness?"

Adele.—"I cannot say that I understand that reason. Pray, elucidate it in a few words."

George.—"I will try. Suppose Spencer should put his reasoning as follows: We cannot have consciousness of that which does not exist; therefore, if matter should cease to exist our consciousness of it would cease also. But we are always thinking and can always think of matter; therefore it can never cease to exist."

Adele.—"I understand now. The very fact of our thinking of matter is a warrant of its continual existence; because, as we are not able to think of anything which does not exist, it follows that if matter should cease to exist the very thought of it would cease."

George.—"Excellent, Miss Adele. And what must we say to that, Doctor?"

Doctor.—"Why, George, laugh to scorn such a pitiful, miserable, childish reasoning, which would disgrace a young Miss learning the A B C of logic. It is a mystery to me how, in the nineteenth century, men can come forward and spout such nonsense, and, instead of finding persons charitable enough to shut them up in a madhouse, meeting with a host of would be educated men, who are ready to fall down and worship them just because that nonsense and arrant absurdity is turned against Religion and God Almighty. If it were true that we could not conceive the non-existence of matter, on the ground that 'nothing' cannot be the object of thought or consciousness, as Spencer is pleased to call it, it would follow that we could never conceive the ideas of negation, privation, absence, death, darkness, black, and a hundred more similar ideas. Every one knows that we form negative ideas by means of the positive, and that we contemplate, so to speak, the negative in the positive. For instance, I have the idea of an object which is lying before me. By a mental operation I remove that object, and thus I acquire the idea of negation and absence. I can, therefore, easily suppose matter to be removed, and thus apprehend its destruction or annihilation."

Adele.—"But, Doctor, can we prove by true, real, positive argument, that matter must have been created?"

Doctor.—"Not only that, but we can prove that real, true science has demonstrated by inference that matter must have been created according to the Christian sense of the word. But it is sufficient for to-day. Enough is as good as a feast. We will resume the subject at the next meeting."

THIRD ARTICLE.

MODERN SCIENCE PROVES THAT MATTER MUST HAVE BEEN CREATED.

Doctor.—"George, what is the subject of our conversation to-day?"

George.—"Why, that matter was created by God in the Christian sense of the word; that is, from no previous existing materials, but by a pure act of His omnipotent will. And I think it will not be hard to prove that, as, from my studies of the real results and consequences of modern science upon the subject, I am ready to show that it has really been created."

Adele.—"Let me put the question properly, so that I may follow your demonstration. You undertake to prove that matter has really been created, and you feel strong enough to accomplish the task from the results and consequences of modern science. Is that what you undertake to do? Think well on it, for I will hold you to your promise."

George.—"Well, I don't think I undertake a very hard task, so I am sure I can fulfill my promise; but you must allow me to quote a passage from the *Encyclopædia Britannica* about matter which is edifying and interesting to a degree: 'If we knew thoroughly the nature of any piece of matter, the deduction of its properties would be a question of mere reasoning. But as we not even know what matter is in the abstract, the converse operation is (at least for the present) the natural and necessary one. *We must endeavor from the experimentally ascertained properties of matter to discover what it is.* The properties of matter may be arranged in several classes, thus: 1st. Properties of matter in itself, such as inertia. (*Encyclopædia Brit. Art. Matter.*).'"

Doctor.—"Mark well, Adele; it is freely admitted by the scientists that they know nothing at all about the nature of matter, as it is evident from the passage quoted, and as it could be proved by any number of testimonies of the best and the greatest among them. And they are perfectly correct in the consequence they draw from that admission: that, therefore, all we know about matter must be inferred from the properties, which by experience we observe to be found in matter. Hence we must conclude that to attribute to matter a certain nature in evident conflict with its principal and most widely known properties, would be to make a mockery of logic and of human intelligence."

Adele.—"I understand perfectly; so long as by admission of all scientists we know nothing about the nature of matter, and so long as all we can know about it must be inferred from the properties we observe in matter, it follows that it would be absurd to assign to it a nature in direct opposition to its best known properties."

George.—"True; and now I call your attention to one of the most commonly admitted properties of matter, upon which all natural philosophers agree without one dissentient voice; and about the scientific importance of which there cannot be the remotest possible doubt. It is *inertia*. I am sure the Doctor can give us a better idea of this property of matter than I could ever attempt to do."

Doctor.—"I prefer to give it in words of well-known authorities. Prof. Silliman, in his 'First Principles of Natural Philosophy,' says: '*Inertia or Inactivity.*—No particle of matter possesses within itself the power of changing its existing state of motion or rest. Matter has no spontaneous tendency, either for rest or motion; but as equally acceptable to each, according as it may be acted on by an external cause. If a body is at rest a force is necessary to put it in motion, and conversely. It cannot change from motion to rest without the agency of some force.' Ganot's 'Elementary Treatise on Physics,' page 12: 'The inability of matter to pass by itself from the state of rest to that of movement, or to modify the movement by which it is animated, is called *inertia*.' The first law of Kleper about motion is founded on this property of matter, and reads as follows: 'Every body continues in its state of rest or of uniform motion in a straight line, except in so far as it is compelled by force to change that state.' It is explained by Prof. P. G. Tait, of Edinburgh: 'This law tells what happens to a piece of matter which is left to itself, that is not acted upon by force. It preserves its state whether of rest or of uniform motion in a straight line. This property is commonly called inertia of matter, in virtue of which it is incapable of varying in any way its state of rest or motion. It may be the sport of forces for any length of time; but so soon as they cease to act it remains in the state in which it was left until they recommence their action on it. Hence whenever we find the state of a piece of matter changing, we conclude that it is under the action of a force or forces.' (*Enc. Britt.*, *art. Mechanics, by Prof. Tait.*)"

Adele.—"I am sure something very serious is going to be the upshot of so many preliminaries and of so much care and trouble of explaining the property of inertia. But as I am very anxious to understand it well, I would beg leave to put a question. I would like to ask, by the inertness of matter do we understand absolute and unqualified inactivity?"

Doctor.—"No. The real and objective existence of matter is and can only be known to us by the changes which it causes in us, either directly or by modifying other objects which act upon us in their turn. If, then, matter were supposed to be completely inactive, or devoid of all external activity, we should have no natural means of knowing it. Then again, it is impossible to suppose matter to be devoid of all action, either internal or external. Because there can be no finite substance without attributes. Now, what attributes can we predicate of matter? Extension? But, without impenetrability, extension would simply be an imaginary attribute. Now, impenetrability necessarily implies resistance, which is somewhat an active element. The inertness of matter, therefore, cannot be supposed to mean absolute and unqualified inactivity."

Adele.—"I am glad that matter has at least the force of resistance not to let any other body take its place."

Doctor.—"It has more than that. It has the force of resistance to a change of motion, and to the passing from rest to movement, or from movement to rest; and to counteract by such resistance in the external motor or agent part of that motion communicated, equal in quantity to that part which takes effect; also to receive the movement and to transmit it to others according to an invariable law."

Adele.—"Then I don't see why philosophers have calumniated matter, and given her the ugly character of a lazy, inert, indolent, good-for-nothing old thing."

Doctor.—"No, Adele, they have not slandered it in the least. The real inertness of matter consists in the fact that it can never *spontaneously* and *of itself* begin movement, or cease from it; it can never spontaneously change its velocity or speed, or change its direction. In this all scientists have done her justice."

Adele.—"Well, and what do you infer from this absolute inability of matter to start its movement or cease from it?"

Doctor.—"I infer that on that account it cannot be self-existent, and must necessarily have been created."

Adele.—"I cannot say that I follow you."

Doctor.—"Listen then to the argument which follows from that universally admitted fact. If matter, if each portion of matter which we call a body, must receive its movement from an external agent, it follows that the principle of movement is not and cannot be in matter, nor in any portion of it; that matter must depend for its action upon an external agent; that it can never act except and solely under the impulse of an external agent; again, that supposing the absence of an exterior force to impress such movement, matter would be absolutely and irredeemably motionless and good for nothing. Now, it is a contradiction to suppose a thing on the one hand subject to and dependent upon another for its movement, and, on the other hand, to suppose it altogether independent, free, sovereign, absolute as to its existence; for, mark it well, all this is supposed when we assert the self existence of matter. To be self-existing means to be independent, absolute, sovereign, free, as to existence from any outward or external cause. Hence to assert matter to be self-existent is to claim for it freedom, independence, sovereignty from all causes whatever as to existence."

Adele.—"And is it a contradiction to say that matter is absolute, independent of all causes whatever as to its existence, and to affirm, on the other hand, that it is absolutely helpless in itself and dependent upon an external cause for its action?"

Doctor.—"To be sure."

Adele.—"Why?"

Doctor.—"Because, if a thing is dependent as to its action, it must also be dependent as to its existence, since a *thing acts as it exists*. If its existence is independent of any external cause it will act independently of any external agent; if it be dependent and subject as to its existence it will act as dependent and subject. Scientists admit that we must infer the nature of matter from its qualities and properties which come under our observation; we find the action of matter dependent upon an external agent; therefore its nature also and existence must be dependent upon an external principle."

Adele.—"You mean to say this: Does it not seem quite ludicrous to make matter so grand and lofty as to proclaim it no less than self-existent, and then to behold the very men who exalt it so much setting aside all regard for its grandeur and lofty majesty, mercilessly and pitilessly pulling it down from the high throne to cast it on the ground? Matter so great, so sublime as to be self-existent, free, independent, sovereign, absolute; matter so low, so mean, so paltry, such a miserable slave, as to be unable to move an inch without the impulse of the first living being which may choose to kick it! And what is worse, it is so chained to absolute inaction and sloth as to remain in its indolence and helplessness for all eternity unless, like the poor wretches on board a slave ship, who are forced to dance and to be merry for fear of their dying for want of exercise, it be aided and impelled to move by some hard task-master or some kind external power. That is self-existence with a vengeance!"

Doctor.—"And this is the more absurd because, as I have already alluded, the action of a being is in conformity and in full keeping with the existence and nature of the being. You cannot gather grapes out of thistles. A thing cannot act except as it is, and it were absurd to expect a thing to act either as above or contrary to its nature. What is the action of a being? Its movement. And can any one suppose a thing to move in any way except in that shaped and determined by its existence and nature? This is so true, so in accordance with the common sense of mankind, that they are continually inferring the nature of a thing from its action, and are perfectly confident that in doing so they cannot be mistaken. Now, the action and movement of matter necessarily and absolutely depends upon the action of an external agent and cause; consequently, its existence and nature must be dependent upon an external cause, and cannot be admitted to be self-existent without contradiction. And you will remark that this argument proves not only the impossibility of matter being self-existent, but also that it must have been created by one truly and really self-existing, infinite Power."

Adele.—"Pray explain that."

Doctor.—"We have seen that matter depends upon an external cause for its existence and its movement. Now, it is natural to inquire next what sort of a power or cause is this upon which matter depends, and in answer we may make a twofold supposition. Either this principle upon which matter depends for existence and movement contains in itself the reason of its own existence and action, or, like matter, it borrows it from another. This latter supposition cannot be maintained because it explains nothing, and throws the question back as one could ask: From whence does this principle borrow its existence and movement? and the answer would have to be from a third, a fourth, a fifth, and so on forever, without ever accounting for the existence and movement of matter. Hence to account for the existence and movement of the latter we must absolutely and necessarily take refuge in the admission of a Being who contains in Himself the reason of His existence and action."

George.—"What are you laughing at, Miss Adele?"

Adele.—"Why, the supposition of a number of beings, every one of which has a borrowed existence and movement to account for the existence and movement of matter, brought vividly before my mind an anecdote I read some time ago in a French book. A free-thinker was boasting in a gathering of ladies and gentlemen that he did not see any necessity whatever for the existence of an infinite self-existing Being to account for the universe. One of the ladies present politely and charmingly asked him if he would allow her to put him a question."

"'I shall consider it a great honor,' he replied.

"'Will you be so kind,' continued the lady, 'as to tell me which was first, the egg or the hen?'

"'Why, the egg, of course,' answered the free-thinker.

"'Charming!' said the lady; 'but pray, who hatched that first egg?'

"'Beg your pardon,' retorted the free-thinker, 'I must have been distracted; the hen, of course, must have been first.'

"'Then will you allow me to suppose,' insisted the lady, 'that the first hen did not come from an egg; and in that case, if the first hen did not come from an egg, pray from what did it come?'

"'Madam,' replied the free-thinker, 'you would make one forget the respect due to your sex, with your hens and your eggs.'

"'Of course,' replied the lady, raising her voice so that every one in the room could hear, 'you unreasonable boasters, without the supposition of a self existing infinite power, you cannot account even for the existence of an egg or a hen, and without God you pretend to account for the myriads of lofty, vast, wondrous worlds, rolling in grandeur and majesty above our heads. A filip for your pretended science!'"

Doctor.—"This self-existent, infinite, living power, Christians call God, praising and adoring Him as the source and fountain of all existence as well as of all other good."

George.—"Well may we exclaim with Mrs. Hemans:

> "O Thou, th' unseen, th' all-seeing Thou, whose ways
> Mantled with darkness mock all finite gaze;
> Father of worlds unknown, unnumbered, Thou
> With whom all time is an eternal *now*,
> Who know'st no past nor future—Thou whose breath
> Goes forth and bears to myriads life or death,
> Look on us, guide us, wanderers of a sea,
> Wild and obscure, what are we 'reft of Thee?'"
>
> —*Mrs. Hemans' "The Skeptic."*

FOURTH ARTICLE.

IDEA OF SELF-EXISTENCE—DID CHRISTIANS EVER UNDERSTAND WHAT THEY MEANT BY GOD?—COMPLIMENTS OF HERBERT SPENCER.

Doctor.—"We may now turn our attention to the attributes and perfections which can be logically deduced from the idea of a self-existent Being, and thus to explain all the perfections of God."

George.—"I am sorry to interrupt you, Doctor, but I fear the so-called modern science is in your way there. I need not remind you that Herbert Spencer and his followers have pretended that the idea of a self-existing Being is wholly and utterly inconceivable, and that, therefore, the thing itself is impossible."

Doctor.—"I am fully aware of what you say, George, but Spencer's reasoning is so childish, so silly, so ludicrous, so utterly wretched and pitiful, that I had come to the conclusion to pass over the whole thing with silent contempt. But as you mention it, we may as well take it up and examine it. If it has no more beneficial result than to amuse Adele, our time will not be entirely thrown away."

Adele.—"I shall be infinitely obliged to Mr. Spencer for any little fun he may afford me."

Doctor.—"Tell us, George, what dire and lamentable consequences will follow if we maintain the idea of a self-existent Being?"

George.—"I will quote Mr. Spencer: 'In the first place, it is clear that by *self-existence* we especially mean an existence independent of any other, not produced by any other' (First Principles. Appleton edition, 1874, page 31)."

Doctor.—"To be sure we mean that very thing—and what then?"

George.—"The assertion of self-existence is simply an indirect denial of creation." (*Ib.*)

Doctor.—"Breakers ahead, George. When you are reading our modern scientists and infidels you must be on the alert and have the eyes of Argus, else by some sly manipulation they will slip in some vague, indistinct, general assertion, which, if you fail to detect at the proper time and place, will give you trouble afterwards. Now look closely at the proposition, 'The assertion of self-existence is simply an indirect denial of creation.' Mark what I say: in reference, and only in reference, to that being of whom we predicate the self-existence, certainly the assertion of self-existence is an indirect denial of his creation. In reference to all other beings, certainly not Mr. Spencer takes the expression, 'an indirect denial of creation, in a general sense, as applicable to all and every being, and taken in that sense the proposition is false. Because from the fact that I predicate the self-existence of one being, and thereby suppose the denial of the creation of such a being, it does not follow that I mean to deny all creation in general. Go on, George."

George.—"In thus excluding the idea of any antecedent cause, we necessarily exclude the idea of a beginning."

Doctor.—"Of course we do."

George.—"Spencer gives the reason for this."

Doctor.—"Spare us such transcendental effort of genius, George. Why, any tyro in logic would be ashamed of such attempt at display. Come at once to the conclusion."

George.—"Self-existence, therefore, necessarily means existence without a beginning, and to form a conception of self-existence is to form a conception without a beginning. No, by no mental effort can we do this."

Adele.—"Why?"

Doctor.—"Adele has taken the word out of my mouth. Dear me, what a display of the cheapest metaphysical lore! Self-existence means an existence without beginning! Did any one ever hear anything so wonderfully cute, rare, precious and unique? To form an idea of self-existence is to form n idea of an existence without beginning! How profound! Why was not Herbert Spencer born a few centuries back! He would have shed floods of light on what he and his associates, equally deep as himself, call the dark ages! And now, 'by no mental effort can we form the conception of an existence without beginning.' Why, without such a mental effort the whole Christian world has formed such a conception. Among Christians of every age there were, literally speaking, the greatest and the noblest geniuses of the human race, colossal intellects, alongside of which the puny brains of our modern infidels must sink into utter insignificance, even as a pebble which we crush under our feet is utterly lost in comparison with the Egyptian pyramids. Spencer, with a coolness commensurate with his ignorance, dares to assert that such men for instance as St. Augustine, St. Thomas, Leibnitz, Michael Angelo, Galileo, Bacon, Shakespeare, Bossuet, Fenelon, Milton, Kleper, Newton, Napoleon, only imagined to conceive what in reality they did not conceive, and were the victims of mystification and self-delusion. But let us hear the wonderful reason which, according to Spencer, prevented all Christians from conceiving what they really and truly did not conceive."

George.—"To conceive an existence through infinite past time implies the conception of an infinite past time, which is an impossibility."

Adele.—"Stop, if you please, Mr. George. The only word I understand in your whole quotation is pastime, and I am sure I find it anything but pastime or amusement."

Doctor.—"It is not such a hard task to understand it. Listen. We learn in mathematics that an infinite number is impossible, because a number is necessarily a collection of distinct units. If it were not a collection of units it would be a unity, but not a number. If those units were not distinct, but the same and identical, the same inconvenience would follow: we should have a unit, but not a number. Number is therefore a collection of distinct units. This renders the conception of an infinite number absolutely impossible, for the simple reason that we can always add to or subtract from it—addition or subtraction—which is in direct contradiction with the idea of the infinite."

Adele.—"Why?"

Doctor.—"Because the infinite implies the idea of something complete, finished, perfected, to which we can neither add nor subtract from, whereas number means a collection of distinct units capable of increase or diminution; hence the two ideas exclude each other and cannot agree together, and an infinite number is as inconceivable as that of a square circle or a triangle with four sides."

Adele.—"Let me see if I catch your reasoning. What is a number? A collection of distinct units capable of increase or diminution, of addition or subtraction, because whatever number we may imagine we can always add to or subtract from it certain units. On the other hand, the idea of the infinite is that of something absolutely perfect and complete, to which one can neither add nor take from. Hence the two ideas exclude each other, and the two together cannot be conceived."

Doctor.—"Excellent, Adele. Now, Herbert Spencer pretends that to conceive an existence without beginning is to conceive a number actually infinite."

Adele.—"How?"

Doctor.—"Thus: Suppose the existence without beginning to have undergone movement and a succession of acts, it is clear that we have a number of acts without beginning or end. And what is that but a number actually infinite—or, to use Spencer's expressions, an infinite past time? Of course I need not say that such a thing is impossible."

George.—"Then, Doctor, you agree with Spencer that to conceive of an existence without beginning is an impossible task, because it implies the conception of a number actually infinite?"

Adele.—"What, uncle! I cannot conceive God as self-existent, because that would be attempting to form an idea of infinite past time."

Doctor.—"I see both of you are upon me at once. But don't be afraid, I am conceding what is true in the argument of Spencer, and at the same time putting in the most striking light possible the monstrous and colossal ignorance of the same, or his evident dishonesty and bad faith. Mark it well. To conceive of an existence without beginning, subject to a succession and change of movements and acts, is an impossibility, because that would be really supposing a number that is a collection of distinct units actually infinite.

"But such an existence has only existed in the fertile imagination of Herbert Spencer. Christian philosophy never as much as dreamt of such a thing. The existence without beginning, as understood by the Christian world, differs as much from the existence without beginning imagined by Spencer as light from darkness, white from black, the infinite from the finite differ from each other; and Spencer was either a fool or a knave when he asserted that Christians conceiving an existence without beginning meant an existence for all eternity subject to a succession of movements and acts; in other words, subject to a succession or collection of different acts, which would be an infinite past time."

George.—"So the idea of self-existent being, of course without beginning or end, absolutely excludes all succession of acts or movements; otherwise we should have the impossible supposition."

Doctor.—"Certainly, it excludes all number. The self-existent being must necessarily be one pure, simple, absolute actuality or act; otherwise we cannot conceive it. Suppose for a moment that it could be two acts—first, the act of existence; next, the second act or movement. Whence would this second act come? From the first act? Then it was there already, as the first act could not give itself what it had not. From an external agent? Then, in that case the first act would not be self-existent any longer; because, as we proved in another conversation, one who is dependent upon another for its action is dependent also for its existence, since a being acts as it is; if it is independent in its existence it acts independent of any one; if it is dependent it acts under dependence."

Adele.—"I think I understand the whole argument, and if I had the greatly exaggerated philosopher before me, I would say: My dear Mr. Spencer, you have played a part unworthy of one of your nation, so fond of fair play. First, you have imagined that Christians, by a self-existent being without beginning or end, meant a being subject to movements and changes following each other in rapid succession; then you have argued that the supposition of such a thing is to suppose a number actually infinite, and have easily come to the conclusion that therefore the conception of self-existent being is impossible. Now, Christians, by a self-existent being, have always and everywhere meant an existence absolutely complete and perfect, free and independent of all possible change and succession; they exclude from such existence all composition, collection or number, and they have purposely called it most Pure Act, or Actuality itself, to eliminate from it all possibility and capacity of or liability to progress, improvement, change of state, or modification of any kind whatever. Therefore the idea of self-existence, as such, implying the idea of absolute, independent, most finished and complete perfection, is assuredly intelligible and conceivable."

George.—"Very good indeed, Miss Adele; if Mr. Spencer were accessible to you he would not get off very easily on the score of self-existence."

Adele.—"Nay, more, I would tell him and his compeers that, by their idea of self-existence, they have themselves offered the best argument for the overthrow of their whole system."

George.—"I don't exactly catch your meaning."

Adele.—"Didn't you say that the very essence of Spencer's system consists in admitting an indestructible matter which has had no beginning, and which develops itself and gradually assumes all the forms of the universe?"

George.—"Certainly, that is the outline of Spencer's system, and of all those who are called material Pantheists."

Adele —"Very well, if their system is the hypothesis of a matter self-existent, which had no beginning of course, and which gradually unfolds itself, that is, is subject to movement and change of states; all that is admitting a number actually infinite, or the conception of an infinite past time, as he expresses it, which according to him is absolutely and utterly impossible. Therefore, to my poor mind, the whole system of Spencer and compeers is inconceivable and absurd by their own admission."

Doctor —"You are perfectly right, Adele, and if these gentlemen had a grain of logic and consistency in them, or a tittle of love for truth, they would soon find out the utter worthlessness, inconsistency, contradiction and absurdity of their pet theories. A self-existing matter, or matter without a beginning, must be supposed to be either absolutely inert, stationary, immovable and dead, or subject to successive motion. In either supposition Spencer's system is absurd. If we assume matter as stationary and inert, it will remain in that state for all eternity for want of some agent to set it in motion, and, mind you, Spencer admits no other principle; matter, then, will remain in its inertness forever, and neither the different forms nor the movement of the universe can be explained. If we suppose matter subject to successive motion it will not be any better because successive motion without a beginning means an infinite past time; an infinite past time is absolutely and utterly inconceivable; therefore a self-existing matter undergoing movement from all eternity is a sheer absurdity and nonsense, and Spencer's system is scattered by himself to the four winds of heaven. But, for God's sake, let us leave darkness so heavy and oppressive and turn to light. George, please read the page I have marked in Fenelon. I know you can translate as you go along."

George.—"The self-existent Being exists in a supreme degree, and hence is possessed of the fullness of being. It is not possible to suppose the supreme degree and fullness of being without at the same time supposing the *infinite;* because the finite is neither full nor supreme, as we are free continually to add to it. Hence the self-existing Being must be the infinite Being."

Doctor.—"Mark, Adele, what Fenelon, with all Christian theology and philosophy, means by a self-existing Being. They understand by it one who has a real and downright actual possession of the fullness and completeness of being in the highest, supreme, and absolute degree. They mean *Being Itself*, and not a certain kind of being with the capacity and aptitude of receiving more being. Now, to suppose such a being is to suppose the Infinite; because you can neither add to nor subtract from the absolute fullness of being. What would you add to it? Perfection? It *is* the absolute fullness of perfection, and if you could add more to that you would call in question and destroy the supposition of its being the absolute fullness and completeness of perfection."

George.—"If He is an Infinite Being He is infinitely perfect, because being, goodness, and perfection are one and the same thing."

Adele—"Hold on, George, this seems to require some explanation. How can being, goodness, and perfection be one and the same thing?"

George.—"Well, are goodness and perfection something or not? If you cannot say that they are nothing they must be something, therefore they are the same as being. The only difference in these ideas is that being means that which is really existing, whereas goodness and perfection mean being, which is the object sought after by a faculty. Hence goodness and perfection suppose a relation that being has to a faculty, which longs for it. Take for instance light. Now, considering it as a real something, it is called being; but, if we look upon that something as the object sought for by our vision, it is called the good and the perfection of our eye. Being, therefore, good and perfection, are, so far as reality is concerned, one and the same thing."

Doctor.—"Continue the passage of Fenelon."

George.—"From the idea of a necessary or self-existing being follows the simplicity and unity of God. His simplicity, because nothing made up of parts can be either infinitely perfect or infinite at all in any sense. His unity, because if there were two necessary and independent beings, each one would be less perfect by this divided power than if one should unite in Himself the whole.

"He is immutable, for He who is self-existent can never be otherwise understood. He contains always the same reason for self-existence, which is His essence. Hence He is immutable in His existence. He is no more capable of changes with regard to the manner of being than He is with reference to His existence itself. The moment He is conceived to be infinite and infinitely simple, we cannot attribute to Him any modification, because modifications are limitations and boundaries of being. To be modified in a certain fashion is to exist in a certain fashion to the exclusion of all other ways. The infinitely perfect, therefore, cannot be subject to modification, and therefore cannot change." (*Fenelon De l'Existence de Dieu.*)

Doctor.—"The idea, then, of a self-existent Being, as understood by Christianity, is the only possible and reasonable idea of self existence, that is, a Being existing by Himself, without beginning or end;

without succession or change in His existence or in His manner of being; but absolutely immutable, the fullness and plenitude of being, the Infinite, the most pure and simple Act, the concentration, so to speak, of all conceivable actuality, reality and perfection. Take away such an idea of self-existence—in other words, take away the Christian idea of God—and you proclaim absolute materialism, the death of all being and of all intelligence, as we have proved that if we remove such idea we have nothing left but to fall back upon the idea of a self existing matter without beginning, subject to change and succession; that is, to the absurd and inconceivable supposition of an infinite past time. In spite then of modern science, we may conclude—

"God is still God and
His faith shall not fail us."
—*Longfellow*, "*The Nun of Nidaros*."

FIFTH ARTICLE.

FORMATION OF THE UNIVERSE—BEAUTIFUL HYPOTHESIS OF LA PLACE.

Doctor.—"In our former conversations we have come to the conclusion that matter, or the primitive substances out of which the inorganic world was fashioned, was created by the Almighty from no pre-existing materials, but simply by an act of His all-powerful will. We demonstrated also that matter could not be self-existent, that the only self existent being is God. We also defended and vindicated the real notion of a self-existent being from the attacks of an ignorant and silly philosophy, and pointed out the principal attributes of God. We have now reached that stage in our discussion when we can occupy ourselves about the formation of the universe, or rather of the inorganic world."

Adele.—"Shall we discuss it according to science?"

Doctor.—"To be sure. Our method shall be to get the best results or hypotheses of science on every subject under discussion, and afterwards we shall compare those results or hypotheses with the respective dogmas of our religion, and we shall find that whenever they come in contact no conflict or opposition whatever is to be observed between them. George, what does science say upon the formation of the inorganic universe?"

George.—"It is useless for me to remark that science has not as yet ascertained with sufficient certainty or evidence how the inorganic world was formed. It has only brought forward guesses, conjectures, and hypotheses."

Adele.—"Why do you take such care to repeat with the Doctor the epithet *inorganic?*"

George.—"Because, as I understand the Doctor, he wants to treat first of the inorganic world, the universe, which as yet does not manifest any life in its bosom."

Doctor.—"Precisely. We cannot treat of every question at the same time, therefore for the sake of clearness and not to mix up matters we will speak first of the lifeless, inorganic world, and afterward proceed to treat of life when we see it springing up in the universe. Go on, George."

George.—"Well, as I have remarked, science has not pronounced the last word, as the French scientists would say, on the formation of the universe. It only offers hypotheses and guesses. The most probable among these is the opinion of La Place, which he developed and defended in his book, 'Celestial Mechanics.'"

Adele.—"If we can have no better we will take his opinion."

Doctor.—"Certainly La Place has given upon the formation of the universe a very remarkable theory based upon mathematical conclusions of the highest value, and which the immense progress realized by science, since the great astronomer, have helped to confirm, to develop, and to complete."

George.—"I will explain it in my own way."

Adele.—"Yes, provided you make it clear to me."

George.—"Never fear. It has been proved by mathematical demonstration, as well as by observation, that all kinds of fluid mass, that is, a mass whose molecules can slide one upon the other, like liquids and gases, tend by themselves to take a spherical form. Thus the bubbles of air or gas which rise up from the bottom of a liquid to vanish at the top upon the contact of the surrounding air; also the drops of oil projected into water till the moment when their specific lightness makes them mount up and spread themselves over the surface; also the parts of mercury which roll over a glass, the tiny drops of dew hanging on the leaves of trees and flowers; all these take and represent a spherical form or shape."

Adele—"That is not always true. Suppose I fill a glass or any other vessel with water, surely it does not take a spherical form, but the form of the vessel which contains it."

Doctor.—"The law always holds good, Adele; and the instance to the contrary does not prove anything. It does happen sometimes that the weight of the fluid mass and the force of attraction which draws it down may surpass and overcome the effect of the molecular attraction. But suppose any given fluid mass, and eliminate from it the influences of all other causes, such as the attraction exercised by the earth, the sun, and the stars, which people the universe, and such a mass, small or large, will always take a spherical form."

George.—"Now, let us carry ourselves in thought to the origin of time, to the beginning spoken of in Genesis. God reigns alone and enjoys in Himself a boundless felicity. No material creature has as yet troubled, so to speak, the silence and solitude of nothingness God creates. In the bosom of nothing arise the atoms, and matter is already existing in its germ. It is nothing more than a mass of imperceptible and imponderable fluids, so small and so tiny that our own hydrogen gas, which is fourteen times lighter than air, would seem to be lead in comparison with this first and ethereal essence of all matter. This impalpable fluid, which senses a thousand times finer, more delicate, and more piercing than ours, could not detect this fluid ; or, so to speak, this shadow, or trace of a fluid, is that which may be supposed to constitute space."

Adele.—"Pray, before you go any further, will you please to tell me: Does this imponderable fluid—which is supposed to be material, of course—rest on any place? Does anything uphold it? In one word, where is it located?"

Doctor.—"Sportingly, Adele, you have raised a very difficult question, but this is the place to dispose of it, and we may as well do so. You must understand that it is not necessary to the essence and properties of a body to be located in any place. Suppose God had created one single atom, where would this atom be located? Nowhere. Where would it be? In itself. What would uphold it? God's infinite power. This, I admit, is hard to understand, and it surpasses the power of language to express how many errors and fictions have passed through the brains even of scientists as to this point; but after all the thing is very simple. Either we must admit that a body which is a mass of molecules, or a group of atoms which forms a molecule, or an atom itself, must be conceded to be able to exist in itself irrespectively of any other body or molecule or atom wherein it may be located, or the existence of an atom is impossible. Because the existence of an atom necessarily requiring another atom to be located in it, would imply a number of atoms actually infinite, which is absurd."

Adele.—"Why?"

Doctor.—"Because if one atom cannot exist without another on which to rest, this second would require a third, the third a fourth, and so on forever, and either you would never stop, or, to stop, you would require a number of atoms actually infinite, which we have seen is an impossibility."

George.—"Dear me, Doctor! you have lifted a load off my mind. I never understood space till this moment, because I always imagined that a body must be located necessarily in another body, and therefore I could never explain to myself what space is, and could only fashion to myself monstrous, immense, boundless phantoms; where located, if at all, I did not and could not conceive. I see now what floods of light Catholic philosophy can shed upon the most difficult and intricate questions. We will then suppose that an imponderable and impalpable fluid which forms space is located nowhere, but exists in itself, upheld by the creative hand of God. Now let us take any of the points of the space at random. Two atoms meet and join together; they thus united form a mass larger than their own separate mass. Immediately the law of universal gravitation goes into effect. The atoms nearer to this group, this first nucleus, are attracted towards it, adhere to it, and form a more considerable mass, say a molecule; at any rate, an infinitesimal sphere of attraction. Once the movement commenced, nothing will stop it. It will go on increasing, the centre of attraction growing in power by the fall of the atoms which enhance its mass; these are attracted and precipitated with force directly proportionate to the mass ever on the increase. In consequence of this number of light shocks on all the points of this sphere in the process of formation, the latter yields to a movement of rotation upon itself. It revolves on its axis, never ceasing to attract the atoms nearest to it and spread through the ether, or the atoms on its surface towards its own centre. Thus its intensity grows from the surface to the centre at the same time that its volume extends from nearer to nearer."

Adele.—"You could not describe this process of formation better than if you had been present at the scene. How old are you, Mr. George?"

Doctor.—"Go on, George, and don't mind her."

George.—"This phenomenon, ever going on and increasing in velocity during thousands of centuries, this sphere, fluid-form, will, in the end, occupy an immense volume. Then, in consequence of the centrifugal force, which tends to throw off at a distance the parts more distant from the axis of rotation, a time will come when this sphere will extend itself and grow in diameter on the plane of the great circle perpendicular to its axis, whilst diminishing in the direction of this axis. Flattened at the poles and increasing at the equator, it will pass from the spherical form to the spheroidical and elliptical form to make a distinct whole, a gaseous mass, an immense lens, the smallest diameter of which could only be measured by milliards of miles."

Adele.—"Dear me, I can hardly fancy the immense and colossal proportions of such a vast spheroid swimming and floating in ether."

George.—"It is a law well established in natural philosophy that movement, light, heat, magnetism, and electricity, are different manifestations of the same agent; movement is tranformed into heat; heat into light, etc. This is called the law of the equivalence between movement and heat. Therefore, the time will come when this gaseous sphere, heated by the ever-increasing movements of its atoms and of its molecules towards the centre, and of its mass around its axis, will become luminous. It will be at first a shadowy glimmer, vague, undecided, hardly phosphorescent, indistinct from darkness, less marked than the imperceptible glimmer of certain nights of summer known as the *zodiacal light*. But it will go on increasing. Increasing also in density, the central mass will go gradually contracting, and diminish in volume. However, the force of inertia will preserve to each of its parts, to each of its atoms, the velocity acquired in the movement of rotation; from which it follows that this velocity, being exercised incessantly in accordance with a circumference more or less restricted, the movement of rotation will go on increasing. In consequence of such increase of the rotatory movement, a movement will arise when the centripetal force, that is, the force which tends to hurry the atoms and molecules toward the centre, is overcome by the centrifugal force at the circumference of the equatorial circle. A ring is then detached from the ellipsoidal, which will find itself reduced to the spherical form. This ring, though detached from the principal mass, continues its movement, and turns around the spheroidal, which has originated it. It is not absolutely even as to its intensity and volume in all its parts; but it exhibits a little swelling on one point; a little shrinkage on another; it narrows down on its weakest point, as far as to crack, in order to concentrate on the opposite side. The ring thus becomes a crescent, whose two horns incessantly endeavor to approach the swelling, upon which, in consequence of the same effort, they impress a rotatory movement around itself. Soon, however, mixing with it, they end in rendering the primitive ring a new sphere, immense in itself, but small in relation to the original sphere, around which it moves, as well as upon its axis. Things happened on this second sphere in the same manner as in the original one, though in much less time, in consequence of the smallness of the mass and volume of the new globe. In the course of myriads of centuries the original spheroid, being concentrated and condensed more and more, throws off another ring, and then a third, and so on. Each of these rings becomes a satellite spheroid, which, being capable of throwing off rings detached at its equator, can engender other subordinate satellites. Thus has been formed the planet Neptune, with one satellite; Uranus with its four satellites; Saturn, encircled by a triple ring, concentric to the exterior orbits of its eight moons. All the planets which gravitate around the sun, like our earth, have been thus detached successively from the original spheroidal nebula set in motion by the action of God Almighty."

Doctor.—"Very good indeed, George. You have explained the hypothesis of the formation of the universe as clearly as could be done. But I want to recapitulate the whole theory, to make it easier for Adele to understand."

Adele.—"I am sure I am very much obliged."

Doctor.—"Well, George, tell us how the atoms are joined together to form the original colossal nebula."

George.—"The law of universal gravitation brings the first atoms together and forms the primary mass, which goes on increasing as other atoms are attracted, and as the mass increases."

Doctor.—"And what gives the first mass a rotatory motion, that is, a motion around itself?"

George.—"The rotatory motion is produced by all those little shocks which it receives from the atoms which are precipitated upon it on every side with a force and violence proportionate to the mass which attracts them."

Doctor.—"How is the sphere changed into a spheroid?"

George.—"The centrifugal force causes the parts more distant from the axis of rotation to push off, and a moment arrives when the sphere swells towards the equator and narrows and flattens down at the poles. This gives it a spheroidal form."

Doctor.—"How is it that it becomes luminous?"

George.—"By the law that all the forces of nature can be reduced to movement, that is, by the law of the correlation and equivalence of forces. Movement under a certain condition becomes heat; heat becomes light. A time, therefore, will arrive in the life of the nebulosa when, being heated by a movement ever increasing in rapidity, it will pass to the luminous state."

Doctor.—"What increases the velocity of the spheroid?"

George.—"The contraction which it undergoes in its mass and volume, in consequence of its becoming denser and denser. The volume, therefore, being diminished, the movement of rotation becomes more rapid."

Doctor.—"What causes a ring to be thrown off from the original mass of the spheroid?"

George.—"The increase in the velocity and rapidity of its movement by the contraction of its mass will cause, at some time or other, the centrifugal force to overcome the centripetal, and hence a ring will be detached from the original mass. This ring will undergo the same process as the original mass."

Doctor.—"You could not recapitulate more accurately the explanation of theory. I will add, to finish our conversation and to complete the theory, that thousands and millions of attractive centres have been formed under the divine impulse in the infinite cosmical depths produced by the creative word. Thousands and millions of partial nebulose have been thus developed from more than gigantic clusters of complex nebulose; and to-day, aided by the spectroscope, the telescope of astronomers discovers, in the most inaccessible depths of the infinite, nebulose of every dimension and of every form, and at any degree of development. Thus has the universe been formed and continues to be formed."

Adele.—"The whole hypothesis is a beautiful and grand idea. Would that it were confirmed by facts and observations."

George.—"It is coherent in every one of its parts, and conformable to all the laws so far discovered. At any rate, science at the present has nothing better to offer, and we must rest content."

Adele.—"And now I want to describe the whole formation of the universe in my own way, and see if I cannot do better than Mr. George."

George.—"Let us see."

Adele.—"Why, I suppose an immense quantity of tiny, small, little things called atoms, all floating in that imponderable fluid called ether. Am I right so far in assuming that such were the first elements out of which the universe was to be formed?"

George.—"Perfectly."

Adele.—"Very well. How am I to make them join together so as to exhibit one mass? Easily enough, if we call into play the law of attraction. This law causes the two first atoms which are nearest to each other to be attracted together and come closer one against the other. As the mass increases in bulk it increases its attraction, and other atoms come to join company, and so forth until an immense mass is the result."

Doctor.—"Very good, indeed."

Adele.—"Now I must set that mass in motion; must I not? No, I must first remark that all those atoms arrange themselves in a spherical or round form; that we know by experience of fluid bodies. Well, the fall of so many atoms on the original mass of two on every side give it a shock on all sides, and hence the rotatory motion of the original sphere. This motion is quickened and quickened until that immense mass not only becomes luminous, but also, in consequence of the centrifugal law, some parts more distant from the axis of the rotation are thrown off, and a new ring is formed which, on account of the law of inertia, retains its rotatory movement, and thus a new star or planet or satellite is formed, and so on without end. There! You have the whole thing in a nutshell."

SIXTH ARTICLE.

TRUE SIDE OF THE SYSTEM OF EVOLUTION.

George.—"Doctor, we talked over the hypothesis of La Place and other eminent scientists upon the formation of the universe. Now, I want to know if a Christian can, consistently with his belief, hold and maintain such an hypothesis?"

Adele.—"I was going to put the same question."

Doctor.—"To be sure he can. What should prevent a Christian from maintaining the hypothesis of La Place?"

George.—"Well, I don't exactly know. It seems to me that La Places' hypothesis implies the truth of evolution."

Adele.—"How?"

George.—"Don't you see that according to that hypothesis we start from a few atoms which float in ether, and which, by the law of attraction, come together to form a molecule, and this attracts more atoms or molecules until the whole thing starts into a rotatory movement in consequence of the shocks it receives from all points from the atoms falling on it, and by the continued motion of myriads of years; and by the ever-increasing attraction it swells into an immense nebulosa, the proportions of which defy the power of the strongest mind to imagine. Then this same immense nebulosa, being acted upon in the course of other myriads of centuries by the law of centrifugal force, throws off ring after ring to form the starry worlds whose name is legion. This is merely evolution from the minimum to the maximum."

Adele.—"I see now."

Doctor.—"Well, and what then? You imagine two things, George. First, that evolution of one kind implies the truth of the whole system of evolution. Second, you seem to believe that the Church condemns all kinds of evolution. Now, both these two mistakes require to be set right."

Adele.—"With your leave, I would like to have the terms explained to me before we go any further. Gentlemen, I have a certain kind of an idea as to evolution, but I would like to form an adequate conception of it."

Doctor.—"Well, listen to me, both. There are three systems of evolution, two of them false and one true. The first is what may be called evolution in its most comprehensive and universal sense, and may be defined as that system which holds that everything in the universe was evolved from the minimum, or the least kind of being. Suppose an atom of such insignificance as to be almost akin to nothing, and suppose, moreover, that not only all the myriads of worlds of the mineral kind were evolved out of that infinitely small atom, but also that life sprang out of it; not life limited to the vegetable kind, but also sensitive life, intellectual life of the highest and the supreme kind; this would be evolution in the first sense in its most universal acceptation. This is the system of Herbert Spencer, and in fact of all pantheists who do not differ from each other except on the nature and kind of that infinitesimal small beginning. For those who hold that beginning to be matter, like Herbert Spencer and others, are called material pantheists; those who hold it to be an idea are called idealists; those who maintain it to be an idea and something together are called by other names."

Adele.—"I understand perfectly."

Doctor.—"The second kind of evolution is that which makes all kinds of life be evolved and drawn, as it were, out of protoplasm."

Adele.—"What is a protoplasm?"

Doctor.—"Protoplasm, or, as Huxley calls it, the physical basis of life, is a certain amount of matter which science observes to be the necessary foundation of all life. As the foundation of all kinds of living things, a certain amount of oxygen, hydrogen, carbon and nitrogen is necessary. These substances, however, to constitute protoplasm and to be the foundation or basis of all life, must be combined by nature, which alone has the secret. No artificial or scientific combination or manipulation of those substances has ever been able to produce an infinitesimal amount of protoplasm. You must be satisfied for the present with this amount of information, as we shall return to the subject. Now, evolution, in a more restricted sense, is that system which teaches that all kinds of life, vegetable, sensitive, or animal, even intellectual life, orginates in and is developed out of protoplasm. This is the system of evolution more generally embraced. The third and true system of evolution is that which admits distinct species in creation—or distinct kingdoms, as some would call them—the mineral, the vegetable, the sensitive and the intellectual. In consequence of this doctrine it allows any amount of evolution and development within the species, but denies that the evolution or development may arrive to that point that one species may develop into another. Thus, for instance, it willingly grants that the first mineral substances created by the Almighty, acting under the influence and the pressure of the laws established by Him, can develop into the magnificent worlds which are rolling in space; but denies that those same mineral substances can develop themselves so far or combine in such a way, by their own unaided efforts, and under the same physical laws, as to spring into life and be transformed into the vegetable world. This kind of evolution within the species is taught by all Christian philosophers and theologians, and by true scientists, and it is that which is demanded by the law which God follows in the creation and government of the world, and which is called the law of wisdom."

George.—"Will you please to explain this law, Doctor?"

Doctor.—"The law of wisdom is simply the law of reason and common sense, and that is that an intelligent being should not act except for a reason which accounts for his act; if one acts without a reason, or a reason not sufficient to account for his act, he is said, by the common consent of mankind, to have acted foolishly and not as an intelligent being."

Adele.—"But don't we perform many actions without any reason at all?"

Doctor.—"Oftentimes we have the reason for what we do, only we are not conscious of it. But suppose we do something without a reason, then we don't act as reasonable or intelligent beings. This can happen as to man, who is an animal besides being reasonable, but can never happen as to God."

Adele.—"Why?"

Doctor.—"Because God is intelligence and reason itself. If He could act unreasonably He would act against his nature, which is impossible."

George.—"I see."

Doctor.—"Now, this law of doing a thing always for a sufficient reason, when applied to finding a proportion between an end and the means which must obtain that end, is expressed by saying that the law of wisdom is to follow the minimum means to an end. For instance, you want to go to a certain place. You must take the shortest road, which is the straight one, otherwise any amount of walking other than is claimed by the straight road is superfluous, over and above, without a reason, and foolish.'"

Adele.—"I don't see how all this applies to evolution."

Doctor.—"Listen. God has created the first substances, which are also forces. It behooves His wisdom to let those forces be exercised and developed into anything of which they are capable by their nature and by the physical laws which govern them. If by allowing those forces full play they can develop themselves into the immense worlds we so much admire, they should be allowed to do so, and it would be wasting energy and power to aid them in what they can do by themselves; it would be contrary to wisdom to do what they can do unaided. God's wisdom, therefore, obliges Him, so to speak, not to interfere in the development of the natural forces, except only when an end is to be obtained which they could not themselves bring about."

Adele.—"I understand now. If all the primitive matter under the laws of gravitation, of inertia, of centripetal and centrifugal forces could be evolved into the myriads and tens of myriads of stars which stud the heavenly space, they must be allowed to do so; to add strength, or energy, or power to them, would not make those stars more vast nor more beautiful; it would be a waste of energy, a foolish throwing away of power."

Doctor.—"This is true evolution. But suppose that we want life to appear in those grand worlds, and suppose, for the present, that no amount of self-development of the mineral kingdom could produce life, then what is to be done?"

George.—"I suppose it requires an act of the Creator, an intervention of the first cause, to supply what is lacking in the mineral substances in order that they may spring into life."

Doctor.—"It is so; if no amount of unfolding of the mineral kingdom can, on the supposition, spring into life, then if life be wanted an act of the Creator must, by its fiat, evoke life out of the mineral kingdom, supplying whatever mysterious agency is required to exhibit and represent the phenomena of life."

George.—"Then, if I understand aright, Catholic theology not only admits evolution within the species, but absolutely requires it, on the ground that the wisdom of God, which creates and governs the universe, is bound to follow the essential law of its nature; law which is expressed in different ways, as, for instance, that one should act for a sufficient reason; that one should use the minimum means to an end; that in the use of force no amount of it should be allowed to go to waste, and so forth. This law, so variously expressed, applied to the present subject, clearly indicates that if God had created substances which were at the same same time able to act, and subjected these forces to certain laws, after having given them the first impetus to action, it behooved His wisdom to let those forces have full play and development, and let them be evolved into whatever they could produce; God's action and influence upon them being limited only to whatever is necessary to be supplied by the first cause to enable secondary causes to act."

Adele.—"I don't understand the last clause of your speech, Mr. George."

Doctor.—"I will explain it to you, Adele. A creature is, by its own nature of creature, a finite being, indifferent to be or not to be, because if it were not so it would be necessary; its existence would be required absolutely by its own essence and nature; in one word, it would no longer be a creature, but God. Now, if a finite being is indifferent to be and not to be, even after being created, it does not by that fact change its nature; it remains naturally indifferent to be or not to be; again, it must be also indifferent to act or not to act, because, if it were not so, it would be already in act, and always in act, and never with the possibility to act; in other words, it would be God again. Three moments of God's actions are required, in order that the creature may act: 1st, that moment which creates the substance; 2nd, that moment which continues to keep it in existence; 3d, that moment which brings the creature from the possibility to the very fact of acting. This is absolutely necessary for any creature to act. This God must always supply. After supposing that, we by all means must admit that God let each species develop itself as much as possible, and this is called evolution within the species. And we will, if you please, stop here for the present."

Adele.—"But shall we not discuss the other two kinds of evolution?"

Doctor.—"Yes, in its own proper time. The subject which will claim our immediate attention is the history of the formation of the planet in which we have the honor to be located."

SEVENTH ARTICLE.
HISTORY OF THE FORMATION OF THE EARTH.

Adele.—"Doctor, our next subject, if I remember rightly, was to be the history of the formation of the earth. How am I to understand that?"

Doctor.—"Very easily; we said that our earth was a ring detached from the original mass of matter, or the nebulosa in which all the stars and planets have originated. Very well; we want to follow up the process which the earth had to undergo from the moment its original matter was thrown off from the nebulosa, up to the time when it took a proper solid form, and was ready for life."

Adele.—"In other words, I suppose you would call its being detached from the original mass the birth of the earth, and then the process it had to undergo you would style its infancy, its youth and its manhood, so to speak."

Doctor.—"Precisely. Now, George, I understand you are well up in astronomy and geology. Please let us have the history of the formation of the earth."

Adele.—"Wait one second. I decline—respectfully, of course—to hear anything on the subject unless I am promised that I shall hear no strange, uncouth names, such as I was obliged to listen to when I was in the seminary. Why, my head aches at the very thought of that ordeal."

George.—"Never fear, Miss Adele, I will put everything, as far as I can, in honest, straightforward, genuine Christian language. Will that do?"

Adele.—"Provided you keep your word."

Doctor.—"You will understand better, Adele, if George will allow me to put him question after question."

George.—"Certainly."

Doctor.—"Well, in what state was the earth the moment it was detached from the original mass of matter?"

George.—"It was in a luminous and incandescent state, like the mass from which it was detached."

Doctor.—"What happened to it next?"

George.—"In the course of centuries the cold of the spaces between the stars affected the incandescent mass of the earth, and reduced it from the state of gas to the liquid state."

Adele.—"What do you mean by the cold of the spaces between the stars?"

George.—"Did we not in one of our conversations say that what we call space is formed by *ether* which God created at first, and with which He filled, so to speak, the immense void? Well, we will suppose the original mass of substances which formed the nebulosa to have occupied part of that space. Ring after ring is thrown off from that original mass, each one of which takes its place at a distance from the nebulosa and from the other rings. It is evident that there are empty spaces between the original mass and the rings, and between one ring and the others. These spaces are called intermediary spaces, or spaces between the stars or rings. Now these spaces, being void of all heat, necessarily transmit their cold to the rings which they surround, and, gradually affect them. Thus it happened to the earth, and from its heated and incandescent state of gas it was turned into an incandescent and liquid mass of fire."

Doctor.—"What was the next step in the formation of our planet?"

George.—"The whole mass, having become liquid through the gradual cooling of its molecules, would be changed into a sea of lava whirling around in space; but this state was one of transition. After an indefinite number of centuries the loss of heat was sufficient to cause a formation of a light covering, or scoria, like a thin sheet of ice over the surface of the fiery sea. This first scoria was succeeded by a second, and then by others; next they would unite into continents floating on the surface of the lava, and finally would cover the whole circumference of the planet with a continuous layer. A thin but solid crust would then have held and imprisoned within it—an immense burning sea."

Doctor.—"Did that crust remain unbroken?"

George.—"It was frequently broken through by the lava boiling beneath it, and then was again united, the cooling process also tending to slowly thicken it. Finally, after millions of centuries, it became so firm that the eruptions of the liquid mass within ceased to be a general phenomenon, only taking place occasionally and where the crust was thinnest. The surrounding atmosphere, impregnated with vapors and various substances maintained by the extreme heat in a gaseous state, would gradually get rid of its burden; all kinds of matter, one after another, would become detached from the burning aerial mass, and precipitate themselves on the solid crust of the planet. When the temperature was lowered sufficiently to enable it to pass from the gaseous to a liquid state, metals and other substances would fall down in a fiery rain on the terrestrial lava."

Doctor.—"What would be likely to happen next?"

George.—"Next, the steam confined entirely to higher regions of the gaseous mass would be condensed into an immense layer of cloud, incessantly furrowed by lightning; drops of water, the commencement of the atmosphere ocean, would begin to fall down toward the ground, but only to become vapor on their way and again ascend; finally, these little drops reached the surface of the terrestrial scoria, the temperature of the water much exceeding 100°, owing to the enormous pressure exercised by the heavy air of those ages, and the first pool, the rudiment of a great sea, was collected in some fissure of the lava. This pool was constantly increased by fresh falls of water, and ultimately surrounded nearly the whole of the terrestrial crust with a liquid covering; but at the same time it brought with it fresh elements of future continents. The numerous substances which the water held in solution formed various combinations with the metals and soils of its bed; the currents and tempests which agitated it destroyed its shores only to form new ones; the sediment deposited at the bottom of the water commenced the series of rocks and strata which follow one another above the primitive crust."

Doctor.—"Thus—to capitulate all that George has said—you see before you, Adele, a vast sphere of water, an ocean without shore, resting on a basis of granite gneiss, etc.; a basis hardly consolidated and quivering under the ignited liquid which rages in its bosom; above this boundless ocean an immense atmosphere very thick and opaque, according to all probability the theatre of continual phenomena of magnetism, electricity and meteoric light. Such is the state of the earth at the period at which we have arrived."

Adele.—"Now, gentlemen, will you please to tell me, are all these things you have narrated quite certain and demonstrated, or have you imagined them?"

George.—"We have proceeded, Miss Adele, on the nebular hypothesis of La Place, which of course is only an hypothesis. As we cannot have certainty and scientific demonstration, we must take that supposition which best explains the formation of the universe. Upon that hypothesis, then, we have considered the earth as a ring thrown off from that immense burning mass of gases. Now, considering that ring, the nucleus of our earth, to be in that state, and supposing it to be subject to well-known physical and chemical laws, we have come to the conclusion that such must have been the process undergone by the earth to reach the period of consolidation."

Doctor.—"George, what do geologists call this period in the life of our planet?"

George.—"They call it primitive epoch, or azoic age."

Adele.—"Look out, my friend, you begin to forget your promise."

George.—"I will explain in a moment. Geologists call this period so because the soil which constitutes it forms the basis of all the mineral strata of the globe. In fact, wherever it has been possible to excavate deep enough, micaschist has always been found to rest upon granite. Granite is therefore the general material of the earth. This epoch is called azoic—that is, lifeless—in consequence of the absolute absence of all vestige of either animal or vegetable life. This absence of life is the characteristic trait of this epoch; so you see, Miss Adele, I have not broken any promise to use no harder words than is absolutely necessary to explain the results of science."

Doctor.—"What is the epoch next to the azoic called?"

George.—"Transition epoch. It is so called because it serves, as it were, as some sort of passage between the total absence of life to the first manifestations of vitality. The carboniferous period is generally referred to this epoch of transition."

Doctor.—"Now, George, we must pause here, because before we give heed to the appearance of life upon the globe we must face the momentous problem and the great question whether life can spring up or be evolved from matter or the mineral world without any particular intervention of the Creator. For the present, to impress upon Adele's memory all we have said with regard to the formation of the universe of our own globe, we will recapitulate all in a few questions."

Adele.—"I will put questions and George will answer me."

George.—"Be it so."

Adele.—"What was the first thing God created?"

George.—"Ether, an imponderable substance, which constitutes the boundless spaces. Also all the other ponderable substances which were to form the universe and which may be classed under the comprehensive word of matter."

Adele.—"In what state were all these substances?"

George.—"Both imponderable and ponderable substances were in a state of confusion and chaos. Darkness as black as death reigned over this mixture."

Adele.—"Did they remain in that state?"

George.—"No. Under the impulse and movement of the Creator the ponderable substances were disengaged from the imponderable. Centres of attraction and impulsion were formed at innumerable points of space. They were the germ and the beginning of the cosmic nebulose."

Adele.—"Did the darkness continue?"

George.—"No. From the concentration and rotatory movement of the nebulose heat was produced; and in the course of time the increasing elevation in the temperature produced light, and the nebulose cast the first glimmering of phosphorescent and indistinct light."

Doctor.—"Wait, George, I want you to remark that there is nothing on earth to prevent us to understand the first verses of Genesis in accordance with the scientific theory we have been explaining. 'In the beginning,' says Moses, 'God created heaven and earth,' that is, the imponderable and ponderable substances out of which the universe was to be formed. 'And the earth (the sacred writer expresses a part for the whole) was void and empty (all the imponderable and ponderable substances are mixed up), and darkness was over the face of the deep.' We have said that all matter was in absolute darkness. 'And the Spirit of God moved over the waters.' God giving movement to matter from which the centres arise which are the germ of the nebulosæ. 'And God said, let light be made, and light was made.' Movement produces heat, heat develops the phenomenon of light in the nebulosæ. Hence Science is no way in conflict with Revelation, or *vice versa*. And remark well, both of you, that in those three verses no time is specified wherein the creation of matter and the formation of the universe, till the appearance of light, took place. Scientists may take as many millions of years as they list without revelation begrudging them one single instant.'

Adele.—"What happened next to the nebulosæ?"

George.—"They are gradually condensed. They break up and give origin to stars, which finally become incandescent and dazzling, and perfectly distinct from the surrounding darkness, that is, the space which does not receive their light. Our own earth counts as one of those suns."

Doctor.—"'God,' says Genesis, 'divided light from darkness. And He called the light Day, and the darkness Night, and there was evening and morning one day.' We are not obliged by our religion to understand that word day in any other sense than that of an indefinite period of time, as long, or as short, as science may require."

Adele.—"What happens next?"

George.—"From the gaseous state our earth passes to the state of incandescent liquid; then its surface tends to become solid by cooling. Around this crust which is being formed there gathers an immense and dark atmosphere, saturated with rocky, metallic and watery vapors. These vapors progressively and gradually cool and precipitate themselves on the crust of the earth. Their aquatic vapors solved into water. Hence the purification of the atmosphere, which then becomes distinct from the terrestrial spheroid, properly so called, though as yet charged with thick clouds."

Doctor.—"This formed the second day or period spoken of in Genesis: 'And God said, let there be a firmament (an expansion, a spreading) amidst the waters, and let it divide waters from waters.' (The atmosphere thick with vapors we have spoken of.) 'And God made a firmament and divided the waters which were under the firmament from those that were above the firmament.' And God called the firmament Heaven, the atmosphere distinct from the Earth and purified."

Adele.—"What followed after this?"

George.—"The crust of the earth became solid all over, covered with the waters which had fallen. Appearance of the first islands produced by the upheaval of the central fire."

Doctor.—"This was part of the third day. 'And God said, let the waters that are under the Heaven be gathered together into one place and let the dry land appear, and it was so done. And God called the dry land Earth, and the gathering together of the waters he called Seas.' But as on this day also Life is evoked by the almighty voice of the Creator, we must transfer the consideration of the problems it raises to other entertainments."

EIGHTH ARTICLE.

SPONTANEOUS GENERATION OR EVOLUTION IN ITS GENERAL SENSE.

Doctor.—"Now we can approach the great problem of life before we go another step in our scientific and religious chit-chats."

George.—"I never took hold of any subject before with as much interest as I will this, and expect to be enlightened by your great knowledge and experience."

Adele.—"And I will listen with all the attention I am capable of."

Doctor.—"In the first place, we will try to understand what is life, and then inquire whether life can spring up, or be evolved from the mineral world only, without any special interference of the Creator. Now, George, please to tell me, for I know you are acquainted with all scientific theories, what are the essential conditions and properties which science attributes to life? You see I want to give you an idea of life from scientific observations and general scientific results, and not from mere philosophical reasoning. The latter will come in if science does not reason properly from the facts which observation presents. In the first place, tell me what is the physical basis of life?"

George.—"It is what is called protoplasm."

Doctor.—"What is protoplasm, according to its chemical composition?"

George.—"I will give it in the words of Professor T. H. Huxley: 'A solution of smelling salts in water, with an infinitesimal proportion of some other saline matters, contains all the elementary bodies which enter into the composition of protoplasm.' (Lecture on the Physical Basis of Life. Page 21. New Haven: Charles C. Chatfield & Co.) This as to the protoplasm of animals. As to the protoplasm of plants I will quote Huxley again, No. 23 : 'Carbon, hydrogen, oxygen and nitrogen are all lifeless bodies. Of these, carbon and oxygen unite in certain proportions and under certain conditions to give rise to carbonic acid. Hydrogen and oxygen produce water; nitrogen and hydrogen give rise to ammonia. These new compounds, like the elementary bodies of which they are composed, are lifeless. But when they are brought together under certain conditions they give rise to the still more complex body, protoplasm, and this protoplasm exhibits the phenomena of life.' Carbonic acid, therefore, water and ammonia, brought together under certain conditions, constitute the physical basis of the life of the plant or its protoplasm."

Doctor.—"Pray, George, can an animal make protoplasm ?"

George.—"I will answer with Huxley. An animal cannot make protoplasm, but must take it ready made from some other animal or some plant, the animal's highest feat of constructive chemistry being to convert dead protoplasm into that living matter of life which is appropriate to itself. Therefore, in seeking for the origin of protoplasm we must eventually turn to the vegetable world. p. 22 "

Doctor.—' George, can the vegetable world make protoplasm ?"

George.—"No; 'the plant can raise the complex substances, carbonic acid, water and ammonia, to the same stage of living protoplasm, if not to the same level.' But it can do no more. 'A plant supplied with pure carbon, hydrogen, oxygen and nitrogen, phosphorus, sulphur, and the like, would as infallibly die as the animal in his bath of smelling salts, though it would be surrounded by all the constituents of protoplasm.' Page 22."

Doctor.—"Then we may conclude with Huxley: 'All the forms of protoplasm which have yet been examined contain the four elements, carbon, hydrogen, oxygen and nitrogen in *very complex union*. To this complex union, the nature of which has never been determined with exactness, the name of protein has been applied.' Adele, please to fix the signification of *protein* strongly on your memory, because it will play a great part in our discussion."

Adele.—"I will. I must remember 'that peculiar chemical composition consisting of at least four elementary bodies, viz.: carbon, hydrogen, oxygen and nitrogen, united into the ill-defined compound known as *protein*, and associated with much water, if not always with sulphur, and phosphorus in minute proportions.'" (Huxley, *Encyclopædia Britannica*. Art., Evolution. American edition; vol. 8, page 654).

Doctor.—"Then mark well, both of you, that according to the well admitted facts and observations of science, life is impossible without *protein*. George, do you know of any one denying this fact ?"

George.—"None of the modern scientists that I am aware of has ever denied this absolute physical necessity of protein to obtain life."

Adele.—"Then I am to understand that protein is admitted by all modern scientists to be absolutely necessary as the first germ of life."

Doctor.—"Certainly; now let us go on and investigate the process of life. Describe this process, George."

George.—"Well, then, the germ, as Huxley describes in the article you have quoted of *Encyclopædia Britannica*, passes step by step from an extreme simplicity, or relative homogeneity, of visible structure, to a greater or less degree of complexity or heterogeneity, and the course of progressive differentiation is usually accompanied by growth."

Adele.—"Can you not speak more intelligibly, and without using such big words?"

George.—"I have been quoting Huxley; and, after all, his language is not so very hard. He means that the germ passes from an extreme simplicity of structure to a more complicated one, and consequently from being of a certain size it gradually assumes larger dimensions."

Doctor—"Tell us, George, how is this growth effected."

George.—"By into susception, as Huxley calls it."

Adele.—"What does that mean?"

George.—"*Taking in* other substances. And it is to be remarked that 'the substance by the addition of which the germ is enlarged is in no case simply absorbed, ready made, from the not living world, and packed between the elementary constituents of the germ. The new element is in great measure not only absorbed but assimilated, so that it becomes part and parcel of the molecular structure of the living body, into which it enters."

Doctor.—"George, explain more clearly how the germ passes from a great simplicity of structure to a more complex one."

George.—"In all animals and plants above the lowest the germ is an enucleated cell, using that term in its broadest sense, and the first step in the process of evolution is the division of this cell into two or more portions. The process of division is repeated until the organism, from being unicellular, becomes multicellular. The single cell becomes a cell-aggregate, and it is to the growth and metamorphosis of the cells of the cell aggregate thus produced, that all the organs and tissues owe their origin." Page 654.

Adele.—"Well, as I understand the whole matter, we know by experience and by the results of observation what is the phenomenon of life. First, my friend protein, or protoplasm, is necessary. Without him nothing can be done to start life. Next, he begins to move and to grow, and this he cannot do by himself alone, but must take in nutriment and food from without. This he uses not simply as an addition to him, like putting on a suit of clothes, but he appropriates it to himself, makes it its own flesh and blood as it were, and thus from being unicellular he becomes multicellular, a thing made up of tissues or organs, and so forth. Am I right?"

Doctor.—"Let you alone for recapitulating. Now, 'in the investigation of the phenomenon of life, the first question which arises is whether we have any knowledge, and if so, what knowledge of the origin of living matter.' George, what answer does science give to that?"

George.—"I will answer with Huxley in his article in the *Encyclopædia Britannica*, entitled Biology, Vol. 3, page 595. 'In the case of all conspicuous and easily-studied organisms, it has been obvious, since the study of nature began, that living beings arise by generation from living beings of a like kind; but before the latter part of the seventeenth century, learned and unlearned alike shared the conviction that this rule was not of universal application, and that multitudes of the smaller and more obscure organisms were produced by the fermentation of not living and especially of putrefied dead matter by what was then termed *generatio equivoca vel spontanea*, and is now called abiogenesis, that is, equivocal *vel* spontaneous generation.'"

Adele.—"Hold! What is meant by that other queer word which they use now—abiogenesis, I believe you called it?"

George.—"It is simple enough. Genesis means generation, and *abio* from not living—generation from non living matter."

Doctor.—"Well, according to all observations and experiments of science, what are we to think; can living matter spring up from non-living matter?"

George.—"I will give the words of Huxley in the same article: 'The fact is that at the present moment there is not *a shadow* of trustworthy direct evidence that abiogenesis does take place, or has taken place within the period during which the existence of life on the globe is recorded.' Page 596. And in the article on Evolution, vol. 8, page 653, the same scientist says: 'In the immense majority of both plants and animals it is certain that the germ is not merely a body in which life is dormant or potential, but that it is in itself simply a detached portion of the substance of a preëxisting living body; and the evidence has yet to be adduced which will satisfy any cautious reasoner that *omne vivum ex vivo* (every living being from a living being) is not as well established a law of the existing course of nature as *omne vivum ex ovo* (every living thing from the egg). Professor John Tyndall, in two articles published in the *Monthly Science*, vol. 12, gives the whole history of the experiments directed to find out whether abiogenesis can be proved by facts or not, and he concludes, page 482: 'These and other experiments, carried out with a severity perfectly obvious to the interested scientific reader, and accompanied by a logic equally severe, restored the conviction that even in these lower reaches (air dust particles of being), life does not appear without the operation of antecedent life.'"

Adele.—"Just wait an instant, Mr. George. I heard once somebody talking about something or other which Professor Huxley had discovered, and which was going to settle the whole difficulty about this matter, some kind of link, a go-between inorganic matter and life. What is it they called it? I believe it was something like basilius, or babitius, or ambitious."

Doctor.—"Stop, Adele, you mean bathybius."

Adele.—"Yes, to be sure, what about bathybius? Was it not something between life and not life—something that might serve as an explanation how life can come from non-living matter?"

George.—"Well, this thing which was discovered by Professor Huxley, and which was christened by him under that name, was supposed to be a mineral substance which could spring up into life, the missing link between the mineral and the vegetable world. Now, Huxley himself owns that the whole thing is a fraud and a deceit. I quote from an address of the professor, reported in the *Popular Science Monthly*, vol. 15, page 862: 'I thought my young friend Bathybius would turn out a credit to me. But, I am sorry to say, as time has gone on he has not altogether verified the promise of his youth. In the first place, as the president (of the society he was addressing) told you, he could not be found when he was wanted; and in the second place, when he was found all sorts of things were said about him. Indeed, I regret to be obliged to tell you that some persons of severe minds went so far as to say that he was nothing but simply a *gelatinous precipitate of slime*, which had carried down organic matter. If that is so, I am very sorry for it; for whoever else may have joined in this error, I am, undoubtedly, primarily responsible for it.' So you see that Professor Huxley, the discoverer of this grand link, fairly and honestly gives it up, and abandons all kind of paternity and responsibility of the poor waif so hastily christened and held up as the grand proof of life springing from matter."

Doctor.—"Well, now, let us draw our conclusions from our conversation; it is evident that, according to the most accurate and severe observations and tests of science, abiogenesis is impossible, or, in other words, that life cannot spring up spontaneously from the mineral or inorganic world. The conclusion of all this is that evolution in its general sense is proved by science to be impossible. For evolution in that sense assumes life to have sprung up from non-living matter. Now, every experience and every observation of the best scientists, Pasteur, Tyndall, Huxley, and a host of others, has put in the best and clearest light the impossibility of such a thing. Therefore, evolution in its general sense is out of the question. But it is comical in the highest degree to observe how this fact embarrasses those evolutionists who have sense and honesty enough to admit the fact of the utter failure of any experiment directed to prove spontaneous generation. They are between two fires; on one hand, they admit that no experiment has proved abiogenesis to have taken place in a single case; on the other hand, they hang on evolution as a mother on a pet child, and they cannot, for the life of them, see how to get out of the difficulty."

George.—"Huxley gets out of it in a very singular way."

Adele—"Let us have it."

George.—"I quote his words from the article on Biology we have so often mentioned (page 596): 'If the hypothesis of evolution is true, living matter must have arisen from non-living matter; for, by the hypothesis, the condition of the globe was at one time such that living matter could not have existed in it, life being entirely incompatible with the gaeous state.'"

Adele.—"Dear me! what a comical way of getting out of a scrape! You men are the worst hands at helping yourselves when you are driven in a corner; why, a woman would have invented a hundred ways much better than the pitiful get off of Mr. Huxley. He says: 'If evolution is true, life must have sprung from no living matter.' Suppose I turn the tables against him, and say: Every experiment has demonstrated that it is impossible to eke life out of non-living matter; therefore the hypothesis of evolution which demands such impossibility cannot be true."

Doctor.—"You would argue very correctly, my dear. The very fact that every possible experiment has rejected the hypothesis of any living matter springing from non-living matter ought to make them guarded, and make them modify the hypothesis of evolution, and restrict it within certain limits. Instead of that they start by supposing evolution to have been proven and demonstrated, and from that supposed proof they deduct that life *must* have sprung from non-living matter, in spite of the fact that science has demonstrated the impossibility of such a thing. 'The fact is,' we may repeat Huxley's words, 'that at the present moment there is not a shadow of trustworthy, direct evidence that abiogenesis does take place, or has taken place, within the period during which the existence of life on the globe is recorded,' page 596."

Adele.—"But to really and honestly get out of the difficulty, could they not adhere to the Christian doctrine, and say that when the earth or any other planets or stars which may contain life were ready to admit of and to sustain life, the Almighty caused life to spring forth; in this way they could reconcile both the hypothesis of evolution, in a sense restricted within each species or natural kingdom, and also the fact demonstrated by science that life cannot come from inorganic matter."

Doctor.—"That is the only way to get out of the difficulty—science demands a Creator who with His fiat may evoke life out of inanimate matter. No other supposition is admissible. But some of these gentlemen are determined to have no interference on the part of God; they want to do without Him, and therefore they make all possible effort to prove, what cannot be proved, that life can spring up naturally and spontaneously from inorganic matter. Professor Haeckel admits it in so many words, with which we will close our conversation: 'Not wishing,' he says, 'to have recourse to miracles and mysteries, in order to account for the apparition upon earth of the first organized beings *we are forced* to fall back upon the generating virtue of matter itself.' Haeckel's 'History of the Creation.' Now, for miracles and mysteries, read *God Almighty*, and we find that these gentlemen are forced to have recourse to a wholly imaginary, gratuitous power of matter to engender life—a power which observation has not justified in the remotest possible way, just because they will have none of God and His creative power. There is frankness for you with a vengeance! And the wonder is that people listen to such barefaced, impertinent, absurd infidelity."

NINTH ARTICLE.

EVOLUTION IN ITS GENERAL SENSE—VERDICT OF REASON.

Adele.—"Look here, gentlemen, in our last conversation we ascertained from the results of science that abiogenesis, or spontaneous generation, is not possible, and we inferred from that fact that evolution, understood in a general sense—that is, evolution which makes the whole universe, with all the different species we find in it, to spring from non-living matter, is scientifically untenable. Now, I would like to put a question: Has reason nothing to say in this matter? Has logic and common sense no opinion to give on such hypothesis?"

Doctor.—"Certainly it has; but I wanted first to argue the question from the standpoint of science and observation, and afterwards take up the subject, and let reason pass its verdict upon it. If we had done otherwise they would say, as they are continually saying, right or wrong, that we argue the question *à priori* from preconceived notions of our own, which have no foundation in real nature, and then build upon such flimsy notions a whole structure of reasoning as shaky and tottering as the foundation on which it rises. But as we can now reason upon facts fully admitted and demonstrated by every scientist of note, our structure will have a solid foundation. From the idea of *life* then, as exhibited by science, I want to demonstrate that evolution in its general sense is an utter impossibility and absurdity. I may define life to be a spontaneous, uninterrupted movement. Mark the definition: first of all, life is a movement to mark the first difference which flashes before our eyes between living beings and inorganic beings. Secondly, we have called it a spontaneous, or internal movement, to mark the second difference existing between living and nonliving beings. The inorganic world is subject to movement; if I loosen the hold I have of a book it will fall to the ground; the earth moves, the air stirs, the wind blows, the light and sound travel, the locomotive dashes on. In fact, all the different forces of nature can be reduced to one single force, and that is movement. But, mark well, when the inorganic body moves the impulsion comes to it from without, and never from within. It is the necessary consequence of the law of inertia to which the mineral world is essentially subject; of itself and of its own nature, as it is admitted by all natural philosophers, it is indifferent to movement or to quiet; hence, once started upon moving, it would move forever, if it did not encounter on its way obstacles which counteract and exhaust the impulsion. And what would stop it if no external obstacle were supposed? Certainly no internal reason emanating from its essence, which is absolutely indifferent to quiet or to movement. Therefore if inorganic bodies move, their movement comes to them from an external agent, and never from any internal principle of action; it comes from without, and never from within; hence we have defined life to be a spontaneous, or internal movement."

Adele.—"But what do you mean by the word uninterrupted?"

Docto..—"I don't take that word uninterrupted as if organic beings were not subject to dissolution or death. For we know that all organized beings in this world are born, grow, and die. At least, we may take this much for granted at present, without entering now into the question whether any living being really perish forever. By that word uninterrupted, therefore, I want to express the idea that between the commencement of life in all organic beings, and its dissolution by death, that spontaneous internal movement is never broken, but goes on affecting and modifying the being without ever ceasing. Therefore we may define life in the abstract to be spontaneous, uninterrupted movement."

Adele.—"But is this definition a product of your imagination, a figment of your fancy, an abstruse ideal notion which has no foundation in fact and in reality?"

Doctor.—"Not at all. I have drawn it from the most universally admitted facts of observation and of experimental science. I have built it upon the generally acknowledged essential difference between living beings and non-living matter. This latter does not move; when it does move, the impulsion to movement comes to it from without, never from within; whilst moving it is not interiorly affected by the movement or by any obstacle to its continuation which it may find in the way—no alteration having taken place in it either when impelled to move or when forced to stop; whereas, in a living being the movement is from within, and the internal movement affects and transforms the being, and this movement is never interrupted until death comes to the organism either from internal causes or from violent causes from without."

George.—"Why, Professor Huxley gives the distinctive marks of living beings from non-living in the same manner as you have given them, and the definition of life almost in the same words. I will quote the passage: 'Consider how differently this living particle (*Englena*, a living germ) is from the dead atoms with which the physicist and chemist have to do. The particle of gold falls to the bottom and rests —the particle of dead *protein* decomposes and disappears—it also rests; but the living protein mass neither tends to exhaustion of its forces nor to any permanency of form, but is essentially distinguished as a disturber of equilibrium, so far as force is concerned, as undergoing continual metamorphosis and change in point of form. Tendency to equilibrium of force and to permanency of form are the characters of that portion of the universe which does not live in the domain of the chemist and physicist. Tendency to distinct existing equilibrium to take on forms which succeed one another in definite cycles is the character of the living world. What is the cause of this wonderful difference between the dead particle and the living particle of matter, appearing in other respects identical—that difference to which we give the name of life? I for one cannot tell you. It may be that, by and by, philosophers will discover some higher laws of which the parts of life are particular cases—very possibly they will find out some bond between physico-chemical phenomena on the one hand and vital phenomena on the other. At present, however, we assuredly know of none; and I think we shall exercise a wise humility in confessing that for us at least this successive assumption of different states (external conditions remaining the same), this *spontaneity of action*—if I may use a term which implies more than I would be answerable for —which constitutes so vast and plain a practical distinction between living bodies and those which do not live, is an ultimate fact, indicating as such the existence of broad line of demarcation between the subject matter of biological and that of all other sciences.' Huxley's Lay Sermons. Appleton & Co., 1876. Page 76."

Doctor.—"Nothing could be said better, or in more choice words. We will adopt, then, the definition of life given by Huxley, which consists in *spontaneity of action*. Now, George, please to give me the idea of the principal stages, or, we might call them, functions of life."

George.—"I will reply with the same scientist: 'Whatever forms the living being may take on, whether simple or complex, *production, growth* and *reproduction are* the phenomena which distinguish it from that which does not live.'"

Adele.—"So that the principal functions or stages of life are three: the first is production. What is meant by that, uncle?"

Doctor.—"Why, is meant that first function by which the living germ or *protein* is developed into an individual being of its kind. For instance, we will take the germ of an oak; when its protein has been evolved into a tree called oak, no matter how small it may as yet appear, the first function of life has been exercised and an oak has been produced. The oak goes on increasing until it reaches the full perfection which oaks generally attain, and we have the second function of life, *growth*. Finally, something is separated from the oak, an acorn which contains the protein of a new oak; the third condition or function, life, is verified *reproduction* or *generation*. Now, Adele, please to tell me, for we have alluded to this before, are these three principal functions of life possible simply from the fact that the living germ is possessed of spontaneity of action?"

Adele.—"Certainly not. It must draw from without whatever it needs for its production, growth, and reproduction; and this it does, not by simply adding external objects to itself, as one would put on a covering, or as molecules of the mineral kind are added to other minerals, but changing the forms of these objects, appropriating them to itself, and transform them into itself."

Doctor.—"We may conclude, then, by saying life, to be that spontaneity of action in a germ by which it becomes an individual of its kind, grows to a certain definite growth, and reproduces itself. Now, what we want to know is if that spontaneity of action can originate in dead matter—or, in other words, if a piece of dead matter, immovable, inert, can of itself, and without supposing any other element in it than is to be found in an individual being of the mineral kingdom, spring into action? Is this consistent with reason? Is it possible?"

Adele.—"I think not."

Doctor.—"And why?"

George.—"I am anxious to see how ladies can philosophize. Please tell us why?"

Adele.—"Why, the thing appears to me very simple. You want life—that is, spontaneous action—to spring up from dead matter, and from dead matter alone; that is, without the interference of any one, or without supposing any other element in matter, except what is found in a mineral pure and simple. That is the supposition, is it not? Well, I say the thing is impossible, because no being can give or exhibit what it has not got; matter is dead, immovable weight; therefore it cannot give or exhibit movement or action. If action could be supposed to spring from dead, inert matter, it could only be because we could imagine matter, though immovable and inert, to be endowed with a power, a potentiality to action. But even in such supposition the thing is impossible, because matter could by no manner of means actualize that power by itself dormant and latent in itself. How could it issue from the dormant state into that of movement and action? By the interference of a strange agent? No. By itself? But don't you see that to do that it would be already in movement and action? Therefore, it is evident that matter could never of itself pass from the state of potentials into that of movement; and if life is spontaneous act or movement, no dead matter can ever of itself spring into or exhibit life."

George.—"I did not think you could reason so closely and so stringently, Miss Adele."

Adele.—"The point is, am I right?"

Doctor.—"You are perfectly right, and there is no escaping the force of your argument. Life is internal action or movement, which effects certain definite results, as for instance the production of an incipient individual of a certain species, the growth of that individual up to a defined stage, and the power of reproduction. On the other hand, before the appearance of life, the earth presented nothing but dead, immovable, inert matter. Now, the question is, how did life—that is internal spontaneous action and movement—appear? How did that dead, inert, inanimate matter become alive and glowing with action and movement? How was matter, till then absolutely devoid of action and movement, and consisting merely of an aggregate of atoms and molecules holding together in juxtaposition to each other simply by the law of attraction and cohesion, which does not at all exist or originate in the molecules themselves, but acts from without—how did it come all at once to be invested by a principle which takes hold of those molecules, dissolves them, as it were, and, grasping and appropriating from the surrounding earth and air whatever it stands in need of for its special purpose, initiates a cell, and from that nucleus cell start other cells until it forms a regular organism of a special kind, and then, continuing the appropriation and assimilation, exhibit an individual of its kind in its full growth and capable of reproducing itself? That living principle which evidently did not appear in dead, inanimate matter before, must have come there from without, and without the aid of external agent, since to actualize its own power, to bring itself from potentiality into real act, matter would have to be already in action. Let me illustrate: We will suppose a pebble;

there it lies on the sand by the seashore, immovable, inert, dead. The waves pass over it playfully and caress it, but it remains unmoved and insensible to those caresses. Now, you would want that pebble to spring up into a rose tree. It is evident that it is not now a rose tree. To become that beautiful plant it would have to give itself that spontaneity of action by means of which it would select that aliment from the surrounding surf and air, and assimilate them to itself, and thus acquire the nature and qualities of an incipient rose tree, and continue the process until it had acquired the full growth of a rose tree, and then be able to let fall buds and seeds to reproduce itself. It is evident that that immovable, inert pebble shows not the least sign or inclination to such action or movement. You say it is by an act of the Creator, or it must have lain dormant in the inanimate matter. It could not have lain dormant in inanimate matter and rise up by itself, because it would have to be active already before it had been evoked from the dormant state. Therefore the living principle in matter, the cause of life in the living world, must either have been created by God Almighty from nothing and placed in matter, or it must have been evoked from matter by a special act of the same Creator. In either case, we require a special act of the Creator to account for the appearance of life upon the earth, and evolution, in a universal sense, is proven by reason to be untenable and false."

George.—"I see by your last words that to account for life it is not necessary to suppose a new creation from nothing. That principle, which united to inanimate matter as the soul to the body, need not be created anew. It may be evoked, evolved, drawn from the capabilities of matter itself by a special act of God, which special act is necessary, because no being can pass from the state of rest and immovability into action and movement except by the impulse of an external agent."

Doctor.—"We may conclude it is impossible to account for the appearance of life in the universe without a special interference of the Creator, and this conclusion, both of true science and right reason, is so true that those would-be scientists, who will have none of God, not being able to satisfactorily account for the appearance of life, are obliged to assume life as a necessary postulatum of science. I will quote a few testimonies: 'The existence of a spontaneous generation,' says Clus, 'if we could succeed to demonstrate it, would prove of great service in our efforts of physico-chemical explanations. It even appears to be a necessary postulate to 'explain scientifically the first apparitions of organisms.' (Treatise on Zoölogy, page 2.) 'He who does not believe in spontaneous generation, or rather the secular evolution of organic matter from inorganic matter, admits the miracle. It is (spontaneous generation) a necessary hypothesis which none can shake, either by à *priori* arguments or by experiments of the laboratory.' *Soury Le. preuves des transformism.* What are you laughing at, Adele ?"

Adele.—"At your scientists, who make it their boast that their science is founded on facts and observation, and now assuming a hypothesis in direct contradiction to facts and observations. You men have the very greatest capacity of swallowing."

Doctor.—"Enough of the subject."

TENTH ARTICLE.

WERE ALL LIVING BEINGS EVOLVED FROM THE LOWEST FORM OF LIFE, OR WAS EACH SPECIES OF THE VEGETABLE AND ANIMAL WORLD EFFECTED BY A SPECIAL ACT OF THE CREATOR ?—TRANSFORMISM AND DARWINISM—WHAT IS A SPECIES?—CAN A SPECIES BE DISTINGUISHABLE FROM ANOTHER ?

Doctor.—"Having demonstrated in our two last conversations that life cannot spring from dead matter, but that it must have been evoked by the Creator—as Darwin freely admits in these words: 'There is a grandeur in this view of life, having been originally breathed by the Creator into a few forms or into one'—we may pass to the discussion of that great problem, were all living things evolved from one or from a few forms of life, or was each species of the vegetable and animal kingdom effected by a special act of the Creator?"

George.—"As I understood you, Doctor, in one of our conversations, this question is an open one."

Adele.—"What do you mean by an open question?"

George.—"I mean that we can hold either the one or other of the two propositions without meeting any opposition from revelation."

Adele.—"Do you mean to say that I can maintain the opinion that all living beings were evolved from one of the lowest forms of life without contradicting any truth of our religion?"

Doctor.—"George is right, Adele, if we exclude man from the list of living beings. With that exception we can hold, as we intimated in one of our conversations, we can maintain either the one or the other opinion."

Adele.—"Then why do we discuss the question?"

Doctor.—"Just to see what real science has to say about it. You remember, Adele, what is meant by evolution, restricted in the sense in which we examine it now?"

Adele.—"Certainly. Evolution, as admitted by the different scientists of modern times, is that system which maintains that all living beings, from the lowest to the highest, have been evolved from one or two of the lowest forms of life."

Doctor.—"Very good. Of course there are different ways of explaining the system, but all those who admit the creation of the first form or forms of life agree in that general idea. We will pass over the accidental differences in the systems of the various evolutionists and transformists, and examine the idea common to them all—that all living beings, vegetable as well as animal, were evolved, developed, from one or few of the lowest forms of life. George, please to tell us what are the main arguments or proofs upon which the system is supposed to rest?"

George.—"Why, Doctor, you know evolutionists claim that the whole bevy of natural sciences is in favor of this. First they allege general experience and observation of the mutability and changeableness of natural species; then they invoke in their favor geography, paleontology, geology, embriology, comparative anatomy, pathology, and a host of other sciences."

Adele.—"I hope you do not exaggerate, Mr. George."

Doctor.—"He is right, Adele. Evolutionists claim at least half a dozen sciences in support of their pet system. I am afraid we shall have to devote one or two conversations on each one to do justice to the subject. The first thing to be investigated is whether observation and experience bear out the assertion of evolutionists with regard to the mutability and transformation of natural species."

Adele.—"Excuse me, gentlemen; it seems to me you are committing a slight oversight; you are talking of forms and species without defining what you mean by those words. Would it be presuming too much on your condescension if I ask you to throw some light on those expressions?"

Doctor.—"We are coming to it, Adele. Suppose I enter a botanic garden; a beautiful sight stretches out before me—a great multitude of plants and flowers of every size, of every shape, of every color. At first I distinguish nothing in particular, but by degrees I observe that the garden is divided into so many beds, each filled with a number of plants, which appear to be of similar structure, of similar form and shape, though each plant is more or less distinguished from the others in some peculiarity of size, of shape, of tints, which, without at all destroying the general resemblance, mark the individuality of each. Moreover I observe that each bed of plants is totally different from the adjacent beds. Am I right in inferring that each bed contains a special kind of plants?"

Adele—"Certainly."

Doctor.—"Well, then, we begin to surmise what is meant by a species. When I see a number of plants, each exhibiting the same general organs and structure, the same form and shape, I naturally infer that they must have a common type, as they appear to be fashioned after the same design. George, what would Huxley call it?"

George.—"He would call it a morphological species."

Adele.—"Pray, explain."

George.—"Here are Huxley's words: 'When we call a group of animals, or of plants, a species, we may imply thereby either that all these animals and plants have some common peculiarity of form or structure, or we may mean that they possess some common functional character. That part of biological science (science of life) which deals with form and structure, is called morphology.'"

Doctor.—"From the Greek words *morphe*, form, and *logos*, discourse."

George.—"That which concerns itself with function, physiology"

Adele.—"Well, let us have the definition of species according to form and structure of animals and plants."

George.—"'A species is nothing more than a kind of animal or plant distinctly definable from all others by certain constant morphological peculiarities.' (Lay Sermons, page 258.) Thus, for instance, horses form a species, because the group of animals to which that name is applied is distinguished from all others in the world by exhibiting all those combined characters of structure and form which everybody knows."

Adele.—"I understand a species in the morphological sense. Now, I want to have a clear idea of a species according to those actions or functions which it exercises."

Doctor.—"A species, considered in relation to the acts or functions it exercises, is a group of animals or of plants, which are able to generate others like themselves, and to transmit to their offspring the same power of reproduction."

George.—"'In all living beings,' says Huxley, 'the primitive impulse is tending . . . seems to be to mould the offspring into the likeness of the parent. It is the first great law of reproduction that the offspring tends to resemble its parent or parents more closely than anything else.'" (Page 262.)

Doctor.—"Then by combining both ideas together we may give a full definition of a species by saying that it is a group of animals or of plants presenting the same structure and form, and capable of producing offspring like themselves and with the same power of reproduction."

Adele.—"But, uncle, can there be no variety among plants or animals belonging to the same species?"

Doctor.—"Certainly a number of external circumstances, principal among which we enumerate change of climate, nourishment, artificial training, and others, may produce certain varieties in the structure and form of individuals of the species, without altering at all their essential qualities. These varieties may influence the function of reproduction and appear in the offspring. Now, two things may occur: after one or a few generations the variety may disappear; or it may become fixed and permanent in the course of generations; so that we may have a number of individuals exhibiting the essential requirements of the species, but always with a certain special variety of their own. In the latter case we have what is called a *Race*, which may be defined, in the words of Quatrefaces: 'A number of individuals resembling each other belonging to one species, having received and transmitting, by means of generation, the characters of a primitive variety.' " ("The Human Species," page 39: Appleton, 1881.)

Adele.—"Who is Quatrefaces, uncle?"

Doctor.—"One of the greatest of modern scientists, Professor of Anthropology in the Museum of Natural History of Paris."

George.—"Also a member of the Academy of Sciences and author of many works in natural history."

Doctor.—' Now we must approach that great question which has such important bearing on the subject which we are discussing— that is to say: Is there a certain unerring, unmistakable criterion or sign by which we may tell one species from another, and where is it to be found? Do you understand, Adele?"

Adele.—"I think I do. We suppose, mankind supposes, that there are a multitude of species in the vegetable and animal world. Now you want to find out whether there is such a thing as a mark or criterion by which, without fear of mistake, we can distinguish one species from another."

Doctor.—"Right; now, George, what is agreed upon among scientists with regard to the matter in hand?"

George.—"That if there be such sign, it is not to be found in the morphological species—that is, species with regard to its structure and form. 'As it is admitted on all sides,' says Huxley, 'that races occur in nature, how are we to know whether any apparently distinct animals are really of different physiological species or not, seeing that the amount of morphological difference is no safe guide?'"

Adele.—"Then, if there is any such reliable test or criterion, we must seek for it in physiology—that is, in the function of the plant and the animal. And is there such a thing, Mr. George?"

George.—"I answer with the same Huxley: 'The usual answer of physiologists is in the affirmative. It is said that such a test is to be found in the phenomena of hybridization in the results of crossing races as compared with the results of crossing species.' Page 272."

Adele.—"What do you mean by that long word?"

George.—"I mean the offspring of parents, one of whom belongs either to a different species from the other, or to a different race. 'So far as the evidence goes,' continues Huxley, 'individuals of what are certainly known to be mere races, however distinct they may appear to be, not only breed freely together, but the offspring of such crossed races are perfectly fertile with one another. Thus the spaniel and the greyhound, the dray-horse and the Arab, the pouter and the tumbler breed together with perfect freedom, and their mongrels, if matched with other mongrels of the same kind, are equally fertile. On the other hand, there can be no doubt that individuals of many natural species are either absolutely infertile if crossed with individuals of other species, or if they give rise to hybrid offspring, the hybrids so produced are infertile when paired together. The horse and the ass, for instance, if crossed, give rise to the mule, and there is no certain evidence of offspring ever having been produced by a mule and female mule.'"

Doctor.—"Now mark the conclusion which follows from this common universal experience. 'Here, then,' says the physiologist, 'we have a means of distinguishing any two true species from any two varieties. If a male and a female, selected from each group, produce offspring, and that offspring is fertile with others produced in the same way, the groups are races, not species. If, on the other hand, no result ensues, or if the offspring are infertile with others produced in the same way, they are true physiological species' (page 273). We may conclude, then, that the generality of scientists, evolutionists included, admit that there is such a thing as an infallible criterion to distinguish one species from another, and that is infertility or barrenness. If two individuals of two different groups brought together produce no offspring, or a barren one, they belong to two different species. If two individuals of two different groups when brought together produce offspring, and an offspring with the same power of reproduction, they belong to two different races, but to the same species."

George.—"But, Doctor, you must surely know that Huxley does not admit your criterion in those words. 'The test would be an admirable one if, in the first place, it were always practicable to apply it; and if, in the second, it always yielded results susceptible of a definite interpretation.'"

Doctor.—"I was perfectly aware of those words of Huxley, but count them as absolutely worthless, and so would Huxley himself if he were not determined, at all hazards, to pave the way for his pet theory of evolution by abolishing all distinction of species. But let us examine them. What is the first reason?"

George.—" 'The test is not always practicable. The constitution of some wild animals is so altered by confinement that they will not breed, even with their own females, so that the negative results obtained from crosses are of no value; and the antipathy of wild animals of different species is ordinarily so great, that it is hopeless to look for such unions in nature'—page 273."

Doctor.—"The reason then of Huxley is that the test is not practicable, because, forsooth, it cannot be applied in all and every case. Such a reason proves nothing at all, for the question is not whether we can test the criterion in every possible case, for that is not at all necessary, and if it were it would render all natural science absolutely impossible; but whether, in all the cases in which the test has been applied, the result has ever been different from one expected by the test; and I say—all scientists say—that in the thousand and tens of thousands and millions of cases where the test has been applied, in all time and place the criterion has never failed."

Adele.—"But, uncle, what did you mean by saying that if it were necessary to apply the test to all and every case it would render all natural science impossible?"

Doctor.—"You will understand it, Adele, if you will remark that all natural sciences are founded on observation and experience, from which general laws are deduced. Let us take physics, for instance. It is that science which observes the external phenomena of bodies and endeavors to investigate the causes which produce them and the laws which govern them. By observing, for instance, in sufficient number of cases, that the molecules of a body attract each other, the natural philosopher has deduced the law of molecular attraction. By observing by repeated experiments in a sufficient number of cases that all the known causes of external phenomena, such as movement, light, heat, electricity, can be reduced to movement, the natural philosopher has concluded the law of the correlation of forces. Now, of course you understand that what makes a science is not the knowledge of a number of disconnected facts, but the knowledge of the principles in which such facts originate and the laws which govern them. But if the natural philosopher were to wait before deducting a law governing a phenomenon from sufficient number of observations till he has observed all the possible cases bearing on the same, he would never arise to that law which governs it, and hence science would become impossible. It is sufficient, therefore, in order to deduce a law said to govern a certain class of phenomena that a sufficient number of repeated experiments warrant the conclusion, and that whenever the experiment has been made the phenomenon has been manifested always as if governed by such law. Now, coming to our subject, Huxley says that the criterion to distinguish a species from another is not reliable, because it is not applicable always and in all cases. We might as well say that the law of universal gravitation is not reliable or infallible, because one could not apply it in the case of the heavenly bodies, as not exactly within our reach, or of those bodies that cannot come under our observation. It is not necessary that we should make the experiment in every case, but it is amply sufficient that the test be applied to a multitude of cases and always found to be reliable."

Adele.—"Oh, I am glad I put the question, as I understand now a good many things I did not understand before."

Doctor.—"Let us have the second reason, George."

George.—"The second reason is, that the test does not always succeed in the cases where it can be applied. 'For example,' says Huxley, 'cases are cited by Mr. Darwin of plants which are more fertile with the pollen of another species than with their own.' Page 274."

Adele.—"Do you mean by pollen those granules of dust which fall from the flower in bloom to fertilize the ovules?"

George.—"Yes, certainly; and Darwin says that certain plants are more fertile with the pollen of another species than with their own, which, of course, takes all reliability from the criterion of a species."

Doctor.—"I beg your pardon, George, but your great lights of science forget themselves in this particular as in many more; but they are so accustomed to contradiction that the most glaring one can hardly arouse their attention, and they stand in no fear of their admirers; for such read their works, if at all, with such carelessness and such blind trust as to be prepared to swallow any number of inconsistencies, provided it bears the parentage of Darwin, Huxley & Co."

Adele.—"Something terrible is coming, I am sure.

Doctor.—"George, please to answer me. Have Mr. Darwin, Huxley & Co. any criterion or test whereby to know and to detect one species from another?"

George.—"Not that I am aware of."

Doctor.—"And they reject the criterion of all physiologists, ancient and modern?"

George.—"They do."

Doctor.—"Then how do they know one species from another?"

George.—"I am sure I cannot tell."

Doctor.—"Then these great lights, after telling us that there is no criterion to safely tell one species from another, with great seriousness and magisterial tone talk of one species being different from another, and how one species of plants is more fertile with the pollen of another species. Gentlemen, are you aware of your contradiction? How can you talk with such assurance? How can you call one species different from another, when you maintain there is no safe guide to know that?"

Adele.—"Dear me! It is a pity to see such pet idols, so exalted, so far above the multitude, exhibit such a miserable spectacle of silly reasoning, and of contradiction and inconsistency!"

Doctor.—"It seems incredible, yet it is so. Here are our greatest evolutionists contending most strenuously that there is no certain criterion to tell one species from another, and then flatly contradicting themselves by urging certain alleged facts of plants of one species being more fertile with the pollen of a different species!"

Adele.—"Then we may conclude that the criterion admitted by all physiologists and scientists, and called admirable by Huxley himself, stands, in spite of the two silly objections brought forward by the latter, and we may take it as an infallible rule that two plants or animals which produce offspring like themselves, which in their turn can do the same, belong to the same species, no matter how different in race; and that two plants or animals which produce nothing, or an offspring infertile and barren, must belong to two different species."

George.—"Species, then, are easily distinguishable one from another."

Doctor.—"We must rest here at present."

ELEVENTH ARTICLE.

EVOLUTIONISM IS CONTRADICTED BY HISTORY.

Doctor.—"George, what is the consequence which follows from the criterion we spoke of in our last conversation as to the theory of evolution?"

George.—"If I apprehend it rightly, why a most fatal one. If we admit that plants and animals of one species cannot propagate with plants and animals of another species, and that the forced union of an individual of one species with another of a different species either results in nothing or in an individual perfectly barren and infertile, it is evident that there cannot be a change, a transformation of one species into another, and that evolution in that case is easily disposed of."

Doctor.—"Excellently said, George. But we will not take advantage of that criterion. We will proceed as if it did not exist, and as if physiologists had not concluded it from secular experiences of numberless experiments and facts. We will do the work over again, and examine whether there are in nature fixed species which can never be transformed into others; or whether from facts we are justified to maintain that species are not fixed, but are in a state of passage and transition."

Adele.—"So we won't mind what we said in our last conversation, and we will investigate from facts whether we are to cling to that criterion and its consequence or whether we can hold the evolution of one species into another."

Doctor.—"Just so; we will begin the inquiry from history. I say that history, as far back as we can go, always exhibits species as fixed, permanent, and unalterable. George, what do historical monuments say?"

George.—"If we limit ourselves to historical monuments I must freely own that they are all against evolution and transformists."

Adele.—"We will judge of it when you have brought them forward."

George.—"I take them from the book of Mr. Faivre, 'La Variabilité des espèces et ses limites,' Paris, 1868, p. 162: 'The lava which covered in the year 76 of the Christian era the cities of Pompeii and Herculaneum enveloped, without altering them, remnants of organic life at such an epoch. In the house of a painter they have found a collection of shell-fish, and in the shop of a fruiterer vases filled with chestnuts, olives, and nuts. In spite of the eighteen centuries which have intervened between us and that event no appreciable change has been found in the forms of those remnants and the fruits of our own time. Aristotle, who lived over two thousand years ago; Galien, who lived in the second century of our era, have given descriptions so entirely exact of animals and plants as to their exterior or anatomical qualities that one would think they were traced by the hand of some modern naturalist."

Adele.—"Well, the alleged testimonies have some respectability, as they are a couple of thousand years old."

George.—"But the monuments of ancient Egypt present a more respectable front."

Doctor.—"George, before you go on, I would like to call your attention to the fact that, if there be a country in the world which could be said to be most favorable to the evolution of species, that country is certainly Egypt.'

Adele.—"Why?"

Doctor.—"Because the richness of its *flora* and its *fauna*, the fertility of the soil, the elevation of its temperature, together with the abundance of humidity, the industry of man also, attested by so many gigantic works, all conspired to excite the energy and activity of organisms, and must have highly favored evolution."

George.—"And yet in spite of all these causes organisms have remained fixed though so many centuries have passed, and they appear as the present ones."

Adele.—"The subject begins to be highly interesting. You maintain that vegetables and animals of modern Egypt are the same in form and shape with the animals and plants of ancient Egypt."

George.—"To be sure, a comparison between them will prove the assertion. Every one knows, for instance, that the ancient Egyptians were great experts in embalming bodies, and that they laid in their sepulchres not only human bodies, but also the bodies of animals of all kind; all these testimonies of past ages, known under the name of mummies, have been preserved without alteration till our time. In the expedition to Egypt, commanded by Napoleon, at the end of the last century, the scientists who formed part of it gathered a great number of such mummies and brought them to France, where they became the object of the most earnest examination of the most celebrated naturalists of the time. Cuvier, Lamarck, Lacépède studied them in their smallest details, as far as concerned higher animals. The celebrated entomologist, Latreille, did the same with regard to insects, and all discovered a perfect identity of characters between the animals thirty or forty centuries old, and those of our own times."

Adele.—"I disliked to interrupt you, but really I must have the explanation of that long word entomologist?"

George.—"I beg your pardon; that word is taken from two Greek words: *entomon*, insect; and *logos*, discourse. Hence entomology is the science of insects, and he who studies them is an entomologist."

Adele.—"Many thanks; go on, please."

George.—"The equality between the animals of those times and those of our own was so great that even Lamarck himself, though a partisan of the mutability of the species, was obliged to admit it. The ox, the dog, the cat, the monkey, the ichneumon, the crocodile, the sacred pilulary, the domestic bee, are to-day what they were forty centuries ago. On examining the animals engraven on the obelisks transported from Egypt to Rome, Cuvier has likewise observed this equality between animals of our time, such as the *ibis*, a kind of wading bird, with a long slender bill and long broad wings, or the vulture, the falcon, the Egyptian goose, the rail, the lapwing, the asp, the cerastes, the hippopotamus, and many others."

Doctor.—"Yes; and since that time new researches and new comparisons have been made and they have all corroborated the preceding observations. They have found in the cellars or vaults—called hypogea—of ancient Thebes and of Memphis figures, very easily discernible, of the Egyptian giraffe or camelopard, the male lion, the crocodile and others, exactly like to those of our own time. And not only the species but even the races have remained perfectly intact. The greatest part of the varieties of dogs represented on the *bas reliefs* in the Egyptian tombs yet exists to-day in that country or its adjacent places. One can easily recognize the dog in the bazaars of Cairo and of the other cities of contemporary Egypt, the dog of Dongolah, which is met with in the villages of Nubia, the large greyhound of the north of Africa, etc."

Adele.—"Very interesting, indeed."

George.—"Plants have not changed any more than animals. Very able botanists such as Kunth, Jussien, Candolle, and very recently Professor Unger, have made such examination. Kunth, observing fruits, seeds, fragments of plants found in tombs, has recognized wheat dates, papyrus, the palm-tree, the orange, the pomegranate, the vine, the fig, the acacia of Farnese, and others. 'The remains which have been examined belong,' says Kunth, 'all of them to vegetables which are met with to-day in those countries; the most exact comparison having discovered no difference whatever.' Bonastre, Passalacqua, Candolle confirm the indications given by the learned German professor. Unger, on examining the bricks used in the year 3400 before our era, in the building of the pyramid of Dashour, has extracted from the straw and the sand, of which they were partially formed, some organic remnants the preservation of which permitted a very attentive study; in these remnants he has recognized, among the cultivated plants, wheat, barley, pease, flax, and among other vegetables the radish, the chrysanthemum, or golden flower of the harvest. Time had not rendered these forms unrecognizable."

Doctor.—"Alongside of these proofs, derived from the remnant of long past ages, we may place others drawn, so to speak, from the living annals of nature. There are found, here and there, trees the longevity of which, altogether extraordinary, is attested either by tradition or by their colossal dimensions. Botanists reckon their age with sufficient certainty from their height, the volume of their trunk, and the number of layers of which they are composed. We can mention among these veterans of the vegetable kingdom the gigantic chestnut tree of Etna, which, at the time of Pliny, the naturalist, was already strong and vigorous, and which they calculate to be twenty centuries old; the Baobab of Cape Verd, measured by Adanson, which would carry an age of five thousand years; the famous California Seguoja, whose head rise nearly three hundred feet in the air and whose circumference measures about ninety feet, and to which naturalists have given the trifle age of sixty centuries; the cypress of Oaxaca, under the shadow of which Cortes sheltered himself and his little army, claims also an age of forty centuries. Now allowing a certain margin and latitude in the reckoning of the respective ages of these veteran trees, it is no less certain that they have seen generation after generation succeed each other almost without number. And the fact stands that trees of the same kind growing round about them or in their vicinity do not differ one important iota from the ancient representatives of their species."

George.—"I want to refer to another fact, Doctor, which bears very great analogy to the preceding ones. There have often been found in the ancient tombs of the Egyptian mummies grains of wheat. The Count of Sternberg had the happy thought of sowing these grains, and the result was that in spite of their three or four thousand years of age they bloomed and bore fruit; and it has been found that the plant which grew from that seed is identical with the wheat with loose ear. From which we must conclude that the species existed in ancient Egypt, and that it has been transmitted without alteration to the present time."

Adele.—"Well, gentlemen, what do you infer from all the facts of history which you have so happily quoted?"

Doctor.—"We draw the general conclusion which gives a death blow to all evolution and transformism so far as history is concerned—that all facts of history relating to the vegetable or animal kingdom triumphantly prove that there has been in the course of thirty, forty, fifty or sixty centuries no alteration of any importance in the species of plants or animals; those known to us to have existed six thousand years ago being the same as those existing under our own eyes."

George.—"The words of the great Cuvier come in *apropos*: 'I know,' he says, 'that some naturalists reckon very much on myriads of centuries which they accumulate at once by a stroke of the pen, but in matters of this kind we cannot judge of that which a long time may effect, except by mentally multiplying that which a shorter time does.' Now three, four, six thousand years have effected no transformation in animals and plants. Hence the right conclusion must be that a longer time, no matter what, may not produce any."

Adele.—"I would like to hear how transformists get over this difficulty, which seems to my poor judgment a very weighty one."

Doctor.—"Oh, very easily indeed! Catch them sticking at a trifle. They have hit upon a very ingenious invention. They alone have discovered that species pass successively through two phases; one phase, during which they are subject to very rapid variations; the other phase, immeasurably longer than the first, during which they are found to be fixed and vary no longer."

Adele.—"Very nice, indeed! That seems to assert tranformism in other words. Well, and what are we to think of this second theory or explanation?"

Doctor.—"That it is a gratuitous hypothesis, resting on no facts whatever. To establish it, it would be necessary to bring forward facts of the actual passage of the species through this phase or period of change, and to do that it would be necessary to trace up their genealogy, till the species from which they are derived mark the point which has separated the two periods, and exhibit them in that transitory phase when they are endeavoring to attain a definite and fixed form. They have neither done this nor can they do it. In the second place, they ought to be kind enough to explain why species, at other times variable so far as to pass from one into another, are no longer so. The laws of nature are not so subject to change, and to make us accept this passage of species from a state variable and restless to one fixed and permanent, transformists ought to allege at least some plausible reason. Thirdly, they cite the example of certain species which actually give birth to a number of varieties, and affirm that all species have travelled through this unstable state; but if it be so, we claim the right to ask an explanation, a reason, a motive, why the latter are yet in that state of change, and others living under the same climate, on the same soil, and under conditions of life.exactly identical, have reached the permanent and fixed period. Until they have accounted for this satisfactorily, we shall rest in the testimony of history as to the immutability of species."

Adele.—"I have certainly great opinion and respect for science, and a certain quantum of the same respect for scientists of every shade and color. But the more I hear from them the stronger grows my inclination to laugh, not at real science, as at scientists so called. Here it seems to me that these celebrated great evolutionists. and transformists have made up their minds to maintain, right or wrong, at all hazards, their system of evolution. Very well; you come to them with history in hand and say: My friends, you hold that species vary one into another, that one species is gradually transformed into another. History—let me call your attention upon it—history is against you; it shows that species of plants and animals are the same to-day as they were thirty, forty, fifty, sixty centuries ago. This is proven by millions of facts and observations and comparisons made by the best, the most expert scientists of our century and of the last. What is the answer of evolutionists to that argument? Why, we were perfectly aware, they say, that history proves the fixedness and permanence of species. That is no news to us; but you must know that species pass through a double period, one of change and transformation, which occurred before historical times, and the other of fixedness and permanence, which fortunately began with history and continues to remain so. Hence you can account for changes required by our theory and for the permanence exacted by the facts of history. You ask them, what proofs have you of the existence of that prehistorical period? What proofs? they reply. Why, are we not entitled to some confidence on the part of our readers? Is not the principal right of a scientist to draw largely on the imagination? And when he is in a corner, to have recourse to some remote period about which nothing is known or can be known? Pray, gentlemen, would not all this provoke the risibility of the most serious judge, not to speak of the same in a poor, heedless girl like your servant ?"

TWELFTH ARTICLE.
EVOLUTION IN CONTRADICTION WITH PALEONTOLOGY.

Doctor.—"You remember, Adele, that evolutionists claim half a dozen sciences in support of their system. One of these sciences upon which they rely as their staunch supporter is paleontology. I suppose you understand the word."

Adele.—"Not a bit; pray, give me its meaning.'

Doctor.—"It comes from the Greek, as usual: *paleos*, ancient; *onta*, beings; and *logos*, discourse—the science of ancient things. But modern scientists, strictly speaking, understand by paleontology that science which treats of fossil remains both animal and vegetable."

Adele.—"Now, uncle, if you will be so kind as to throw a little light on the words *fossil remains*, I shall understand the whole thing perfectly."

Doctor.—"Of course you understand what remains signifies. The original signification of fossil is *something dug out of the earth*; but now it is restricted to express the petrified remains of vegetables and animals; so that by the words fossil remains we intend to signify those remains of vegetables and animals which by being buried into the earth a long time have become petrified, or become stony, and appear so when dug out."

Adele.—"I understand now. Paleontology is that science which treats of those remains of plants and animals which, by being buried into the earth and remaining there for ages, have become petrified or stony."

Doctor.—"Very good. And do you see the great advantage to be derived from that science ?"

Adele.—"Not exactly."

Doctor.—"The remains of plants and animals, preserved in the bosom of the earth, enable us to go beyond historical times even as far back as the first appearance of life, and they are therefore of the greatest advantage to scientists as so many truly prehistorical monuments. Now, evolutionists claim that these fossil remains prove the theory of transformation of one species into another. But before we come to speak of this we must take a peep at geology and get a little information about a point or two, else what we are going to say would be a sealed book to you. Of course you understand that geology means the science which studies the earth, and the formation, nature and location of its different components ?"

Adele.—"Certainly I understand that. I remember, when I was at school, to have learned that the earth is composed of different materials, and that such materials are found at certain depths, others are seen higher up, and others higher still, and that to investigate the nature of such materials, the manner according to which they formed, how they came to be located where they are found, is the special study of the geologist."

George—"Very cleverly said indeed, Miss Adele. It is evident that you did not lose all your time during your school days."

Adele.—"Spare your irony, if you please, Mr. George."

Doctor.—"Then you are aware that all these different materials appear formed into beds or strata; some horizontally; others, especially those found at much lower depth, are more inclined. In various places they are found bent serpent-like, as the leaves of a book violently pressed down. Now that part of geology which treats of the nature, formation, and location of these beds, the depth at which they are discovered, and the form and appearance of the same, is called stratiographical geology, that is, description of the strata or beds of the earth, their nature and formation, and shape. George, please to tell us now how geologists have tried to classify these different beds, or strata."

George.—"I will do my best. Of course every one understands that all these materials out of which, as far as men have been able to discover, our mother earth is composed, were formed but very slowly and gradually, some of them requiring millions of centuries to be constructed."

Adele.—"Why do you say as far as men have been able to discover?"

George.—"You know, of course, that man has only been able to reach, as it were, the outward covering, the crust, so to speak, of the earth; all his endeavors to dig reaching only a very small portion of the earth's depth; hence the reason why we must say as far as man has been able to discover; for if we could descend deeper and deeper into the bowels of the earth many a profound mystery would be unravelled to us on things we hardly have a suspicion of."

Adele.—"I see."

George.—"Geologists have divided all the different materials they have been able to discover into so many groups, which they call epochs, eras, or periods, in view of the time of their formation; each group being assigned a special name appropriate to the time of its formation, the depth at which it is found, and to some particular remains found in its bosom."

Doctor.—"Very good, George. Tell us now, how many such epochs or periods are admitted by geologists?"

George.—"They assign seven principal epochs. The first is the Azoic."

Adele.—"What do you mean by that?"

George.—"Geologists mean by the Azoic epoch those layers or beds of minerals in which are found no relics whatever of either plants or animals that is no relics of life. These beds are composed of rocks, of granite porphyry, and the like, and which are the result of other elements, such as silez, albumen, potassium, soda, magnesia, and iron."

Adele.—"The first epoch, then, is easy to understand. Its layers are principally granite rocks, and in them no trace or relics of animals or plants are to be found."

Doctor.—"Please to fix the individual peculiarities of each epoch in order that you may understand at once what is meant when in our discussion each epoch is referred to."

Adele.—"I will, with pleasure, if every age or period is as easy to understand as the Azoic. What next, Mr. George?"

George.—"We may refer to this Azoic epoch, the beds called Laurentian and Huronian, because found on the borders of the St. Lawrence and Lake Huron in Canada. In these have been found traces of an organism, or rather structure, resembling that of a polypus. Such formation was believed by some to be organic, and by others to be simply mineral. This fossil was christened by the name Eozoon, that is, the dawn of life. It is now classed in the Protozoic age, that is, the period of embryo and rudimental animals."

Adele.—"I like that name—dawn of life, or Eozoon. What is the next epoch?"

George.—"The Paleozoic, so-called because in it we find unmistakable vestiges of life. It is divided, according to the order of the formation of the different beds, into the Cambrian, Silurian, Devonian, Carboniferous and Permian periods."

Adele.—"I suppose you will condescend to throw a word of explanation on each of those epithets?"

George.—"With pleasure. The first system of beds is called Cambrian, relating to Cambria or Wales, where those beds are found. Some are composed of clay, generally of black color, and others of mixture of very fine sand and clay. Very clear vestiges of vegetables, zoophites, or animal plants, and shell-fish are found in them."

Adele.—"Very good, indeed, and very clear."

George.—"The next beds, which are an extension of the Cambrian, and which are composed of slate, of brown free-stone, and of fine sand and clay, contain many fossils of *alge*, an order of plants comprising sea weeds and moss; also, of cephalopoda, a kind of mollusk or shell fish, having a circle of eight or ten tentacles around the mouth, such as the cuttle fish; also, immense deposits of corals."

Adele.—"How did these beds come to be called Silurians?"

Doctor.—"Because they were best developed in that part of England and Wales formerly included in the ancient kingdom of the Silures, an old people of Britain."

George.—"Next come the Devonian beds, because found in Devonshire. They lie right over the Silurian beds, and are composed of old red slate and carboniferous chalk. Remains of moss and mushrooms, and of fishes having the whole body covered with scales, have been discovered in these layers. The next is the carboniferous resting on the Devonian beds, and containing stratas of anthracite; that is, hard coal and pit coal; it has also its remains of the vegetable and animal kingdoms. The Permian contains the new red slate, some chalky magnesia, bituminous clay, and some minerals of bronze or iron; also, fossils of the vegetable and animal kind."

Adele.—"Now we have disposed of the Primary epoch, if I don't mistake; let us pass to the Secondary."

George.—"That is the reason why it is called with the Greek word Meozoic, or middle epoch. It is divided into two principal groups, called the Triassic and Jurassic. The first was called by the scientists of Germany, where it was best developed, on account of its tripartite character, *Trias*—that is, triple group. The second is called Jurassic, from its admirable development and exposure in the range of the Jura. The first contains new red slate, variegated slate and chalky shells, and other components. In it are found all the remains of plants which come under the general name of coniferae, such as fir trees, pine, cedar, juniper, and so forth; the animals are represented by an extraordinary abundance of shell fish and of all kind of Saurians, a general name applied to the family of lizards. In the Jurassic period, which is composed of clay, inferior, medium and superior, of different color, and of slate and other materials, we find that the remains of fern appear rather small, and the coniferae assume very large proportions, and are found in great abundance. We meet also with marine reptiles, and especially with that very singular one called pterodactyle, from the Greek words *pteron*, wing, and *dactyle*, finger, with winged fingers. For that animal has been looked upon as a bird, a bat, and a flying reptile; because he exhibits the head and neck of a bird, the structure and wings of a bat, and the skull flattened like a reptile, and a bill with no less than sixty teeth, ready to do execution at a moment's notice on any unfortunate little animal that may come within his reach."

Adele.—"He must be a beauty to look at."

George.—"It is in the deep strata of this Jurassic period where are found the first rudiments of the mammalia. This Secondary epoch has been called the age of the reptiles.

"In the Tertiary epoch, we find deposit of rocks of chalk, of granite, porphyry, slate and remnants of pulverized shells and corals. The mammalia predominate at this epoch. It is subdivided into three periods, the Eocenes, that is, the dawn of the new world; the Miocenes, the middle new world; and the Pliocenes, the world newer still."

Adele.—"Well, what remains or fossils are found in each of those periods?"

George.—"In the first are found many coniferous plants, such as palm tree, oaks; and among the animals many pachyderm—that is, animals with thick skin; from two Greek words, *pachis*, thick, and *derma*, skin; for instance, the rhinoceros, the elephant and the anoplotherium, ancient animal, and which had a certain resemblance with the rhinoceros and the tapir, which last in his turn is allied to the rhinoceros and the hog. The monkey now makes his first appearance on the scene."

Adele.—"My compliments to his high and worshipful mightiness!"

George.—"The next period, or the Miocenes, is formed of the product of the acacias, platanus, and poplars; and of enormous mammalia, the most remarkable among which is the dinotherium, from the Greek *dino*, terrible, and *therion*, animal, the terrible animal; the mastodon, from *mastos*, nipple, and *odontos*, teeth; a huge mammiferous quadruped, now extinct, allied to the elephant, and so-called from the conical projections upon the surface of his molar teeth."

Adele.—"I am glad he is gone. He would frighten one to death by his ugly appearance."

George.—"The Pliocene beds contain plants, the forms of which resemble very much those of our own time, though we find none of our present ones in the Tertiary epoch. The mastodon disappears to make way for the horse, the camel and the hippopotamus."

Adele.—"We begin to feel at home now. But what is the hippopotamus?"

George.—"He is a kind of aquatic animal, and might be called river horse. The next epoch is the Quaternary. It contains sediments and deposits of anterior materials mixed up, of volcanic products mixed with ancient substances. The *flora* is like ours and the *fauna* contains the so-called elephant, primigenius or mammoth; the hippopotamus major, and other species now extinct, together with the savage beasts, which are yet living in some parts of the earth. At this epoch appear human remains and products of human art and industry. This epoch is called also glacial."

Adele.—"Let me see, now, if I can remember all that has been said. The crust of the earth resulting of various materials and of beds and layers of such materials, formed at different times, has been divided by geologists into different epochs. The first and the lowest formation is called the Azoic, because no appearance of life, either vegetable or animal, is to be seen in it. It consists of beds of granite and porphyry. Next comes the Laurentian and Huronic period, which is called Protozoic, because the first traces of life is found in its beds. Then comes the primary period, called Paleozoic, consisting of the Cambrian, Silurian, Devonian, Carboniferous and Permian. In them remains of plants of the lowest kind, such as moss, sea-weed and fern, are to be observed together with the fossils of shellfish. Then comes the Meozoic or middle epoch. Life begins to take larger proportions in them, as we find remains of the coniferæ or family of large trees as the fir, the pine, etc., and the fossils of the whole tribe of lizards and reptiles. In the Tertiary period the life of plants appear in much large proportions, and in the animal kingdom enter upon the scene for the first time the mammalia, and the evolutionists' great and best friend and ancestor, the monkey. In the Quaternary period we have the *flora* in great luxuriance, much akin to our own *flora*. Many of the extinct huge mammalia, alongside of others, which remain alive to-day, and for the first time remains of man and of his skill and enterprise. What do you think, Mr. George, of my recapitulation?"

George.—"It is classical, indeed."

Doctor.—"Well, now that we have disposed briefly of that part of geology which was necessary to the understanding of our argument, we must return to the subject of evolution. You recollect, Adele, the argument we made from history?"

Adele.—"Certainly. We proved that all the species and plants, which are found to have lived thirty or forty centuries ago—that is as far back as we can go—are exactly the same with those which we have at the present time. Hence we concluded that, according to historical documents, species of plants and animals are demonstrated to be fixed permanent and unchangeable."

Doctor.—"Very well; what reply do evolutionists make to the historical argument, George?"

George.—"They laugh at the historical argument, being highly amused at our simplicity as making so much account of thirty or forty petty centuries. It is millions, they say, that must be taken into account in this matter; nay, hundreds and thousands of millions of centuries must have been required to effect the transformation of species. It is in vain therefore, they conclude, to allege history against evolution to prove the immutability of species."

Doctor.—"We will then transfer the question from history to paleontology and to prehistorical times, and give them all the millions and milliards which may suit their fancy."

Adele.—"Very liberal, indeed."

Doctor.—"And we contend that if evolution and transformism be true, and can be so proved by paleontology, the upholders of that hypothesis must show three things. Pay attention, Adele. 1st, they must show by paleontology that changes have really taken place in species. 2d, that species have gradually been perfecting themselves. 3d, paleontology must show also some species in the way of transition or passage medium between the species that is endeavoring to be tranformed, and showing traces and signs of the species which it is going to become. Now, George, let us take epoch after epoch, beginning from the last, and let us see what paleontology has got to say on the first question, Has there ever been any change in species? Or, in other words, does paleontology show any change ever to have taken place in species? Of course, you understand I am not talking of occasional changes, but substantial ones, such as would pave the way to change a plant or an animal from a lower one into a higher."

Adele.—"But I think we have had enough to-day, or you are bound to give me a headache."

Doctor.—"Well, at our next conversation."

THIRTEENTH ARTICLE.

DOES PALEONTOLOGY SHOW ANY SUBSTANTIAL CHANGE EVER TO HAVE TAKEN PLACE IN SPECIES?

Adele.—"Remember, uncle, that in this conversation we have to prove that all the species of animals and plants of our time, and which have outlived the enormous time which has been necessary for all the various formation of the different beds of the earth, have not changed, but are exactly the same as the remains we find in the geological epochs."

Doctor.—"Very good, Adele. Now, George, begin from the Quaternary epoch."

George.—"Of all the species of animals found in that epoch some are extinct; others have emigrated from the regions where remains similar to them are found ; and some have survived, and are to be met with in the temperate countries of Europe, full of life and movement."

Doctor.—"And are any of those found to be different in any important point from those we find in the beds of the Quaternary?"

George.—"None that I know of. Dupont, a French scientist, in his work 'Man in the Stone Age,' gives the enumeration of the mammalia formed in the epoch we are speaking of, and the result is as follows: 'Seven species of the mammoth kind are extinct. Two have emigrated to America, the *Ursus ferox*—the great or ferocious bear; and the *Cervus Canadenses*—the Canadian stag. Five species have emigrated to the Polar regions; two have gone East; three to the Alps, and two to Africa—in all fourteen emigrated.' Of twenty-five species, of which six have been destroyed by man, the rest remain intact and are living in Belgium exactly the same as are found in the Quaternary epoch. I will give one instance, the bat. It was contemporary of the mammoth, with which it was associated in the valley de la Lesse. The renowned Belgian naturalist Van Beneden made a special study of it and compared it with the bat of the present time. He did not find the least difference among these and the bats of the Quaternary period, in spite of the struggle for life which must have been going on among them, whose way of feeding is the same, and who cannot find sufficient insects except on the hot days, and who must have gone through long periods of cold. He has proved that the species buried in caves are absolutely the *fac-simile* of those found to-day. 'They are so like each other that those who are more abundant to-day have left the greatest number of remains.' The same naturalist affirms that it is the same case with other animals living in the same place, mammalia, mollusks and reptiles. 'All these species,' he says, 'are to-day what they once were. The fox has continued to live alongside of the wolf, the weasel alongside of the polecat and muskrat. The remains of all these animals are perfectly similar to those which are living to-day on the spot, and no difference even of size could be discovered among them.' (*Révue Génèrale*, Nov., '71.)"

Doctor.—"Well, George, enough has been said of animals of this epoch. Can you show the same as to plants?"

George.—"The vegetable kingdom of this period furnishes facts as certain and as conclusive against transformism. In the Canton Zurich they have found organic remains mounting up beyond the glacial period. Among them M. Heer, whose authority on the subject of vegetable fossils is incontestible, has found vegetables which are living yet in the Alps. He has recognized the wild pine, the maple, two varieties of the larch, and the hazel tree. These species have run the long course of centuries after centuries without the least modification. We may conclude, therefore, that the verdict of Paleontology, as far as the Quaternary epoch, is decidedly against evolution."

Doctor.—"Well, we have done with the testimony of the Quaternary epoch against the theory of transformism. We must consult the other epochs and see what they may allege against the same. George, what have the Tertiary and Secondary period got to say with regard to the permanence of the species?"

George.—"They give the same answer, that species are perfectly stable and permanent. Professor Agassiz has shown that the polyparies—that is, the houses which polypus construct, such as corals or sponges, and of which the banks of the Gulf of Mexico have been formed—have remained always the same and like to each other for the last two hundred thousand years. According to his calculation, no less than that amount of years has been necessary to accumulate such an enormous quantity of chalky madrepore, which extends itself for the space of two degrees of latitude, and which make up nearly the whole island of Florida."

Adele.—"Now I beg your pardon, Mr. George. I understand what is meant by chalky well enough, but I cannot make out what is meant by madrepore."

George.—"A madrepore is a species of coral having stems like a tree."

Adele.—"Oh! then you mean that the whole island of Florida is formed by such chalky corals, and that it took about two hundred thousand years to accumulate?"

George.—"That is Agassiz's calculation in his work 'On the Classification of Species,' page 80. And he proves that they have remained the same ever since. Pouchet, another scientist, and an evolutionist to boot, furnishes us a very curious and interesting information with regard to ants in the Tertiary, and even the Jurassic period. 'Ants,' he says, 'are older than Mount Blanc. They existed in the Jurassic times *very little different from what they are now*. Whilst an interior sea as yet concealed the space where later on Paris was to be, they swarmed in the regions in the centre of Europe, just emerged from the water. Their remains fill the thick bed of ground at Oeningen on the border of the lake of Constance and at Radoboy in Croatia; the rock is black with ants so admirably preserved, with their paws and their little horns. Professor Heer of Zurich, and Mayr of Vienna, have found more than a hundred species of such ants in the Cantons of Oeningen and Radoboy, *many of which seem to be identical with the actual ones*.'"

Adele.—"I would not suspect that such little tiny creatures would be so serviceable in the question of evolution."

George.—"The same author adds: 'The larvæ called phryganea used to make, as those of to-day, their little case or box wherein to lodge, and which they carry along wherever they go.' (*Revue des deux Mondes*, Feb., '70, page 702.) They have found plenty of them in the tertiary bed of Auvergne, and much more in Gergovie and Chaptuzat."

Adele—"Very clear, indeed, if one knew what is meant by the larvæ of phryganea. But as I am in the dark about that, I must beg for a little light."

Doctor.—"They call larvæ, Adele, the worm of an insect to be transformed in its first state at the moment it issues from the egg.

Phryganea is a generic name, which is given to a number of species of water flies. Go on, George."

George.—"We have the testimony of another evolutionist with regard to the secondary grounds, M. ce Saporta (*Revue des deux Mondes*, Oct., '69): 'The fresh water insect and Mollusks,' he says, 'of the secondary beds differ very little from those of our day; with regard to this, nature has changed very much less than is generally imagined.'"

Adele.—"Such acknowledgments, coming from two evolutionists, as you say, Mr. George, must certainly be treasured up as very important and precious."

Doctor.—"So they must; but to go on with the subject, it is worthy of remark that carboniferous beds yield another example how the most elementary organisms are all subject to this immutability of form. It is very interesting to read the observation which the Count Castracane and other scientists have made on the diatomaceæ. George, please to give us some explanation on these fossils before Adele begins to complain."

George.—"For the knowledge we possess of these beautiful organisms, so minute as to be undiscernible by our naked eye, we are indebted to the assistance of the microscope. It was not till towards the close of the last century that the first-known forms of this group were discovered by O. F. Müller. Now there have been found in Great Britain and Ireland no less than a thousand forms, and Rabenhorst, in the index to his *Flora* of Europe, enumerates no less than 4,000 forms which have been discovered throughout the Continent of Europe. The earlier observers thought them to be plants. Subsequent authors, including Ehrenberg, regarded them as animals; but at present, in consequence of their analogy to other organisms, generally acknowledged to be vegetable, as regards their general structure and reproduction, they are generally classed in the vegetable kingdom."

Adele.—"Is there plenty of such deposits?"

George.—"Various deposits have been discovered in various parts of the world, some the deposit of fresh and some of salt water. Of these the most remarkable in extent, as well as for the number and beauty of species, is that of Richmond, Virginia. It extends for many miles, and at some places it is no less than forty feet deep. The material has long been used for polishing powder, and now is largely employed in the manufacture of dynamite."

Doctor.—"Now, George, please take the *Encyclopædia Britannica* and read the concluding words of the article under that name."

George.—"Here they are. 'It is a remarkable fact that existing species of Diatomaceæ have been traced so far down as the lower strata of the tertiary formation, and though the generation of a diatom in the space of a few months far exceeds in number the generation of a man during the period usually assigned to the existence of the race, *the fossil genera and species are in all respects, to the most minute details, identical with the numerous living representatives of their class.' Enc. Britt.* Volume VII., art. Diatomaceæ."

Doctor.—"Coming now to the secondary formation or silurian beds, we have the testimony of the celebrated Joachim Barrande."

Adele.—"Who is he, uncle?"

Doctor.—"He is one of the greatest paleontologists of our time. He took as an epigraph of his works, 'Nothing but what I have seen,' and never swerved from such a promise. He passed his life in observing and studying a restricted piece of ground in the centre of Bohemia, which was a splendid specimen of stratiographic formation; exhibiting, what is very rarely found, a complete series of beds one upon the other, wherein the scientist could read, in a language sufficiently known at present, the first phases of life in the bosom of the primitive seas. In his 'Silurian system in the centre of Bohemia,' with as much ability as good faith, he has brought forward against the hypothesis of evolution objections so strong that none of the upholders of that theory has ever been able to solve."

Adele.—"That makes me anxious to hear what he has said."

Doctor.—"I suppose you understand what naturalists mean by trilobites?"

Adele.—"Indeed I do not; it is the first time I have had the pleasure to hear such a word."

Doctor.—"Well, the name is applied to an order of shellfish having the forepart of the shell in the form of a large shield and the body composed of numerous parts folding over one another like those of the tail of the lobster, and divided through the whole length of the body into three ranges of lobes by two parallel furrows."

Adele.—"I seem to see it now."

Doctor.—"Well, in three hundred and fifty forms of trilobites, which he examined with the greatest care, and there were species among them of which he handled more than six thousand samples, he discovered that only ten of those species exhibited some variations; the three hundred and forty having remained invariable and unchangeable during the immense time of their specific existence. Moreover, he has discovered and proved that the slight variations by no means affect or change the general character of the species, and, instead of growing more distinct or being more and more accentuated, as the theory of evolution would require, they end in disappearing altogether. Hence during the incalculable duration of the Silurian times none of the three hundred and fifty species of trilobites of Bohemia can be considered as having produced by its transformation or development a single new specific form perfectly distinct and permanent."

Adele.—"That is hard against evolutionism. I really hoped for their own sakes, and not to cause them too much chagrin, that they might have some show in paleontology. But this science seems to be very hard against them, and has no compassion whatever."

George.—"Conclusions similar to those of M. Barrande have been drawn by other scientists, such as Davidson, Carruthers, Pfaff, Gosselet, Grand'Eury, from the Cephalopoda, the Acephala, Brachiopoda of the Silurian formation from the Devonia *fauna* of the Belgian basin, from the reptiles of the beginning of the Triassic epoch, from the Proboscidian of the end of the tertiary era, and for a great number of fossil vegetables of the carboniferous and chalky epochs."

Adele.—"Excellently, indeed; only you will have to explain to me all those outlandish foreign words with which you scientists fill your big mouths, and take great delight in."

George.—"I beg your pardon. I cannot but use the language which is held by those great men. But I am ready to explain. Please say what you want."

Adele.—"What do you mean by Cephalopoda?"

George.—"I mean a certain class of shell-fish which have a circle of eight or ten feelers around the mouth called tentacles, such as the cuttle-fish, the quid, and so forth."

Adele.—"And what is meant by Acephala?"

George.—"A class of shell-fish which have no head, such as the lobster."

Adele.—"And what is the other name you mentioned, commencing with a B? I think Brachiomada, you called it."

George.—"No, I said Brachiopoda, that is, an order of headless shellfish, having two long, fleshy spiral arms."

Adele.—"Now I understand; and you maintain that all such animals, with those elegant names of the Silurian formation, and the others of the triassic and carboniferous times, have never changed, and exhibits species as constant and as immovable as the trilobites?"

George.—"Certainly, and I will quote the words of some of the scientists I mentioned. 'It is twenty-five years,' says Gosselet, 'since I have been studying the fossiliferous horizons of the Belgian basin, and isolating, with great care, one from the other. I have not as yet found neither in time nor in the form the transformation of two types, well defined.' 'One thing is certain,' says Carruthers, 'that the amount of testimonies of the fossil *flora* is opposed to the doctrine of evolution.'"

Doctor.—"Very good, George."

George.—"There is another testimony, that of the celebrated scientist Grand'Eury, who does not hesitate in writing the following words: 'On one side all the facts are in favor of an independent creation; on the other side they are no less contrary to transformism.'"

Adele.—"Where did you get all this information, Mr. George?"

George.—"In a French review, called the *Scientific Revue*, April 1879.'

Doctor.—"We may conclude, therefore, this part of the subject by recapitulating what we have said. Do you remember, Adele, what we undertook to demonstrate?"

Adele.—"To be sure I do. We started by saying that evolutionists claimed that the science of paleontology was in their favor. We then undertook to show that the thing stood just the other way."

Doctor.—"And how have we proved it?"

Adele.—"We have found on the testimony of great scientists, some of them evolutionists, that all the fossil remains of the *flora* and *fauna* of the Secondary, Tertiary and Quaternary formations go to show that the species are absolutely fixed and permanent, and that no change whatever has ever taken place in them. Hence we may conclude, as we did for the historical argument, that the species of plants and animals that have been preserved till our time are the same as those found in prehistorical times in the formations of the different beds, which have taken millions of years to be constructed."

Doctor.—"In our next conversation we will take up the two remaining questions belonging to this part of the subject."

FOURTEENTH ARTICLE.

PALEONTOLOGY DEMONSTRATES THAT SPECIES HAVE NOT BEEN PROGRESSING GRADUALLY TOWARDS PERFECTION—IT AFFORDS NO TRACES OF INTERMEDIARY SPECIES.

Doctor.—"We must now enter upon the second question: Can it be shown by paleontology that the different species of animals and plants have been gradually and slowly perfected? You must understand, Adele, that this continued and uninterrupted progress towards perfection is a necessary principle of evolution, which maintains that all possible form of life has been evolved from the lowest possible form. If such be the case, we must find in the facts of paleontology proofs of the continual uninterrupted effort of nature to lay aside, so to speak, the present form, and to put on another much more nobler and higher, and when this is attained to continue the effort and to seek to throw off the last form to assume another yet higher and nobler. Surely if this struggle, this effort, has been going on for millions and millions of centuries, we must find evidence of it in the buried remains of the geological formations."

Adele.—"I understand perfectly."

Doctor.—"Well, then, George, is there any evidence in paleontology of such presumed progress in the vegetable or animal kingdom?"

George.—"I am sorry to say that there is no such evidence. On the contrary, we fine the very opposite amply and fully demonstrated, that is, that species appear at once in all the perfection convenient to their nature and never change any more. That much I can prove."

Doctor.—"Before we proceed with the proofs I want both of you to pay attention to the following remark: That in the living kingdoms of nature, taken in their harmony and union, there should be a certain progress which is manifested according to the order of times, is evident and admitted without any difficulty by everybody. Man, who appeared last upon the globe, is certainly more perfect than all those creatures who preceded him. The mammals of the Tertiary and Quaternary epochs have an organization much more perfect than the Sauriens of the Secondary, and these, in their turn, are far superior to mollusks, etc. But this is not sufficient to make good the theory of evolutionists. They must show a continual progress which, starting from the minimum form of life from the simplest living cell, rises up, without interruption and without a break, to those living beings which have the most complete organization. Now, the question arises, does paleontology show that the most simple and imperfect forms of life, either vegetable or animal, appear first and in the lowest formations, and gradually assume a higher appearance in those formations which are higher? Secondly, does paleontology show that in the lowest strata nothing is to be found but the simplest kind of life, whereas the more perfect organizations are to be met with only on the superior beds? What do you say, George?"

George.—"I regret to say that paleontology is adverse to evolutionism in those two respects. Of course, every one can see that if all living beings had been developed from the lowest possible form of life, it stands to reason that we should look for the lowest forms of life in the lowest strata or beds, and expect to find nothing more in these beds but the lowest forms of life. Now, the contrary is the fact. I will quote Agassiz, in his work 'On the Species': 'It was believed, not very long ago,' he says, 'that inferior animals had first made their appearance on the earth, and that after them had successively appeared higher types, until man crowned the whole series. It is acknowledged to-day that, on the contrary, there have existed *simultaneously* in the oldest strata representatives of numerous families belonging to the four divisions of the animal kingdom. It has been established by innumerable facts that the hypothesis of a gradual succession of the radiatas, the mollusk, the articulate, the vertebrata, is forever put out of court. We have an indubitable proof that the radiata, the mollusk and the articulate are to be met with together in the most ancient grounds and formations, that the most precocious among the vertebrata are associated with them, and that all of them together continue to be found across the geological ages up to our time.'"

Adele.—"I begin to see the force of the argument. How could we say that all these types of life were perfected gradually and successively, and that they sprang and were developed one from another when they are found simultaneously in the lowest beds?"

George.—"If we rise up to the epoch of the first manifestation of life on the globe, to the Silurian epoch, we find according to Contejean that it is not always the representatives of the lowest which start classes and families. The crinoidea, in fact, hold an elevated rank in the location of the *radiata*, and this family begins by its most perfect types."

Adele.—"I need not remark, Mr. George, that the crinoidea and I are perfect strangers to each other."

George.—"Well, I shall have the greatest pleasure to introduce you to each other. They are a family of nearly extinct animals, so called from the two Greek words: *crinon*, a lily; and *sidos*, from having a radiated, lily-shaped disk, supported on a jointed stem. Again, the cephalopoda, which are the most perfect of the mollusks, and the first fishes, all of the pétérocercal family—that is, those that have the upper lobe of the tail larger than the lower, are far superior in every regard to those which people our seas."

Doctor.—"These facts, now put beyond doubt, very little agree with the doctrine of the transformation of the species, their continual progress and perfection."

George.—"The carboniferous *fauna* offers examples of the same kind. Of course, Miss Adele, you know what is meant by batrachia and labyrinthodon?"

Adele.—"Certainly the contrary, Mr. George."

George.—"The batrachia, from the Greek word *batraces*, frog, are an order of reptiles, including frogs, toads, and salamanders. The labyrinthodon is a genus of reptiles akin to the batrachia, but much superior to the ordinary reptiles under that name, so called because they possess teeth of peculiar, complicated structure."

Adele.—"Now that you have introduced to me such strange company, what do you want to remark?"

George.—"That in the carboniferous formation we find for the first time batrachia; and, strange to say, instead of meeting with the common and the more imperfect of these reptiles at first, we find, on the contrary, that the most perfect, that is, the labyrinthodon, take the precedence and appear first on the scene. How then can life be supposed to have commenced from the least perfect and arisen gradually to the more perfect? Again, as I have remarked, reptiles make their first appearance in the carboniferous beds. Now, among the animals that have preceded them on the globe and those which exhibit the greatest resemblance and affinity to them, and from which it would seem they should have derived their origin, are *fishes*, and consequently the first representatives of the reptile kind ought to have been the serpent, or snake, having no feet, and mostly resembling the class of fishes."

Adele.—"Well, suppose that snakes, being without feet and bearing the greatest resemblance to fishes, should have succeeded the latter. Is that what paleontology shows?"

George.—"The very opposite. The very first to be met with in the beds alluded to are the whole family of lizards, which are more perfect than serpents. Serpents have no feet and can only crawl. The lizard, such as the crocodile, the alligator, the iguana, the chamelion, has four distinct limbs, toes clawed, body elongated, rounded and covered with scales. They are, then, as superior to the serpent as the power of walking is over that of creeping."

Adele.—"That is quite remarkable."

George.—"The *flora* of the Carboniferous period presents the same order of facts against evolution. I quote the celebrated botanist, Grand 'Eury ('Flora Carbonifere,' p. 318): 'A fact,' he says, 'which is the more striking, because it refers to those fossil plants which are the more analagous to living plants, is the greatest perfection of the first in direct opposition to the hypothesis of a progressive development.' He cites Stur, Hooker and Goeppert, in support of his statement."

Doctor.—"Let us pass now to other periods."

George.—"Another most striking fact against that same hypothesis is that the reptiles which characterize the Secondary epoch are certainly more perfect than those of the preceding period, but, strange to say, they are much more perfect than those of the Tertiary and Modern periods. Those gigantic Dinosaurians, well provided with members which allow them to walk, to swim, to fly even, are incontestably superior in organization as well as in shape to our modern reptiles. 'The class of reptiles,' we may then conclude with Contejean, * 'has not obeyed the law of a continual organic perfection. It starts with types of the order of lizards, to be sure, of a medium grade; it afterwards furnishes the most perfect models, such as crocodiles, tortoise, to go down gradually and produce in the last place serpents.'"

Doctor.—"Then we could ask tranformists to tell us what mam-

---

* "Geologie et Paleontologie," Paris.

mals of our own epoch are a progress and an improvement over those of the Tertiary? Are they better organized for walking? Are they better fitted for attack or for defence? Are they superior to these in force, in activity, in shape and structure? It would be highly difficult to maintain and to demonstrate that such is the case."

Adele.—"Then we must conclude again in opposition to transformists, and say: Gentlemen, if your hypothesis were true we should expect as a necessary, indispensable consequence of it the law of a continual organic progress in the species of plants and animals found in nature; we should expect that life, beginning from the lowest and least organization, should advance gradually but surely, and manifest itself in organizations, one more elevated than the preceding ones. Hence it would be but reasonable to expect to find in the lowest and most ancient geological formations only the lowest and the least apparition of organic life, and as we mount up in the stratas and beds, admire higher structures, better and more complicated organisms. Is that the case? Paleontology answers: No, by no manner of means! In the lowest strata we find almost all kinds of organizations living together in peace, sleeping alongside of each other, one would think purposely to aggravate and provoke the patience of our friends, the evolutionists. Isn't it too bad that their beautiful romance must be shattered to the four winds of heaven without pity or compassion?"

Doctor.—"Enough, Adele; let us now pass to the other question."

Adele.—"I forget now what the other question was."

Doctor.—"We did not as yet put it fairly and squarely, though we have alluded to it. Another necessary condition attaches to the transformist hypothesis, and that is the existence of intermediary forms of life in order to explain and make the passage from one species to another possible. Do you understand, Adele?"

Adele.—"I think I do. You say to the evolutionist: Sir, you maintain that one species has been transformed into another. Very well. You will grant that this transformation was not accomplished in a moment and at one stroke. Surely the species, before being changed into another altogether different and more perfect in every thing, must have passed through some other transformations, which may be called *medium* between the one that was to be changed and that which it sought to attain. If so, my dear sir we should find some signs, some remnants, some indications of these medium forms. Is that what you mean?"

Doctor.—"Certainly and paleontology should administer and provide such intermediary forms. Is that the fact, George?"

George.—"No sir. Paleontology does not provide such intermediary forms at all. It was in the Silurian seas where the first beings belonging to a certain family of organic life were discovered. And what do we find? We discover life to have appeared almost on a sudden and from the very first instant under a multitude of forms. We find, at the same time, polyparies, graptolites, innumerable brachiopodes, mollusks, acephalous and gasterepodes mollusk, very great number of cephalopodes and trilobites extremely varied. In one word, the Silurian *fauna* numbers over ten thousand species, and in certain aspects, according to Barrande, it is much richer than the Tertiary *fauna*. Where are the ancestors of such legions? By what intermediary phases have they travelled to reach their present form? How did the first form of life manage to attain to and to shape itself into these ten thousand different forms? How can evolutionists fill up such gaps? The Carboniferous *flora*, which exhibits the greatest display of vegetable life on the globe, had been preceded by the Devonian *flora*, but the same types mark the two *floras*. The Silurian *flora* exhibits nothing but sea-weed, except in those superior stratas which touch on the Devonian *flora*. But what relations of structure and form can be discovered between this humble marine plant and the Devonian vegetables, all of a grand stature, oftentimes of colossal proportions and of very high and complex structure?"

Doctor.—'In the Secondary epoch we meet suddenly with reptiles as strange in the form as gigantic in proportions. Where are the predecessors of these? Without ancestors, as without successors, they appear almost suddenly and disappear in the same manner, without leaving any trace of their apparition on the earth except their enormous remains. Among those we mention the plesiosaurus, a marine monster, with the long neck; the ichthyosaurus, the lizard fish, resembling a crocodile, and having four feet shaped like the fin of a whale; the pterodactyl, or the flying reptile, so called from the fifth toe of the anterior feet being lengthened, so as to serve as the expansor of membranous wings; the megalosaurus, so named from its gigantic proportions; the iguanodons, another reptile monster, varying in length from forty to seventy feet."

George.—"You know, doctor, that some scientists have claimed that the archoepterix, that singular animal which is provided with a tail of twenty vertebra or joints, each one furnished with two lateral wings, is like a transition between the reptiles and the birds."

Doctor.—"I know it, but Huxley and Darwin themselves rank him among birds, and Professor Owen has demonstrated it. Coming now to mammals, we may inquire by what transition are they attached to animals which preceded them on the globe? Do they originate in the fish or in the reptile? For these are the classes which, by their organization, are the nearest to the mammals, and yet by what immense distance they are separated from the latter! Mammals, then, have appeared suddenly, without anything which has presaged their advent. And are those among them which are least elevated in the series the ancestors of those who came after?"

George.—"Some scientists seem to have thought so, and, with your leave, Doctor, I will give the easy process of M. Gaudry, a French scientist, to make our present ox to come from the anthracotherium, an extinct quadruped, belonging to the boar tribe. You want an ox to come from that boar? Well, nothing can be more easily accomplished than that. You must make four slight changes. Listen to his words: 'It seems natural to think that the fine paws of the ruminants may easily be supposed to have been a transformation of the heavy paws of the pachyderms. Four means seem to have been used to arrive at such simplification. The first is the translation or misplacing of the bone. Secondly, the change of the form of the bone. Thirdly, atrophy, or want of nourishment of the bone, which reduces it in size. Fourthly, the joining or soldering of the bone."

Doctor.—"Do this, and you have the heavy, thick paw of the boar changed into the fine one of the ox and steer."

Adele.—"That certainly is a comical way of accounting for a change. You want to change a boar into an ox? Is that all? Why, change the bones of the boar into those of the ox, and the thing is done. My dear Mr. Scientists, I would like to say, would you have the extreme politeness to tell me how you can change the bones of one into those of the other? Don't you think it would answer just as well if you replied to the question—How did the perfect mammals spring from the imperfect?—why, by being changed into them, of course. And if one insisted—But how were they changed? You would retort: Why, by being changed! What can be plainer than that?"

Doctor.—"Let us conclude, then, that paleontology affords no evidence whatsoever of intermediate species between that which seeks to be transformed and the one which it seeks to assume, and that there are insurmountable gaps between one species and another, each one standing apart without apparent ancestors and without descendants. That this, by acknowledgment of Darwin himself, is a deathblow to the doctrine of evolution. 'It is,' says Darwin, 'perhaps the most natural and the most serious objection ever raised against the theory' ('On the Origin of the Species,' p. 346. London, 1869)."

George.—"But he seeks to answer it, Doctor."

Doctor.—"I am aware of that, and for the amusement of Adele we will consider his answer. Give it in his own words."

George.—"'For my part, following out Lyell's metaphor, I look at the geological record as a history of the world imperfectly kept and written in a changing dialect; of this history we possess the last volume alone, relating only to two or three countries. Of this volume only here and there a short chapter has been preserved, and of each page only here and there a few lines. Each word of the slowly changing language, more or less different in the successive chapters, may represent the forms of life which are entombed in our consecutive formations, and which falsely appear to us to have been abruptly introduced. On this view the difficulties above discussed are greatly diminished, or even disappear' (page 384)."

Doctor.—"What do you think of that reply, Adele?"

Adele.—"Why, it is the most convenient reply that can be made. The unknown, the hidden and the absent are the best friends of the evolutionists. You miss the intermediary species to account for our pet theory? You are right, and nothing can be more reasonable; but, unfortunately, we cannot exactly satisfy your curiosity, when the very thing you want was to be found in abundance in the lost pages and chapters and lines of the book. Oh! if we had them we could content you to satiety. But never mind, believe that what you seek was in the lost fragments, and you will see how the difficulty disappears as if by enchantment. Is this what is called Modern Science, uncle?"

FIFTEENTH ARTICLE.

IS THE SCIENCE OF EMBRYOLOGY IN FAVOR OF EVOLUTION?

Doctor.—"The next science which evolutionists claim to be in their favor is embryology."

George.—"'The science of embryology,' says Romanes, 'affords perhaps the strongest of all the strong arguments in favor of evolution' ('The Scientific Evidence of Organic Evolution,' by G. J. Romanes, Humboldt Library, p. 15)."

Adele.—"That is very forcible language, and the author must feel the ground under him to be very solid, to speak so confidently."

George.—"Though in my opinion he abates very much his pretensions when he says: 'From the nature of the case, however, the evidence under this head requires special training to appreciate.'"

Adele.—"I think I see the drift."

Doctor.—"Certainly, and it is a common trick of our modern scientists. First they make the most liberal and unbounded promises of what we should expect from the results of a certain science. Then they regret very much that the thing is necessarily, and by nature of the case, above the general capacity of the reader; and finally wind up by saying in fact, if not in so many words, that the force of the argument really and truly can only be appreciated by themselves, and those who blindly agree with them."

Adele.—"Why, that is very amusing indeed!"

Doctor.—"Well, let us come to the point and see what evidence does embryology bring forward in help of evolution. Of course you understand, Adele, what is embryology?"

Adele.—"I do in a certain way, but I would rather listen to Mr. George."

George.—"Well, I suppose you know that the word comes from the Greek *embrion*, beginning or rudiments, and *logos*, a discourse on rudiments. It is now applied to that science which treats of the rudiments of living beings, and may be defined that science which observes all those primitive cells from which all living beings are developed in order to find the principles and the laws which govern that development."

Adele.—"And what do you mean by a cell?"

George.—"Cells are the first units of living matter in all organic beings. There are several questions about them, but they may prove uninteresting to you."

Adele.—"That depends on yourself and the manner of your explanations."

George.—"Well, I will try to do my best. That cells are the first units of living matter in all organized being, and that the origin of a living cell must come from a preëxisting living cell, is agreed upon by all scientists generally. But whether this small, tiny, infinitesimally little body has an element of internal structure or organization, limited by an external covering and ending, in the interior, in a certain nucleus, is now disputed among scientists. Whatever may be said or mantained about this, it remains as absolutely certain that a cell, whether itself organized or not, is a nucleated mass of living matter originating in another living cell."

Doctor.—" That science, then, which studies the primitive cells out of which all living beings are developed, is the one which is brought to give its testimony in favor of evolution."

Adele.—"How, uncle?"

Doctor.—" Wait a moment, Adele, we have not given sufficient importance to what George has called a round, tiny, infinitesimally small mass of living matter. George, how are the facts of this science ascertained?"

George.—"Principally by the microscope."

Adele.—"Why?"

George.—"In consequence of the exceeding smallness and size of these cells."

Doctor.—"Tell us now, what argument do evolutionists construct from embryology?"

George.—"I will give it in the words of the author just quoted: 'I will observe in general terms that the higher animals almost invariably pass through the same embryological stages as the lower ones up to the time when the higher animal begins to assume its higher characters. Thus, for instance, to take the case of the highest animal, man; his development begins from a speck of living matter similar to that from which the development of a plant begins; and, when his animali'y becomes established, he exhibits the fundamental anatomical qualities which characterize such lowly animals as the jelly fish. Next, he is marked off as a vertebrate, but it cannot be said whether he is to be a fish, a snake, a bird, or a beast. Later on it is evident that he is to be a mammal, but not till still later can it be said to which order of mammals he belongs. Now this progressive inheritance, by higher types of embryological characters common to lower types, is a fact which tells greatly in favor of the theory of descent' (page 166)."

Doctor.—"I suppose, Adele, you understand the force of the argument?"

Adele.—"I am not quite sure. I believe that, from the fact of the embryos of all living beings in their first stage of development being alike and presenting the same characters, they want to draw the conclusion that all living beings come from one form of life."

Doctor.—"Very good. Now we must test the value and the force of this strongest of the strong arguments in favor of evolution according to Mr. Romanes. In the first place, we will ascertain the following question. Is it a fact that the embryos of all living beings in their earliest stage of development are all alike? Now, George, what do you say. Can real, earnest, serious science admit this to be a fact well ascertained, whatever may be the assertions of enthusiastic and fanciful evolutionists?"

George.—"We cannot admit that such is the real fact, because we cannot rely on the instrument by which we endeavor to ascertain such things. We have said that all such embryo cells are examined by the aid of the microscope. But such cells are so infinitely small, so to speak, that they defy the most powerful microscope at least as far as to allow themselves to be studied with any kind of distinctness, accuracy, and in their individual characteristics. Hence their similar appearance under the microscope proves nothing at all as to their real similarity. Suppose one of us should look from a high mountain upon a plain miles away, and should see a number of quadrupeds running on that plain, all that he could ascertain is that a number of quadrupeds which looked all alike were frisking on that plain. He could certainly from such a view tell nothing about their difference and their individual form and character. Should he insist on claiming that that distant view is sufficient to establish their resemblance, and to eliminate and reject all possible difference in them, he would be put down as a fool or a joker. Now, such is our case. The embryo cells appear under the most powerful instrument as those quadrupeds seen from the mountain far away. They can exhibit only a general, vague, indistinct appearance, and thus seem to be all alike. But we have no warrant to conclude that such is the fact, and draw from such supposed fact a scientific conclusion of the greatest possible importance."

Doctor.—"You are right, George, and in confirmation of this I want you to read a passage of a lecture by Rev. Father Secchi upon the subject, which is full of sense and science."

Adele.—"Uncle, who is Father Secchi?"

Doctor.—"He is an Italian Jesuit, one of the grandest intellects of the age, one of the first astronomers and scientists of modern times. His lectures on the sun, which he delivered in Paris, drew the élite of that capital and the very first scientists, French and foreign, who applauded him to the skies. The passage I have marked for George to read is taken from the first lecture on the grandeur of creation."

George.—"'We are placed between two infinites; one extremely great, revealed by the telescope; the other extremely small, shown by the microscope; and as we cannot count the stars in a nebulosa, neither can we count the atoms of a cell nor the organs of an insect. It has been tried to calculate the quantity of atoms necessary to form the thousandth part of the side of an inch of water, and it has been found that it contains three thousand nine hundred billions of atoms. This number, even after the revision of the calculation made by the same microscopist, Soury, is held by him to be only approximately exact.'"

Adele.—"Dear me! it takes my breath away."

George.—"But water is one of the least complicated substances. As to albumen, it is found that the diameter of the last molecule of dry albumen is three hundred and eighty-three times that of water, and the little cube of a thousandth part of an inch, according to calculation, then would contain seventy one billions of these mixed molecules. Now what are, alongside of such dimensions, the distances of the closest lines of Norbert, by which we endeavor to enhance the force of the most powerful microscopes? The very waves of light are too big to enable us to discover such distances. Hence we may draw a very beneficial conclusion to stigmatize those ignorant and impudent naturalists who, in order to sustain their hypothesis of the transformation of species, allege that the primitive cells, from which are developed all living beings, are all equal, strengthening themselves on the fact that their instrument does not reveal any difference between them. Fools! They do not understand that with the most powerful instrument we should perceive those cells only as so many points, as like two tiny points would appear an elephant and a horse gazed at from the height of the most distant mountain."

Adele.—"I am glad that I made the acquaintance of Father Secchi; and I can see the force of his argument very clearly, indeed."

Doctor.—"We will conclude, then, that the embryos of all living beings in the first stages of their development, being in reality all equal as they appear, is not a fact which can be relied upon, because those primitive cells are so infinitely small that no instrument could discover any individual differences. But suppose we grant the fact, George, would it really prove anything in favor of evolution?"

George.—"I don't know, I am sure."

Doctor.—"Your friend, Romanes, has called this the strongest of all the strong arguments in favor of evolution. Before reason and common sense it is one of the most absurd and contradictory things that ever came out of their heated brains. How stands the case? Thus: By their acknowledgment all living beings, plants as well as animals, in the first stage of their embryonic state, are all the same. Very good; let it pass for a moment. How long does that sameness and equality last? By their admission, until the animal must take its own peculiar character. Now, suppose we want to examine the embryos of jelly fish, of a vertebrate, of a mammal. They all start from a tiny speck of living matter, and so far the sameness and equality appears, but does that equality continue? By no manner of means; the first speck begins to present the characters of a jelly fish, and stops there; the second, after taking the character of a jelly fish, proceeds to exhibit the characters of vertebrate, and stops there; the third, after taking the character of both, does not stop there, but puts on the character of a mammal. These are not only facts admitted by all scientists, but by the evolutionists themselves. And how could they deny them? It is upon this that the continuation of all living species is maintained. Then, if the first speck of living matter which starts the three different species of animals just mentioned be the same and identical, if there be no difference between them, if the one has no peculiar character of its own distinct from the others, let evolutionists explain how is it that the embryo of the jelly fish, after starting on equal terms with the embryos of the vertebrate and the mammal, stops when it has been developed into a jelly fish, and no power on earth could make it unfold any further; and again, how is it that the embryo of the vertebrate, after being developed first into a jelly fish and then into a vertebrate, comes to an end of its unfolding, and no created power can make it go a step further; whereas the embryo of the mammal, after going to all the stages of those two, assumes the characteristics of a mammal? Take again another instance—a number of mammals, say the ox, the horse, the dog, the gorilla, man. Let us suppose that the embryos of those five distinct species of mammals are under examination. They all have started from the speck of living matter perfectly the same and identical, according to our friends the transformists. They proceed in the growth and development, and first they exhibit the appearance of a jelly-fish; next the distinct characters of a vertebrate; again, they take up the peculiar and distinct marks of mammalia. So far we may suppose they have gone, step by step, all in harmony and union, and no difference appears in them; when, lo and behold! there is a divergence of the most remarkable nature. The embryo of the ox assumes the distinct characters of that quadruped; that of the horse the distinctive peculiarities of its species; that of the dog the peculiar feature of the dog kind; the gorilla those of the monkey tribe; and man the distinct and singular traits of mankind. How is that divergence, so fixed, so permanent, so immutable, so unalterable, so reliable, accounted for? What causes it, if the speck of the living matter constituting the embryos of all those mammals be one and the same, presenting the identical nature? The only possible answer to the question—the only reasonable answer—is, that though the embryos of all living creatures may at first present some appearance of resemblance in some very general traits, each one is distinct in nature and capacity from the other, as much as each one is numerically different from the other."

Adele.—"I see that our dear friends, the evolutionists, are always the same; from a vague, indistinct general resemblance of the embryos of all living creatures, in the very first stages of their development, they at once jump to the conclusion that they must all be the same offspring of one primitive form of life, and coolly, and with all possible simplicity and unconsciousness, pass over the immensely important fact that the different results must necessarily point out to a different cause and principle."

George.—"We may conclude then that embryology is in opposition to the theory of evolution. First, because the resemblance discovered with microscope in the embryos of all living creatures in the first and earliest stages of their development cannot be relied upon. And secondly, because, even admitting such resemblance, evolutionists cannot explain how embryos end apparently identical, each one in a different species of living creatures."

Adele.—"I am very much afraid that if your friend, Mr. Romanes, heard us treat his strongest of the strong arguments in favor of evolution with so little ceremony, he would count us among those who have not received a special training—which, in good English, means who are too intelligent and too careful not to believe on trust, and with their eyes shut, whatever modern scientists (?) are pleased to impose on the credulity of their disciples."

SIXTEENTH ARTICLE.

ARE RUDIMENTARY ORGANS ANY HELP TO EVOLUTION?

Doctor.—"Before we pass to the other sciences which evolutionists call to their aid in support of their theory, I think it necessary to occupy this present conversation in disposing of the argument which our friends draw from the existence of rudimentary organs."

George.—"This seems to be the place for it, as being very much akin to the subject which occupied our attention in our last meeting —that of embryology."

Adele.—"I am satisfied to locate the subject anywhere, if you will be so kind as to explain what is meant by rudimentary organs."

George—."By such organs evolutionists mean those organs observed in the embryos of many animals, which either disappear upon the growth of the animal or remain undeveloped, and are therefore considered by them perfectly useless."

Adele.—"As for instance?"

George.—"As for instance the examples given by Darwin and his fanatical disciple, Haeckel. 'The boa constrictor,' says the former, 'has rudiments of hind limbs.'"

Adele.—"Pray, what is a boa constrictor?"

George.—"The boa constrictor is one of the largest specimens of serpents, attaining, when fully developed, the length of thirty-five feet. It is so called from the Latin verb *constringere*, to crush, to press, because this animal, on account of its great muscular power, is enabled to crush the largest animals in its folds."

Adele—"Thanks. I suppose it is also poisonous."

George.—"No, luckily, it is perfectly harmless. 'What can be more curious,' continues Darwin, 'than the presence of teeth in foetal (or embryologic) whales, which, when grown up, have not a tooth in their heads; or the teeth which never cut through the gums of the upper jaws of the unborn calves? It is an important fact that rudimentary organs, such as teeth in the upper jaws of whales and ruminants, can often be detected in the embryo, but afterwards wholly disappear. The calf, for instance, has inherited teeth, which never cut through the gums of the upper jaw, from an early progenitor having well-developed teeth.' (Darwin, 'Origin of the Species.') 'In the embryos,' says Haeckle, 'of many ruminating animals, among others our own common cattle, fore-teeth, or incisors, are placed in the mid-bone of the upper jaw, which never fully develop, and therefore serve no purpose.' ('History of the Creation.')"

Doctor.—"Other examples are quoted, as for instance, among birds may be mentioned the ostrich, which is found in Africa, in Asia, and in India, beyond the Ganges, and which is over eight feet high, has wings with long, soft, undulating feathers, of no use for flying; the cassowary, a large, long-legged bird of the same family, inhabiting the island of Java; its wings, armed with strong spines for combat or defence, are shorter than those of the ostrich. In both these animals, then, the wings are rudimentary. Among such organs are also mentioned the eyes, which are found very well developed in some animals, because they are covered with a thick and opaque membrane. Many species of moles, blind rats, serpents, fishes and beetles which live under ground, or in the depth of the sea, are furnished with such eyes, which are of no use to them. Finally, we may mention the imperfect breasts in all the male individuals of the mammalia, and the hair in mankind, both of which are rudimentary, and of no use whatever."

Adele.—"I think I now understand perfectly what is meant by rudimentary organs, but I cannot see what they have got to do with the theory of evolution. How does it help evolution because the calf has the beginning of teeth which never cut through the gums, or because the mole and the beetle have eyes and cannot see, or because Mr. George here has beard which is rather a trouble to him than an advantage?"

Doctor.—"Evolutionists insist that the existence of such rudimental imperfect organs cannot be explained, except on the theory of evolution."

Adele.—"How?"

Doctor.—"The existence of a certain organ in an animal or plant may be accounted for by a twofold hypothesis: either that of design, or that of inheritance and descent. Let us take the eye as an example. Say all mammalia have eyes. Well, we may ask, Why is the eye found in all mammalia, and what is it intended for? You may answer in two ways 1st, the Creator intended that all such animals should be able to perceive all the external objects surrounding them, and it was for that reason that He endowed all of them with the organ of vision. The eye, then, was designed by the Creator to enable its possessors to see. The second answer is: the organ of vision was neither designed nor created, it was developed in proportion, as animals found out how useful the organ of vision might be, and strove after some such contrivance, and succeeded after many an effort and struggle in developing the eye in its greatest perfection. Now, evolutionists contend that the first hypothesis, that is, the supposition of a special creation of organs with a view to attain a certain definite object, cannot account for the existence of rudimentary organs because, as they are useless and of no possible advantage, they certainly cannot have been especially designed for anything; whereas the second hypothesis fully accounts for their existence. Such organs which are found rudimentary in certain animals must have existed in their full perfection in the ancestors of these animals; by degrees, for want of use, they became atrophied and shrunk up, and appear now in the present state, such as they have inherited. George, let us have the confirmation of the statement I have made by the words of some evolutionist."

George—"I will give you the words of Prof. Romanes in his work on evolution: 'Throughout the animal and vegetable kingdoms we constantly meet with organs which, in other and allied kind of animals and plants, are of large size and functional utility. Thus, for instance, the unborn calf, has rudimentary teeth which are never destined to cut the gums. The question therefore is how are they to be accounted for? Of course, the theory of descent, with adaptive modification, has a delightfully simple answer, viz., that when, from changed conditions of life, an organ which was previously useful becomes useless, natural selection, combined with disuse and so-called economy of growth, will cause it to dwindle till it becomes a rudiment. On the other hand, the theory of special creation can only maintain that the rudiments are formed for the sake of adhering to an ideal type.' (Page 11.)"

Doctor.—"We must now examine this new argument, of very great importance in the opinion of the evolutionists; and we will put two questions: 1st. Does the explanation of the evolutionists really account for rudimentary organs? 2d. What is the true and satisfactory explanation? With regard to the first inquiry I may remark, in the first place, that the evolutionist's explanation runs counter to the most fundamental principle of evolution. What is the fundamental principle of all systems of transformation? A continual progress from the minimum form of life to higher and better forms; a continual advance from the simple to the complex; a going upward in the scale of being. I need not quote many passages to prove, what is notorious to all, that the best and greatest among transformists are unanimous in maintaining that the foundation principle of evolution lies in a transition, from the crude to the finished; from the imperfect to the perfect; from the lowly organic beings to the higher grades of organism; from indefinite and vague forms to the definite; from the simple structure to the most complex arrangement of parts. What, then, must be the evident conclusion of such theory? Why, that it can admit of no such a thing as going backward or downward; that retrogression or deterioration in the system is absolutely out of question."

George.—"'A natural selection,' says Darwin, 'works solely for the good of each being; all corporeal and mental endowments will tend to progress towards perfection' ('Origin of the Species,' page 428). And again: 'The continued production of new forms, which implies that each new variety has some advantages over others, almost inevitably leads to the extermination of older and less improved forms' ('Animals and Plants,' p. 18)."

Doctor.—"The consequence, then, of all this is, that rudimentary organs cannot be explained by evolution, because the latter is a continual progress, an advance, a going ahead; the other is a backward movement. What is a rudimentary organ? An aborted and atrophied organ received from ancestral species which had it in perfect condition. Then such an organ proclaims a failure, a retrogression; it is an evident sign of decay, and, as such, contrary to all principle of evolution. Take, for instance, the boa constrictor, which, according to Darwin, once had legs in a perfect condition, and by evolution the species finally lost its legs, leaving the atrophied and shrunken leg bones in the body beneath the skin, and ever since the poor boa has been obliged to drag its ponderous form along the ground, by the most unmechanical and unphilosophical class of movements known in the animal kingdom."

Adele.—"Poor fellow; it would have been better for him if he had never been mixed up with evolution."

Doctor.—"It is asking too much, on the part of evolutionists, from their readers to believe that, according to this theory, the boa constrictor must have travelled through endless ages and numberless successive modifications and changes from legless fish or mollusk till it possessed the quadruped's advantage of legs and feet, and, when it had reached such a convenient state, to put him through another number of efforts and endeavors, through another countless mass of spontaneous variations, for the purpose of losing those useful implements as legs and feet, and for no other object under heaven except to leave little bones under the skin, and to furnish evolutionists with an argument from rudimentary organs. Say the same of the teeth in the embryos of whales, which, when grown up, have not a tooth in their heads; or of the teeth which never cut through the gums in the upper jaw of unborn calves. The ancestors of both must have gone through endless efforts to attain such useful instruments as teeth, and when they had reached the climax and the desired goal, be forced to go back through ages interminable till those teeth got to be atrophied and shrunken, to be transmitted in that useless and unprofitable state."

Adele.—"It is rather hard, I must confess, for those poor beasts. But what is the reason which caused those organs to become atrophied or shrunken?"

George.—"Why, on account of the changed conditions of life, those organs had become useless."

Doctor.—"Why, in most of the cases they quote, those organs

would be of the greatest use to the animals. If the cow, for instance, or the bovine genus, ever had upper incisors, what could possibly have caused their loss? Not, certainly, the supposition of such incisors having become useless; for the absence of such useful instruments has brought about the death of many a bovine animal by being unable thereby to bite off heavy twigs in browsing, to gnaw the bark from saplings, or to crop the stunted grass, which a goat with full incisors would grow fat upon. Such incisors, then, if they ever existed, could never have been atrophied or lost for want of opportunity to use them."

Adele.—"I perceive, clearly, that the reason alleged fails to account for the atrophy of the organs, as it is clear that those organs could have had frequent exercise."

Doctor.—"Then the explanation does not account for the existence of organs in some species in a rudimental state, whereas they are to be found at the present time in full development in the immediate ancestors of such species. Take man, for instance. He is the lineal descendant of the ape. The ape is covered all over with hair in its utmost perfection, and which is of the greatest use and advantage to it. Man has nothing but rudimentary hair. The ancestor keeps its covering whole and perfect; man does not. 'How is it man,' says Darwin, 'differs conspicuously from all other primates in being almost naked—but a few short straggling hairs over the greater part of the body in the man, and a fine down on the part of the woman? There can be little doubt that the hairs, then, scattered over the body, are rudiments of the uniform hairy coat of the lower animals.' ('Descent of Man,' p. 10). Well, how does he explain such rudimentary hairs in man? Certainly not by descent or inheritance, as man's ancestors, according to him, have a uniform hair coat."

George.—"He has attempted a certain explanation."

Adele.—"Well, let us have it."

George.—"'I am inclined to believe,' says Darwin, 'that man, or rather primarily woman, became divested of hair for ornamental purposes, and, according to this belief, it is not surprising that man should differ so great in hairiness from all his lower brethren.' ('Descent of Man,' page 143.)"

Adele.—"It is astonishing to me that none of the young misses of the genus ourang-outang or gorilla never had so much vanity or coquetry as to become divested of hair for ornamental purposes. The young gents of that tribe must rather like hair very much."

Doctor.—"Well, everybody having received that explanation with an explosion of laughter, some of Darwin's disciples took up the cudgel for him and volunteered other explanations. Professor Claparede ('*Revue des cours Scientific*', vol. 8, p. 570) offered a better one. Read it, George."

George.—"Having premised that man perhaps appeared first in some temperate and dry region, and those among men who spread themselves north and south may have found it necessary to protect their shoulders from the cold or the sun with the hide of an animal, he goes on to say, 'and who knows but that the continual friction of the covering upon this part of the body during a long series of generations may not have ended in relative rarity of hair upon the human back?'"

Doctor.—"Besides the ludicrousness of the explanation, the absurdity of it is shown by the fact that no covering or friction will deprive man's back now of whatever rudimental hair may have been left upon it."

Adele.—"We cannot be expected to agree with Professor Claparede."

George.—"Well, there is a better explanation suggested by Professor Grant-Allen. 'Our ancestors,' he says 'half human, and in the way of evolution, acquired the habit of walking erect and of lying on their back, in opposition to all other mammals. It was thus that they lost, little by little, the hair on the back and shoulders, and of those parts which came in contact with the ground.' ('*Revue Scientifique*,' January '86, page 719.) What are you laughing at so heartily, Miss Adele?"

Adele.—"Why, at Professor Grant-Allen and his explanation. It brought forcibly before my mind the fable of the man between two ages by La Fontaine, and I could not repress my risibility. I have no doubt Professor Grant-Allen, in the moments of relaxation from his ardous scientific studies, must have read 'La Fontaine' for amusement, and that same fable must have, unconsciously to himself, suggested the explanation."

Doctor.—"You are a sad girl, Adele."

George.—"And have no fear of scientists or science before your eyes. But let us have the fable."

Adele.—"A man of middle age, whose hair
   Was bordering on the gray,
Began to turn his thought and care
   The matrimonial way.
Two widows chiefly gained his heart;
   The one yet green, the other more mature,
Who found, for nature's wane in art, a cure.
   These dames amidst their joking, and caressing
The man they longed to wed,
   Would sometimes set themselves to dressing
His parti colored head.
Each aiming to assimilate
Her lover to her own estate;

> The older piecemeal stole
> The black hair from his poll,
> While eke with fingers light
> The young one stole the white.
> Between them both, as if by scald,
> His head was changed from gray to bald.
>
> —'*La Fontaine*,' *translated by E. Wright.*

And that certainly would better account for the poor man losing his hair, no matter of what color, than the reason given by Professor Grant for the whole of mankind, male and female, being minus their timely honored ancestral covering."

Doctor.—"Take again the example of the tail. Man's ancestors are furnished with a long, decent, respectable tail. Man, according to evolutionists, has but the very minimum of the rudiments of that organ. How do they explain such a thing, except by that ridiculous suggestion that he has worn it out gradually by sitting down upon it ?"

Adele.—"Is this science or romance, uncle ?"

Doctor.—"It is called science in the nineteenth century; a few centuries back they would have gotten hold of such scientists and shut them up in a mad-house."

George.—"But what is the real explanation for such rudimental organs?"

Doctor.—"In the first place, I want to remark that it is false to suppose that every organ must be of some use and advantage to the individual which possesses it, in the restricted sense that it must serve it for some function or other. It must certainly have been intended for some end, but not necessarily and always for the advantage of the individual, but to follow up the type of the species; or, by variety, to add to the beauty and the adornment of the individual and of the universe. If we take this into consideration, everything can be explained upon theory from design. An organ in a rudimental state may be of no real necessity or use to the individual, but may serve to express fully and completely the type of the species, or it may add to the beauty and ornamenting of the individual, and therefore of the universe. Darwin partly admits this explanation. 'The foregoing remarks lead me to say a few words on the protest lately made by some naturalists against the utilitarian doctrine, that every detail of structure has been produced for the good of its possessor. They believe that many structures have been created for the sake of beauty to delight man or the Creator, or for the sake of mere variety—a view already discussed. Such doctrines, if true, would be absolutely fatal to my theory. I fully admit that many structures are now of no direct use to their possessors, and may never have been of any use to their progenitors, but this does not prove that they were formed solely for beauty or variety' ('Origin of Species,' p. 89)."

Adele.—"Dear me! these gigantic intellects can never string together a dozen words without contradicting themselves. Here is the patriarch of evolutionism admitting that some organs are of no use, and may never have been of any use to their possessors and to their progenitors, and then denies that they were made for beauty or variety. I humbly submit that when a thing is of no use to anybody, what is left to it but to be ornamental ?"

Doctor.—"Let us then conclude: the uniformity of the plan followed by the Creator in His works can easily explain the presence of rudimentary organs in some animals. God has thus impressed upon such as these the signs of relationship with their kind. 'Instead of being an argument in favor of evolution,' says Agassiz—'the rudimental eye discovered by Doctor J. Wyman in the blind fish of the Mammoth Cave—does it not prove on the contrary that this animal, like all others, has been created with all its particular characters by the *fiat* of the Almighty, and that this rudiment of the eye has been bequeathed to it as a memorial of a general plan of structure upon which has been constructed the great type to which it belongs ?' ('Classification of Species,' p. 20)."

SEVENTEENTH ARTICLE.

ARE THE REASONS DRAWN FROM CLASSIFICATION, MORPHOLOGY, ANATOMY, AND PATHOLOGY IN FAVOR OF ORGANIC EVOLUTION OF ANY REAL VALUE ?

Doctor.—"The argument drawn from different sciences will occupy our present and other conversations. These are: Classification, Morphology, Anatomy, and Pathology. An argument and a proof is endeavored to be derived from each of these sciences, which, as they all amount to the same thing and come to the same conclusion, we will treat of and discuss in their combined logical evidence. Please, George, give us the evolutionists' proof, so-called, from classification ?"

George.—"I will answer in the words of Romanes: 'All scientists, who have directed their study upon natural history, have classified all living beings according to the natural affinities which are observed among them. Their system of classification may be compared to a tree in which a short trunk may be taken, as representing the lowest organism, which cannot properly be called either plant or animal. The short trunk is soon separated into two large trunks, one representing the vegetable, the other the animal kingdom. Each of these trunks then gives us large branches, signifying classes, and these give off smaller but more numerous branches, which signify genera, and finally into leaves which may be taken to represent species. In such a representative tree of life, the height of any branch from the ground may be taken to indicate the grade of organization, which the leaves or species present. Now, the framing of this natural classification has been the work of naturalists for centuries past; and although they did not know what they were doing, it is now evident to evolutionists they were tracing the lines of genetic relationship.'"

Adele.—"Let me see if I understand the argument. Evolutionists say, naturalists for ages past have classified plants and animals as two large trunks, branching off from a much shorter but larger trunk, representing some being neither plant nor animal. Those two trunks, that is, the vegetable and animal kingdom, shoot off branches and leaves which represent genera and species of plants and animals. The distance of a branch from the ground is an index of its organic grade of perfection. Now, of course, if such classification was made according to nature and grounded upon observation, nothing better could have been done in favor of evolution, as it represents all living being, plants and animals of every genus and species, as springing up from the lowest possible germ of life. Is that the argument?"

Doctor.—Certainly, Adele, and you have very cleverly caught it. As I intend to consider the whole argument as resulting from all the four sciences we have mentioned. I will not say much now except to observe that the classification as described by Mr. Romanes is cobweb spun out of his fertile and busy brain, a sheer invention of his own, for which he can claim undivided parentage. Why, if naturalists have represented all living beings, plants and animals, under the image of tree, whose trunk branches off into minor trunks, and branches and leaves representing genera and species, they never dreamt to signify that all those genera and species sprang up by generation or evolution from one real form of life, neither belonging to the vegetable nor to the animal kingdom. If they made use of the image of a tree, with trunk, branches and leaves, they merely and simply understood it in a figurative sense."

Adele.—"In such case the argument of evolutionists falls down as a house of cards."

Doctor.—"Neither more nor less. Let them bring forward, if they can, some celebrated naturalist, such as Linnæus, Buffon, Cuvier, who uses it in the sense they take it, that is, in any other sense than as a figure or an image, and then we shall discuss this argument seriously. Pass on to the other sciences, George."

George.—"Next comes morphology or science of form of structure.

The argument they draw from this science is that from the lower tribes of mammals toward the higher organisms, there is such a marked and regular gradation, together with such a general resemblance and such gradual passage from one to another, especially in the genera and species and races of those beings, which are most related to each other as to strike one most forcibly, and to leave no alternative to account for it than the supposition that they are all descended from one prototype in nature. How otherwise account for it?"

Adele.—"So you say that the regular and gradual ascension from the lowest animals to the highest, all resembling each other, implies a common descendance from one single parent?"

Doctor.—"So evolutionists claim, at least, Adele. Let us have a word about comparative anatomy and pathology, George."

George.—"Morphology rather regards the form of the structure of living bodies; anatomy treats of the framework of the organs of the same. Now, as there is a gradual ascent from the lower organisms of living bodies up to the higher, and a general and gradual resemblance in their formation and structure, so there is in the framework, in the bones of the same; and this, of course, must lead us to the same conclusion that they must all have descended from a common parent. 'The similar frame work of bones in the hand of man,' says Darwin, 'the wing of a bat, the fin of a porpoise, and the leg of a horse and innumerable other facts, at once explain themselves on the theory of descent with slow and slight and successive modifications.' Pathology, which is the science of diseases, leads to the same conclusion, as it represents all animals subject more or less to the same diseases, which of course could not happen unless they were endowed with similar organs and pointed to the same common descent."

Adele.—"Very good. I see the drift of the argument furnished by all these sciences, classification, morphology, comparative anatomy, and pathology. They all go to show that in all living beings, especially in animals, from the lowest possible to the highest known to us, there is a gradual successive ascending upwards, one hardly being distinguished from the other and almost insensibly and imperceptibly blending into the other; and that they all exhibit in the forms of their organs and their structure, in the framework of such organs, as the whole system of bones, in the very diseases and failing of their organs and their functions a resemblance so great, a family look so forcible, a relationship so apparent, that the only way to account for such facts is the supposition that all came from a common source and a common parent."

George.—"Bravo, Miss Adele. What a magical hand you have in condensing and recapitulating?"

Adele.—"Nonsense. Uncle, how are we to meet such an accumulation of sciences? Is all what they say true? Are all the facts really as they state them?"

Doctor.—"Pretty much so."

Adele.—"Then you admit the facts?"

Doctor.—"We admit most willingly and cheerfully the facts of the gradual successive and ascending resemblance in all living beings, particularly animals, in the form, in the framework of the structure of their organisms, even as far as the great similarity in their pathological infirmities and evils."

George.—"Then you admit the consequence?"

Doctor.—"What consequence?"

George.—"That they all come from one common parent."

Doctor.—"Most decidedly not."

George.—"Then how do you get over the facts? How do you explain them?"

Doctor.—"I give a different explanation of those facts from that of the evolutionists, as I have an undoubted right so to do, and as I trust those gentlemen will be willing to concede."

Adele.—"Then how is the question to be decided?"

Doctor.—"By testing each respective explanation with logic and common sense and find out which of them will stand the test. We will proceed in this discussion as follows: 1st, we will endeavor to understand the explanation I adopt; 2dly, we will examine what evolutionists have got to say against it; in the third place, we will take the evolutionists' explanation, and investigate whether it does or does not explain the facts. I think all that will embrace the whole ground, and nothing more could be expected."

George.—"And I must confess that no fairer or more equitable method could be desired."

Doctor.—"Now then for the explanation I adopt. It is called the explanation from design."

Adele.—"What is that?"

Doctor.—"I suppose, as we proved in one of our earliest explanations, that God is the Creator of the universe, and I suppose further, that in creating the universe He must have an object in view, because He is infinite intelligence, and no intelligence which acts as such can do so without a knowledge of the object of its action. What can such object be? None other than the manifestation of His infinite nature and perfection, or, in other words, none other than that of communicating existence and perfection to others. Do you understand, Adele?"

Adele.—"You say that the Almighty Creator, being an Infinite intelligence, must have an end in view in the creation of the universe, and that such an end can be no other than the imaging and expressing Himself in created existences and perfections. I understand that far; but why can He have no other end in view?"

Doctor.—"Can you add anything to the Infinite, or take anything away from Him? Can you add to His nature, His knowledge, His wisdom, His goodness, His excellence?"

Adele.—"Certainly not, or He would not be infinite."

Doctor.—"Then, as He can gain nothing by creating, that act must consist and have for its object to bestow being and perfection to such as do not as yet possess either."

Adele.—"I see."

Doctor.—"Next, God in creating must sketch out and express Himself, His nature and perfection in what He effects, because as He is the source of all being, He is also, necessarily, the model, the type, the pattern of all existences. In creating, therefore, He imitates and copies Himself; but, of course, you understand what He creates must necessarily be finite, and, therefore, infinitely inferior to its model."

George.—"I see that well enough. Created means to be dependent upon another for its existence; uncreated and infinite, means to be self-existing; therefore, to suppose a created being equal to the infinite, would be a contradiction in terms, as it would mean a being made by another, and self-existing at the same time."

Adele.—"Gentlemen, I don't see the drift of your explanation yet, but I suppose I shall by-and-by."

Doctor.—"Certainly, please to follow me a moment longer and you will see very clearly into the thing. The amount of being which the Creator may effect being obliged to be finite, and infinitely inferior to God, in order to image Him and His perfections as well as possible, it must necessarily be subject to the following laws—the law of variety, of proportion and affinity, and the law of unity."

Adele.—"I can't say I understand very well."

George.—"Nor I."

Doctor.—"The first law which God must follow in creating is to produce not one class or kind of creatures, but a variety of classes, of kinds and individuals. You understand that much?"

Adele.—"Certainly; but why?"

Doctor.—"Because what He creates is infinitely inferior to the model. Look into yourself, Adele, when you try to express an idea. The idea in your mind is something immaterial, intelligible and spiritual. You want to express it by material sounds. If the sound were of the same immaterial nature with the idea, one sound would fully and completely express the idea, in all cases and under all circumstances; but, as they are inferior in nature and material, in most cases, you must have a variety of sounds to express one simple idea. So it is with creation. The ideal is spiritual and immaterial—infinite in nature. One inferior being, therefore, or one class of them, could never express that idea. Hence the necessity of creating a variety of class and of kinds of beings."

Adele.—"I understand perfectly, now, as a musician, for instance, who wants to express a feeling of tenderness has to make use of various sounds to stamp that spiritual feeling in his composition, and to arouse it in the listeners; so God, having to mirror his immaterial nature and perfection in the universe must make use of a variety of creatures and classes of them."

Doctor.—"Very good. Then you will easily perceive the other laws, that of unity, for instance; because, as that variety is needed to express one ideal, all classes of being must all conspire to ultimately convey that idea of unity. And to attain this God makes use of the law of proportion and affinity, which means that, between one class of creatures and another, though distinct by the law of variety, there must not be a difference so great as to render impossible the unity, but there must be a certain resemblance or similitude between them so as to harmonize them in view of the general end. The conclusion of all this is that it behooved God, in creating the universe, to effect a variety of classes of creatures to express His infinite perfections, and to put such a general softening and shadowing in the varieties of classes as to enable them to represent a whole harmonic universe, whilst maintaining the specific variety of each class. That was God's design, which he effected by creating five distinct kingdoms or classes of creatures, the mineral, the vegetable, the animal, the human and the purely spiritual. Under each of these he created an immense number of species, and of individuals in each species. What I claim is that every one of those kingdoms required a distinct creative act, and that the one could not be evolved from the other. For instance: The vegetable or living world could not be evolved from the mineral, nor the animal or sensitive from the vegetable, nor the human kind from the animal, nor the spiritual world from the human; otherwise, the variety would be extinguished, though I grant that God having created the genus of each kingdom, may have allowed them to evolve within their sphere. Again, having created those five classes, it is no wonder that they should present, in structural form, in the framework of their organism, a successive and gradual ascension and resemblance, because all were made to serve and to express and to mirror the same ideal and pattern."

Adele.—"I perceive the whole thing perfectly and I am charmed with it. What was the necessity of having five distinct kingdoms in nature? To express the grandeur, the unlimited superiority of the ideal and pattern of Creation—the infinite Creator. Why do we find such gradual insensible similarity in all those kingdoms rising up from the lowest to the highest? Why do we admire such family likeness in their form and structure and even in their ills? Because, though distinct and various, they are so fashioned as to imitate the unity of the model."

Doctor.—"Well, that is what is called the explanation from design. George, what have evolutionists to object to this explanation adopted by *all* the highest and best geniuses in every department of science, until Lamark and Darwin and Co. invented this theory of transformation?"

George.—"The great objection they urge against it is that it is not a scientific explanation. 'Nothing can be more hopeless,' says Darwin, 'than to attempt to explain this similarity of pattern in members of the same class by utility or by doctrine of final causes. On the ordinary view of independent creation of each being we can only say that so it is, that it has pleased the Creator to construct all the animals and plants in each great class on a uniform plan; but *this is not a scientific explanation*.'"

Adele.—"Will you be so obliging, Mr. George, as to tell me, in your usual happy and lucid language, what is required for an explanation to be *scientific?*'

Doctor.—"You should have inquired what, according to evolutionists, is necessary for an explanation to be scientific, for in that case he could have a prompt answer, which is: That any nonsense, no matter how ludicrous or absurd, provided it serves to banish God's action from the universe, is accepted and venerated as a truly scientific explanation and extolled to the skies. Say anything you list provided you put God on the shelf and you are sure to be a great scientist. Now, listen to Huxley's answer to the question. It is twofold. The one is that an explanation is scientific when the thing to be accounted for is explained by some general law of nature. 'A phenomenon is explained when it is shown to be a case of some general law of nature.' (Lay Sermons, p. 282, Appleton, '76.) The second part of the answer is that no amount of evidence which we are capable to attain can justify us to maintain that anything is out of the power of natural agents or cause. 'Let us ask ourselves whether any amount of evidence which the nature of our faculties permits us to attain, can justify us in asserting that any phenomenon is out of reach of natural causation' (H.)"

Adele.—"I see, then, that according to evolutionists, no explanation can be scientific unless it excludes God, and no amount of evidence we are able to gather can justify us to say that anything can be done by the Almighty and not brought about by natural forces. But, uncle, do these people admit that God was wanted at all to create matter or all those primitive substances of which the universe is composed?"

George.—"Why do you put the question, Miss Adele?"

Adele.—"Because it seems to me that our friends, the transformists, are in a sad corner again."

George.—"Well, suppose I answer that they do admit, as Darwin did at first, that the materials and the one or few forms of life out of which every living organism is evolved were created by God, what then?"

Adele.—"Why, then, by their leave and yours, I say that their explanation of the existence of primitive matter and primitive living forms is not scientific because it calls in the interference of an agent out of the sphere of nature."

Doctor.—"You have hit the nail on the head, Adele. Evolutionists cannot object to our explanation as unscientific without decrying their own explanation, if they admit primitive matter and living forms to have been created by God Almighty, or must fall into the material pantheism of Haeckel, Spencer, Vogt and Buckner. Listen to the latter's words. He quotes first Darwin's words which say: 'I consider it as probable that all organized beings which have ever lived upon earth, are all descended from a primitive form to which the breath of the Creator has once communicated life. But this conclusion rests on analogy and it is not necessary that it should be admitted or not.' Upon those words Buckner remarks: 'The last assertion is by no means rational and Professor Brown, Darwin's translator (into German) has justly objected to it in a postscript after his translation, as being defective and destructive of his whole theory. For if we must recognize that special acts of creation have been necessary for eight or ten first original couples, why not accept this creation also for all other beings, and why endeavor to explain their apparition by natural causes? Because it is immaterial to a philosopher that the creative act be produced once or several times and once it is admitted, the miracle is substituted instead of the natural law.' (Doctor Bucker, 'Conferences on the Darwinian Theory,' First Conference.) Let us then recapitulate our whole argument. Evolutionists refuse to explain the facts of similarity of all living beings by the hypothesis of design because they contend that it is unscientific and introduces the miraculous and the supernatural in the universe. What have we answered to that, Adele?"

Adele.—"That if they admit creation at all to explain the first primitive forms of life their explanation is unscientific as introducing and calling in the interference of God in nature. If they do not they have the existence of the first living form, whatever it may be, to account for, and they can only do so by accepting the gross and material pantheism of Spencer, Haeckel, Buckner, Vogt, and the like."

EIGHTEENTH ARTICLE.

WHAT IS A SCIENTIFIC EXPLANATION?

Doctor.—"In our last conversation we reasoned on the evolutionists' definition of a scientific explanation, letting it pass for the time being, and only pointing out the consequences which result against their own system from such a definition. I want, in the present conversation, to thoroughly and completely examine it. George, did it ever strike you that such a definition is the very sublimity of pretension and absurdity?"

George.—"I must say it did not. Scientists raise such clamor about the greatness, the solidity of their pursuits, the wonderful depth of their attainments, the sublime privilege of understanding their theories, the very limited mental powers, or rather imbecility, of those who do not hold them for demi-gods, and swear on their word, that no matter how careful a man may be, in guarding himself, he is more or less influenced by such a clamor and becomes biased in their favor in spite of himself."

Doctor.—"It is high time to speak the truth openly and loudly and without much ceremony or glove-handling. For imbecility of true mental vigor and intelligence, only equalled by an overweaning self-complacency and laudation, commend me to your scientists. You will bear me out when we have examined their definition of a scientific explanation. What is it, Adele?"

Adele.—"'A phenomenon,' says Huxley, 'is explained when it is shown to be a case of some general law of nature. And no evidence can justify us in asserting that any phenomenon is out of the reach of natural causation.' In other other words, no explanation is, or can be called scientific, which explains and accounts for a thing by any other cause than that of a general law of nature."

Doctor.—"George, do you see the extreme pretension of such a definition?"

George.—"I begin to guess."

Doctor.—"With infinite modesty our scientists merely suppose that all possible human knowledge and science is included in the physical universe, and that beyond that we neither can, nor must seek for any further knowledge. That is the modest claim of science. The laws of the physical world which govern all bodies inorganic or living are all that can have the name of science. Therefore, that far you can go and no farther; if you seek any farther, if you pretend to have discovered or heard of other and higher principles, higher beings, then you are no longer scientific, you are out of the pale of science. You will the better conceive this when you have read the definition of science by Spencer and Huxley which you will find marked."

George.—"'What is science?' asks Spencer. 'Science is simply a higher development of common knowledge.'" ('First Principles,' p. 18). 'Knowledge,' says Huxley, 'upon many subjects, grows to be more and more perfect, and when it becomes to be so accurate and sure that it is capable of being proved to persons of suitable intelligence, it is called *science*. The *science* of any subject is the *highest and most exact knowledge upon that subject*.' ('Elementary Physiology,' p. 11.)"

Doctor.—"The knowledge of any subject which has become so accurate and sure as to be capable of being proved to any average intelligence is science then according to Spencer and Huxley?"

George.—"Certainly."

Doctor.—"Why, then, if I undertake to account for a natural phenomenon by a cause which is outside of natural causation, and I have such sure and accurate knowledge of that cause as to prove it to any average intelligence, why is it then that my explanation is cried down as not being scientific, except for the lurking, unwarrantable pretension and gratuitous supposition that beyond nature, its phenomena and its laws, there is nothing to learn surely and accurately or capable of demonstration? 'No evidence can justify us in asserting that any phenomenon is out of the reach of natural causation.' In other words, outside nature, its phenomena and its laws, there is nothing more to be learned, or at least to be learned with such a sure and accurate knowledge or evidence as to be capable of being proved to an average intelligence."

George.—"But they say we don't object to your learning anything beyond the physical universe, its phenomena and its laws, or to acquire even a scientific knowledge of this something, if you can. All we want is that physical phenomena, facts belonging to the physical world, should not be accounted for except by physical and natural causes."

Doctor.—"I insist that any explanation of a phenomenon found on a knowledge so sure and accurate as to be capable of demonstration is and must be called scientific, and that the so-called scientists have no right whatever to turn up their nose with utter disdain and disgust when they hear an explanation, derived from other sources than what seems to them natural cause and call it unscientific. If it comes from a knowledge sure and accurate, capable of proof, it is scientific, else all our knowledge and science is limited and narrowed down to the physical world, its movement and its laws. In one word, is science limited only to that sure and accurate knowledge capable of proof of the visible universe, its phenomena and its laws, or can it have some other object? If it is limited to the first, then our knowledge is confined to the universe, its movement and its laws, and the whole human encyclopædia is narrowed down to physical sciences; or it can have some other object, and then we must admit the scientific character and value of any explanation which is beyond the sphere of physical science and natural causation. What you urge about their saying that natural phenomena or facts must only be accounted for by natural causes is a begging of the question. It supposes that the visible universe, its phenomena and its laws, *can and must* be accounted by natural causes. They take that for granted. Have they ever proved it, or attempted even to give an apology for a proof? It is as much as to say the world must be accounted for by the world, nature must be explained by nature; natural causes must be accounted for by natural causes. What is that but saying that the world, the universe, nature are absolutely independent of any other cause, and consequently absolute and self-existent, for that which can furnish of itself a reason for its existence and movement is independent and self existent? I concede that physical facts should be accounted for by physical and natural cause, so far as possible, and that it would be absurd to call in a foreign cause, so to speak, to account for a physical phenomenon, when the natural cause is at hand to explain it: but to say it in a general sense, as embracing all cases, to say in an absolute sense, nature must be accounted for by nature, is the absolute denial of creation, and the assertion of the self-existence of the universe."

Adele.—"But, uncle, what did you mean when you said that scientists have no right to reject as unscientific an explanation which is derived from other sources than what *seems to them natural?*"

Doctor.—"You bring me to a part of the subject which we must mention, and about which our scientists are either laboring under a very gross and sad mistake, or are wilfully and maliciously misleading others. They call every action of God, either in creating the first matter of the universe, or in creating the different species, or in governing and ruling the universe, a miraculous fact, a supernatural interposition of the Creator, a supernatural explanation, an interference of the Creator, and so forth. Read the passages marked, George."

George.—"'The Creator thought fit to interfere in the natural course of events,' etc. 'The supernatural interference of the Creator can, by the nature of the case, exemplify no law.' (Huxley, 'Lay Sermons.') 'If we were childish enough to rush into a supernatural explanation,' (Romanes, 'Scientific Evidence,' page 3). 'To admit creation,' says Buckner, 'is always to substitute the miracle for the law of nature.'" (*Loc. cit.*)

Doctor.—"You see, then, that scientists, with that extreme and incredible ignorance of all true philosophy and religious knowledge so peculiar to them, call supernatural and miraculous what no Christian philosopher for nineteen centuries ever as much as dreamt of considering and calling by any other name than natural. For all Christian philosophy and theology has always understood by natural creation, that act of God which creates from nothing all cosmic substances for a certain end, and endows them with faculties and movement subject to certain laws; act which after creating them, continues to keep them in existence and to aid them in their action and movement towards reaching their end, both individual and cosmical. Christian philosophy considers all those elements comprised in the definition as natural. First, the creative act producing cosmic substances with their faculties and movement subject to certain general laws; second, the continuation of this act in maintaining and conserving those substances in existence; thirdly, the action of God, coöperating with the movement of created substances towards their development and towards their attaining their end, both individual and universal. We Christians call all these natural causes first God, the supreme and universal cause of the universe in its existence and movement, created substances, secondary causes and subordinate agents; but all natural and not supernatural, all according to the general laws established by the Creator, and not by miraculous extraordinary ways outside the established laws. We call all those causes natural and we can prove it, and have proved it by such sublime monuments of Christian reasoning, as would stagger the keenest and boldest intellects among our friends, the scientists. What do they mean, then, when they so confidently spout out that we are having recourse to the supernatural, to an extraordinary interference of the Creator, to a miraculous action when we explain the origin of species by an act of the Creator? They evidently do not know what they are talking about."

Adele.—"They are so childishly afraid, it seems to me, of the supernatural and the miraculous that they scent its presence even when it is myriads of miles away; a dread, a tremor, a chilly sensation, a creeping like a serpent's invasion comes over and makes them shiver at the very shadow of the supernatural. Be calmed, be soothed, gentlemen, be comforted; the supernatural and the miracle are far, far away; they cannot hurt a hair of your venerable and hoary heads."

George.—"Then you claim that the explanation from design is within the reach of the natural, as you claim that the whole creation, implying God as the first cause, and created substances as secondary agents, must all be considered as the natural causes of the universe and of every phenomenon taking place therein."

Doctor.—"Certainly; no Christian philosopher or theologian ever considered them in any other light."

George.—"But supposing all this to be as you state it, Doctor, and, as I have no doubt it is, evolutionists have another escape. They may say: Well, granted that it is not calling in the supernatural, when you admit special creations, but only the natural, you yourself have admitted that when a phenomenon can be explained without bringing the interference of God's action, but by created agencies, we must be satisfied with the latter. Here are the words of M. Romanes: 'Once admit the glaring, illogical principle that we may assume the operation of higher causes, when the operation of lower ones is sufficient to explain the observed phenomena, and all our science and all our philosophy are scattered to the winds. For the law of logic, which Sir William Hamilton called the law of parsimony, which forbids us to assume the operation of higher causes, when the lower ones are found sufficient to explain the observed effects, this law constitutes the only logical barrier between science and superstition.'"

Doctor.—"I think Sir William Hamilton might have used a better word than *parsimony* to express that beautiful law of wisdom expressed by St. Thomas long before him: '*Sapiens operator perficit opus suum breviori via qua potest*'—'a wise artificer performs his intended work by the shortest possible way.' And in one of our conversations, if you remember, we called it the law of the minimum means."

Adele.—"I recollect when we proved that evolution within each species can and must be allowed; because before God should interfere with His creative action in producing a desired effect, He must, in force of that law, allow secondary causes to have all the play they can."

Doctor.—"Decidedly. We therefore admit that law. But what good will that do to the evolutionists? Before they can call it in, in aid of their theory, they must first prove that the existence of all natural species, from the lowest to the highest, can be accounted for fully and perfectly by the admission of a few primitive living forms, out of which all were gradually, successively and in a rising proportion developed. When they have proved that they can call on the law of wisdom, or, if they like better of parsimony, to oblige us to admit their explanation. The whole question then is here: we both admit that law, the evolutionists and their opponents. The former claim that by that law we must not call in the action of God to explain the existence of all cosmical species, because they insist that the hypothesis of a few of the lowest forms out of which all have been developed and evolved fully accounts for them. We, admitting the same law, contend that we are necessitated to call in God's action, because their hypothesis by no manner of means accounts for the existence of all cosmical species. But we insist that our explanation is as natural as theirs, even supposing theirs to be satisfactory, that our explanation is as scientific as theirs, and that they have no right to show their fastidiousness and repugnance to consider as unscientific what does not square with their system, and to create a prejudice against our explanation by that high sounding condemnation. Adele, please to give a summary of our whole conversation."

Adele.—"We set out with inquiring what is a scientific explanation, and we proved that, according to the definition of Spencer and Huxley, every kind of knowledge which is sure and accurate and capable of being proved to a competent intelligence must deserve the name of scientific; that the pretension of Huxley, to the effect that no amount of evidence can justify us to explain any fact by any but a natural cause, is an unwarrantable assertion, as it would reduce all human knowledge to natural sciences; that they have either wilfully or ignorantly called supernatural and miracle what the Christian world has always looked upon and vindicated as pertaining to the natural order; and that, though it be true, that we must not call in God's action when a fact can be explained by created agency, this concession will not help evolutionists, as it leaves the question where it was, whether their hypothesis accounts for the facts. As a consequence of all this we have gained the advantage of removing from one explanation from design the objection of its being unscientific, and of calling in the supernatural and the miraculous?"

Doctor.—"We will in our next conversation see if the evolutionists' explanation of the resemblance of all living beings in form, in structure, and even in their physical ills is satisfactory."

NINETEENTH ARTICLE.

IS THE EVOLUTIONISTS' EXPLANATION OF THE FACTS FROM MORPHOLOGY, ANATOMY AND PATHOLOGY REASONABLE AND SATISFACTORY?

Doctor.—"George, please to state the facts which evolutionists undertake to explain."

George.—"In all living species, but especially in animal species, we find the following general fact: a common resemblance, and as it were, a family look, in the form and structure of their organs, even in the framework of the same. This resemblance begins at the very lowest organic forms, and rises up constantly, insensibly, gradually, step by step; and in proportion as the organisms ascend in the scale and become higher and more complicated the similarity increases, so that you would say that they were all cast at one mould."

Adele.—"Now, give us the explanation of evolutionists?"

George.—"How can such a resemblance be accounted for? Very simply; the organic forms present a family resemblance because they belong, in reality, to one family; they descend from one progenitor, or a few couples which, starting from the lowest steps of organic life, are gradually developed into a higher, and then, into one higher still, until they reach the highest—man."

Doctor.—"Very easily said. We must now examine whether reason and common sense can accept such an explanation; and to do it more orderly and clearly we will investigate the following points: first, what are these progenitors, and what is the amount of capital, so to speak, they start with. Second, by what means are they continually changed from one class to another. When we have fully discussed these two points we shall discover what is to be thought of such explanation."

Adele.—"I understand; we want to know what are these venerable and ancient and primitive progenitors of all organic life, and how they contrive to change from one to another?"

Doctor.—"Now, George, please to tell us what these progenitors are according to best and greatest evolutionists."

George.—"For the sake of clearness and simplicity I will suppose that such a progenitor is only one; first, because logic would force us into it, and secondly, because Darwin himself is not averse to admitting it in those words: 'There is a grandeur in this view of life, with its several powers having been originally breathed by the Creator into a few forms, or into one' ('Origin of Species,' p. 428)."

Adele.—"Well, let it be one, and tell us now his whole history."

George.—"I will not, of course, mention those who maintain that all life has sprung up from dead inert matter. We disposed of that opinion in two of our former conversations. I will give the opinion of those evolutionists who, like Darwin, admit the creation of the first and the most simple form of life. Now, we cannot find in nature any form of life lower or more simple than that which consists of one single cell, and is, on that account, called unicellular. From such a thing as a unicellular living being must all the vegetable and animal species have descended."

Adele.—"It takes one's breath away to have to gulp down such a tremendous paradox. Strong, indeed, must the faith of scientists be. The moving of a mountain, the old test of the great efficacy of that virtue would be a child's play alongside of that."

Doctor.—"Let us examine what the supposition implies. What power or force do evolutionists attribute to this progenitor of all living species?"

George.—"I am not aware that they attribute to, or predicate of it, any particular force any more than what belongs to the nature of any kind of unicellular beings."

Doctor.—"What! Do you mean to say, that, for instance, a tiny little speck, an imperceptible cell, is or can be the parent of the whole vegetable world, from the moss or fern to the most gigantic inhabitants of the forest! That from it also must spring all sorts of animal life! That, starting from the minutest and infinitely small infusoria, it must evolve itself into the radiate, the mollusk, the articulate and the vertebrate, the latter embracing the greatest and the best in the animal world, such as fishes, reptiles, birds, mammals, at the head of which stands, preëminently, man! Do you mean to say that this imperceptible little speck is not endowed with such a native force and energy, such an exterminate hidden power, such a boundless activity as to be able to produce such enormous and colossal results?"

George.—"They certainly do not claim for it any special powers."

Doctor.—"Well, we must bid an eternal farewell to logic and to all principles of ontology. It is a principle of ontology that no effect can be superior to its real cause, that whatever is contained in the effect must be found also in some way or another in the cause, because effect means that which comes from the cause; and how, in the name of common sense, could it come from it if it were not in some way or another in the cause? This great principle of ontology can be illustrated by thousands of examples. Heat, for instance, cannot be more powerful or more raging than the heated body which produces it; movement must necessarily follow and be measured by the amount of force exercised by the motor; a machine of a thousand horsepower could not produce an effect requiring ten times that amount; an ant could not shake up Mount Blanc from its foundation, nor a satellite in our solar system, such as the moon, attract all the planets and satellites as our sun does. How, then, can we dream for a single moment that a cell could evolve the whole vegetable and animal kingdom out of its bosom without endowing it almost with omnipotent power and energy, without making it the condensation, the abridgment, the very quintessence of the whole vegetable as well as animal kingdom, reduced into infinitesimal proportions?"

Adele.—"This reverses the great saying of Horace: 'The mountains bring forth; lo, a ridiculous mouse appears.' We should say: 'The mouse brings forth; there arises a huge mountain.'"

Doctor.—"Then again this primitive form or type out of which all organic species must spring forth must be supposed to be always in a state of transition, in a continual metamorphosis, in an ever-varying change; at one period it is a living vegetable cell; then it is the greatest tree; now it is infusoria, and, after long successive centuries, it begins to put on the appearance of more developed mollusks, from the pecten or marine bivalve to the ascidian or acephalous mollusk; thence to higher forms of structure; first the low articulata, as the astacus or crab and worms, to the strange pagurian hermit who takes refuge in deserted shells of univalves; thence to the primitive forms of fishes, such as the ganoid or star-fish of the paleozoic period; then to the higher forms of lizards, to the amphibia and reptiles and batrachia or toads, frogs, and salamanders; thence to birds of countless patterns, till it reaches the lowest mammals; and thence to a grade next in order, as classified marsupalia, that is, mammals having a pouch for carrying their young ones; and, the development continuing, it comes to more perfect mammals, as rabbits, foxes, wolves, jackals, lions, till it strikes at the lower monkeys, as the lemur, and through them to the quadrumana of the highest type of structure, such as the ourang-outang and gorilla, from which man was developed. Here we have an infinitesimal form of life always on the way, never resting, but moving, passing from one state to another, no sooner has it reached one state than it craves and begins new efforts for another. It is essentially transitory and a bird of passage so to speak. Now such a being may have an existence in the fertile brain of Darwin and his supporters, but never existed in nature, as we have proved from historical and paleontological records, and, as Huxley himself, after stating the documents from the two mentioned sources proving the fixity of species, freely acknowledges. Read the words, George, from his second 'Lecture on Evolution.'"

George.—"'Facts of this kind are undoubtedly fatal to any form of the doctrine of evolution which pos'ulates the supposition that there is an intrinsic necessity on the part of animal forms which have come into existence to undergo continual modifications.' ('Humboldt Ed.,' p. 14.)"

Adele.—"I would like to inquire of evolutionists why should living form or any animal strive to be transformed into another?"

George.—"In order to become more evolved and perfect."

Doctor.—"Evolutionists labor under a very great mistake as to what is, or is not perfection for a plant or animal. I have marked a very remarkable passage from F. Secchi, which I want you to read upon the point."

George.—"'A grave defect is found in the reason of these persons; they are continually talking of imperfect animals becoming perfect. But what is the idea of perfection in such matter? According to right thinkers, that animal is perfect which has all the means necessary to its support and reproduction. Now the monera as well as the battrybius, the mollusks as well as worms, and the radiate as well as the vertebrate, are in this respect completely perfect. Why should they seek for more? It is true that it is said that in the development of the different families of being a progress is remarked, which bears a great similarity to the stages travelled by the fœtus of the more perfect animals; from which one could infer that those less perfect are so many incomplete fœtus arrested in their course. Error and absurdity! because even conceding that similarity, a thing which not so well proven as it is pretended, between the periods of the fœtus not developed and those of the more perfect there is the immense difference that the inchoate fœtus can neither live nor be reproduced except it arrives at completion; and the daily experience denies that an incomplete fœtus can give life to any living creature, whereas these are propagated and multiplied, and nothing is wanting to their own absolute perfection. If, on the other hand, we speak of relative perfection—that is, inasmuch as we call more perfect that being which can be put in contact with greater number of exterior agents and enjoy greater communications with external nature, it is true that there are a great many degrees of perfection, because, of course, the mammal has more extended relations with the exterior world than the polyp, but it is not in the power of the animal to fix or to determine the grades of relation, nor can it arrest its development in any way.' (First Discourse on the Grandeur of the Universe.)"

Adele.—"But let us come to the other more important point: By what means is this primitive type evolved into the whole vegetable and animal kingdom?"

Doctor.—"Understand the question well, Adele. Here we have by the supposition one single cell, from which all vegetable and animal life has to be evolved and unfolded. The question is: How can this tiny living form from being unicellular become multicellular, from having such parts assume different ones, from being what it is become another?"

Adele.—"I perceive perfectly; the very stating of the question seems to be absurd and ludicrous."

George.—"Darwin puts himself that question: 'Looking at the first dawn of life, when all organic beings presented the simplest structure, how, it has been asked, could the first steps in the advancement or differentiation of parts have arisen?' After having said how Spencer would get out of difficulty, he continues: 'But as we have no facts to guide us, speculation on the subject is almost useless. It is, however, an error to suppose that there would be no struggle for existence, and consequently no natural selection, until many forms would have been produced; variations in a single species inhabiting an isolated station might be beneficial, and thus the whole mass of individuals, or two distinct forms, might arise.' ('Origin of Species,' p. 56.)"

Doctor.—"It is the very climax of absurdity, George. These gentlemen have rejected the doctrine of special creation, which accounts for the existence of different species, in order to set up their theory of every species of the organic and animal world having been evolved or drawn out of a single living cell. When we ask, as we have an undoubted right to demand, how that cell from being one thing becomes another, what are the first steps to perform such wonder, we are told that 'speculation on the subject is almost useless.' He should have acknowledged that an answer to such a question is absolutely impossible, because the thing itself is utterly and absolutely impossible. Mark it well. Here is a substance of a certain nature represented by a single cell. We will suppose that it naturally seeks to grow, following the impulse imparted by the Creator into all living beings. Very good; in what direction is it to grow? In the direction and according to the laws of its nature. By what means is it to grow? By appropriating from external objects what is necessary and befitting to its nature; for such is the law of life of created substances. What does not suit its nature it rejects and eliminates; what serves its nature it appropriates and makes its own. What is the result? Growth of that single tiny cell into a large cell, if its nature is to have one single cell, or into several cells, if its nature admits of them, but the growth will always and forever be of the same nature and never of a different one; if the primitive cell belongs to the vegetable kingdom, it will never overstep the boundary of that kingdom, because it is a contradiction that any being should have a tendency to lose its own identity to become another. But to go on, you had better explain to Adele, George, by what means Darwin endeavors to explain how the first cell tries and succeeds to throw off its own identity."

George.—"He does so by means of natural selection. Let us suppose a number of beings representing the lowest form of type and composed of a single cell. There will be among them a struggle to dispute the sources of life. When some of them during this struggle happened to strike some accidental modification which could be turned to advantage they caught hold of it and transmitted it to their descendants, who in consequence of that advantageous modification, which was accentuated more and more, became better favored and succeeded in overcoming in the struggle for life less gifted opponents. Hence these may be called the chosen and selected of nature, and the sum of all these useful variations possessed by a living being tending to secure for it, and its descendants who inherit it, the greatest chance of endurance and propagation is called natural selection."

Adele.—"Well, I easily perceive how Darwin endeavors to explain how in the struggle for life the tiny little creatures of the lowest forms acquire certain modifications which may make them hardier and stronger, and enable them to come off victorious in the fight, and how the sum of all these advantages may be styled natural selection, but I cannot for the life of me understand how the sum of all those advantageous little modifications can change those primitive things into higher species and much more elaborate and complicated structures and organisms."

George.—"I will answer in the words of Darwin himself: 'We must suppose that there is a power represented by natural selection or the survival of the fittest always intently watching each slight alteration in the transparent layers, and carefully preserving each, which, under varied circumstances, in any way or in any degree, tends to produce a distincter image.'"

Doctor.—"He is applying the theory to the organism of the eye, but, of course, it must be understood also in a general sense."

George.—"Natural selection will pick out with unerring skill each improvement. Let this process go on for millions of years, that a living instrument might thus be formed (page 82.)"

Adele.—"Then such powers must be gifted with the highest intelligence to be able to spy every opportunity and to hoard up every possible alteration and change to turn them to the best possible account, being perfectly aware, of course, of the end at which it intends to arrive."

Doctor.—"Fiddlestick, Adele. This power or natural selection is stone blind, perfectly unintelligent and brutish; it perceives no end, nor how to adapt means to the end. It has no design whatever, no aim that it is acquainted with, and only goes on blindly and accidentally without either knowing whence it started nor to where it may possibly be going. George, am I describing it correctly?"

George.—"Certainly. Darwin does not endow this natural selection with any intelligence which may have formed a design, and which it endeavors to realize by adapting means to an end."

Adele.—"Well, then, how does it produce those changes which causes new species?"

George.—"By adapting the various forms of life to their environments, or to the several exterior conditions and stations, of climate, of food, of association with other species, etc."

Doctor.—"Yes, sir; natural selection or the survival of the fittest, accidentally, blindly without design, without an end in view, without being able to discern how this stands to that, must explain the existence not only of the smallest and simplest, but of the most complicated organs, such as the ear, the eye, the brain, the heart, the circulation of the blood, the hand, the foot. This implies such monstrous assumptions that even Darwin has been staggered. 'To suppose,' he says, 'that the eye, with all its inimitable contrivances for adjusting the focus to different distances, for admitting different amounts of light, and for the correction of spherical and chromatic aberrations, could have been formed by natural selection seems, I freely confess, absurd in the highest degree.'"

Adele.—"He has a glimmering of common sense left."

George.—"Haeckel, his great admirer, sees the same difficulty. A difficulty of the greatest importance against the theory of descent, in the eyes of many naturalists and philosophers, lies in the fact that the theory explains the formation of organs appropriated to a certain end by means of blind and purely mechanical causes. Such objection assumes particular importance from the consideration of those organs appearing to be so wonderfully adapted to an object altogether special. In the first rank are to be placed the superior organs of the senses of animals, the eye and the ear. If we were acquainted with nothing else than the eyes and the organs of hearing in the forms of superior animals, this alone would raise great and insurmountable difficulties. How, in fact, to explain that, by the sole influence of natural selection, it has been possible to reach, in every respect, that extraordinary and most admirable high degree of perfection and special adaptation which we observe in the eyes and ears of superior animals."

Doctor.—"Yes, and in spite of Darwin's and Haeckel's silly answer the objection stands absolutely unanswerable. What is the difficulty, Adele?"

Adele.—"How an organ which is a marvel of adaptation of the parts to a definite object can have been produced without a previous arrangement of a creative intelligence, but by certain fatal and absolutely blind forces."

Doctor.—"Correct; and what is the answer, George?"

George.—"It amounts to this; that, for instance, below the most perfect we find a long series of visual organs much more simple."

Adele.—"And what do you conclude from that?"

Doctor.—"It follows that, besides the most perfect eye, which is a prodigy of mechanical arrangement, there is a number more or less complicated and requiring less calculation. But it does not explain how all these arrangements and combinations were made by fatal and blind forces; in other words, it does not explain how a system of the most finished arrangement was not arranged at all."

Adele.—"What sublime geniuses are these evolutionists! Their powers of reasoning must be colossal. Their answer is very much like that of one who should account for his assertion that St. Peter's in Rome is not the work a of great intelligence, by alleging that there are a number of churches in the world that required much less calculation, or that the Strasburg clock was not made by the wonderful skill of a great mechanic, by alleging that there are myriads of clocks in the world which present a much more simple structure. Why don't they send these great lights to study the A, B, C of logic, and, if they are too old for that, why don't they shut them up in an asylum for the aged and the infirm?"

Doctor.—"Let us conclude this part of the subject. We have seen that the great similarity of form and structure of the organ, even as far as the framework, the bones, which is apparent in the organic and animal kingdoms, is fully and perfectly accounted for by the explanation from design; that the evolutionists' sneer that such an explanation is not scientific simply sets in the best and boldest light the incredible ignorance of the same gentlemen as to real Christian philosophy; that their explanation by an intrinsic inherent instinct in the primitive forms to move forward and to progress, or by the natural selection is the height and climax of absurdity and explains nothing whatever. We stand, then, by the doctrine of special creations—all made after the general plan of the Creator."

Adele.—"And we repeat with the pride of a Christian grounded on the highest reason and true science: 'And God said let the earth bring forth the green herb such as may seed, and the fruit tree yielding fruit after its kind. And God made the beasts of the earth according to their kinds, and cattle, and everything that creepeth upon the earth after its kind.' (Genesis, chap. 1.)"

TWENTIETH ARTICLE.

ORIGIN OF MAN.

Doctor.—"As we have demonstrated in several of our conversations that the hypothesis of evolution has no foundation in real science, and that the doctrine of special creations is the only one which can explain the existence and origin of the different kingdoms of nature, the mineral, the vegetable, and the animal, it follows as a necessary consequence that man's origin also must be accounted for by a special creation. But to confirm more and more our argument, and to show how far from the truth are those who maintain that man is the lineal descendant of the ape, I want to devote a few more of our conversations to the object of pointing out all the reasons which show the immense impassable difference which exists between man and the highest types of apes. In this conversation we will point out the physical differences which exist between them, and which show that man cannot by any manner of means have developed from the ape."

George.—"In the first place, they are not agreed from what kind of apes man descends. Darwin refers the reader, who is curious to know the human genealogy in detail, to his disciple Haeckel. Now, the latter considers as the first ancestor of all living beings, the *monera*. From this initial form man has reached the state in which we find him, by passing through twenty-one typical transitory forms. In the present state of things our nearest neighbors are the anthropomorphous or tailless apes, such as the orang, the gorilla, and the chimpanzee. All sprung from the same stock, from the type of the tailed catarrhine apes, and these from the prosimiæ, a type which is now represented by the macaucos, the loris, etc. Now, although the distance between the anthropomorphous apes and man appears to be but small to Haeckel, he has, nevertheless, thought it necessary to admit an intermediate stage between ourselves and the most highly developed ape."

Adele.—"I am glad of that; and who or what is he?"

George.—"A pure hypothetical being, a fancy sketch of Professor Haeckel, of which not the slightest vestige has been found. He is supposed to be detached from the tailless apes, and to constitute the twenty-first stage of the modification which has led to the human form. Haeckel calls it the *ape-man* or the pithecoid man, deprives him of speech as well as of any development of intelligence and self-consciousness."

Adele.—"If such an ancestor is a fancy sketch of the professor, the whole thing is a romance then?"

Doctor.—"Something very like it."

George.—"Darwin makes man descend from a tailed ape. 'The earliest ancestors of man were, without doubt, once covered with hair, both sexes having beards; their ears were pointed and capable of movement, and their bodies were provided with a tail having proper muscles' ('Descent of Man')."

Doctor.—"Well, without entering too deep into the subject, we will assume for a moment that man has descended from the kind of apes which are nearest to us, such as the tailless ape, the gorilla and the chimpanzee of Africa, or the orang and the gibbon of Sumatra and Borneo, and we limit our discussions to these. Of course, if we compare the general structure of the body of man and that of the tailless apes we must own that there is an indisputable affinity between them; they are provided with the same organs, having the same relations with each other; they have a digestive apparatus constructed on the same plan, accompanied by the same annexes. We may say the same of the respiratory and circulary organs and of the nervous system. We find the same muscles, the same bones connected with each by the same relations."

Adele.—"Then where is that impassable difference which renders impossible the descendance of one from the other?"

Doctor.—"That impassable difference is found in the details, in the special structure of the organs, and in the relative development of the parts. George, tell us some of these differences."

George.—"In the first place, an immense difference exists in the posture and carriage of the body of man. He alone, of all animals, is made to stand erect. His whole organization is admirably constructed in view of that; and that position is the result of the whole skeleton and of the form, location and arrangement of the muscles, of the point of insertion of the movable organs, which permit the body to preserve, without labor, the equilibrium in the erect attitude."

Adele.—"It begins to get interesting."

George.—"Thus in man the head rests pretty much by the middle of the inferior face, on the summit of the vertebral column; it is thus balanced in its natural position, and to maintain such position has no need either of powerful muscles or of cervical ligaments. The vertebral column instead of being straight exhibits flexures or bend of the joints, alternately, in a contrary sense, which, by increasing the power of the central part of the osseous frame diminishes equally the muscular mass employed to maintain the erect position of the body. The manner of inserting the thigh-bone in the bone of the basin or bony cavity, which terminates man's trunk, the shape and solidity of this part of the frame, the considerable muscular masses placed behind this articulation, are evidently intended to maintain in equilibrium, in the vertical posture, the superior parts of the body, and to prevent them from bending forward. We may say the same of the muscles of the thigh and the leg, and especially of the muscular mass which forms the projections in the calf, and which constitutes a character special to man. All these muscles are intended to prevent the articulations of the leg and of the foot from bending under the weight of the body."

Adele.—"I see you are at home, here, Mr. George."

George.—"Man's foot is large; the leg is perpendicularly attached to it; the heel is swollen in the under part, the bones of the tarsus and metatarsus, that is, the bones of the heel and of the instep form a kind of an arch which protects against too much pressure the sole of the foot; the toes are short and very limited in movement, the largest of them, the big toe, is placed on the same plane and not against the others. All these arrangements show evidently that the foot has been constructed to carry the weight of the body and to maintain an erect and vertical position."

Adele.—"And do we find the same in the apes most like to man?"

George.—"In apes, on the contrary, we find the same organs, to be sure, but most singularly modified. The head is inserted upon the vertebral column, but not in the middle but behind, and as, on the other hand, the bones of the lower part of the face are very much developed, and the brain on the contrary very small, it follows that the whole mass projects forward, and no equilibrium can be had for a vertical posture; hence these animals are provided with a solid cervical ligament, or fastening, and some powerful muscles to support the head in an oblique posture. The muscular masses of the posterior regions of the basin, and above all the muscles of the thigh, which in man keeps the erect position of the body, are much less developed in the quadrumana. The basin being very narrow and oblique does not help the equilibrium, and the posterior organs are very little adapted for a vertical posture."

Adele.—"But do not the orangs, and the chimpanzees walk erect sometimes?"

Doctor —"They do; but it is evident that such mode of locomotion is not natural to the poor beasts. For their walking is very unsteady; they totter and balance their arms so as not to lose the equilibrium, and from time to time are obliged to touch the ground with their hands to reëstablish it. Besides, their manner of walking erect is not the same as in man, and if they straightened themselves up as man does, they would very soon fall backward. The vertical posture fatigues them and cannot be maintained long. They need the help of a third support, and willingly accept the aid of a staff, which enables them to assume a bending posture so natural to them."

George.—"Then we may conclude with the words of Quatrefages, that 'man is essentially an animal who *walks;* all apes on the contrary are *climbing* animals. In the two groups the whole apparatus for locomotion bears the impress of the two different destinations.' ('The Human Species.')"

Doctor.—"Or with Goaroi, in whose book on the 'Species' are to be found all the above particulars—'of all the beings of creation man alone is organized for a vertical posture, he alone walks erect. It is an essential character which decidedly separates him from all animals. In man the vertical posture results from the special conformation of the frame and of the equilibrium established and maintained, not only by the action of the muscles, but also by the weight of the different splanchnological organs.' ('*De l'Espéce*,' vol. 2, p. 119, Paris.)"

Adele.—"Is it not rather a long word you attached to organs, and for the explanation of which I should be obliged to you?"

George.—"It comes from the Greek, and means organs relating to bowels."

Doctor.—"Now let us pass to another organ, one of the most principal, and which sets in bold relief the impassable barrier which exists between man and apes."

George.—"I suppose you mean the brain, Doctor?"

Doctor.—"No, I mean the cranium, or the bony case which contains the brain."

George.—"Well, I know the labors of Bischoff and Aeby upon

the cranium. I have read the latter's work 'On the Forms of the Cranium of Man and Apes,' wherein the Professor of Berne has put the assertions of Huxley, on the great approach and similarity of man and apes, under the most profound and severe examination."

Adele.—"Well and what is the result?"

George.—"He has accumulated, in view of this, measurements and comparisons, under every possible aspect, of craniums of all the different races of men, and I could say of all peoples, and at the same time of craniums not only of all kinds of apes, but even of mammals inferior to the latter. That work contains hundreds and thousands of measurements, and is, for the extent and variety of researches, infinitely superior to anything which Huxley may have ever written upon the subject."

Adele.—"But what conclusion does it come to?"

George.—"I will give it in his own words: 'From the summary of all comparisons the result is that the total difference of man from the ape nearest to him is greater than that which distinguishes one kind of apes from another, and consequently we do not hesitate for a moment to hold that the human type of the cranium is distinct in the nicest possible manner from the simian type;' and, later on: ' In the whole series of mammals it is impossible to find a chasm which could bear even the most distant comparison to that which separates the ape from man. The human craniums, even the most degraded, are so different in every respect from the simian craniums, the most elevated and are so strictly related to their congenial superiors that even the word simian resemblance should be abandoned.' (Aeby, 'Die Schädel Formen.')"

Doctor.—"Now, Adele, if you want to laugh, you may read the words of Darwin upon this very point. I have marked the page."

Adele.—"'The strongly-marked differences between the skulls of man and the quadrumana (lately insisted upon by Bischoff, Aeby and others) apparently follow from their differently developed brains.' ('Descent of Man.') I see Mr. Darwin does not dare to pass any condemnation or criticism on the exactness of the results of Aeby, but to such numerous and conclusive facts, he opposes simply a supposition of his own. One certainly feels inclined to laugh at such science."

Doctor.—"But, by and by, with a faculty of contradiction peculiar to such scientists, Darwin forgets that he had admitted the strongly-marked differences between the skulls of man and the quadrumana, and has the courage to say: 'Man, in all parts of his organization differs less from the higher apes than these do from the lower members of the same group' ('Descent.') But, George, give us some particulars about these marked differences, especially as to the contents of the craniums—the brain."

George.—"The celebrated German evolutionist, Schaafhausen, says with regard to the brain: 'The assertion of Huxley that men differ from each other as regards the volume of the brain more than do apes, one from another, is erroneous. It rests on some arbitrary measure of certain very rare and very doubtful craniums; whereas the decision should depend on ordinary and medium values. The brain of the Australian surpasses in volume two or three times that of the gorilla, and the brain of an European surpasses five times that of the first.' ('Question Scientifique de Brussels, July, '78 p. 179). Again, 'the human brain not only differs in volume from that of the nearest apes, but it differs also in the revolutions or turnings, which are much more numerous and deeper than those of the brain of animals; and what is more remarkable still, those revolutions in man are developed in a contrary sense from those of apes. Those which in man appear first are the last to appear in the ape. It was Gratiolet who first observed this peculiarity. 'The turnings,' he says, 'of the brain of the ape appear first in the inferior lobes, and last in the frontal lobes. In man the very reverse occurs; the frontal turnings appear first, and the inferior ones last. Continual differences result from this fact during the fœtal life, and man in this respect appears as an insoluble exception.' (Gratiolet, 'Revues des Oeuvres Scientifique,' vol. 1, p. 191.)"

Doctor.—"Well, we may conclude this part of the subject with the words of Professor Burmeister, which recapitulate all we have said upon the immense physical differences between man and the apes, even the best developed and nearest to him: 'Man,' says the professor, 'is distinguished from the ape in the construction of the body by a greater development of the brain, by the structure of the skeleton destined to walk erect, by a stronger development of the brain and by the wonderful typical difference in the design of both the extremities; because in man alone the forward ones are true hands, the backward never; whereas, on the contrary, of the four hands of the ape the posterior only are hands, the anterior are nothing better than paws, and oftentimes without thumb.' (Reusch: 'The Bible and Nature,' vol. 2, p. 227)."

George.—"I cannot refrain from quoting the recapitulation of Huxley's doctrine on the anatomical differences between man and apes, given by Doctor Ed. B. Tylor in the 'Encyclopædia Britannica,' article anthropology: 'The relations are most readily stated in comparison with the gorilla, as on the whole, the most anthropomorphous ape. In the general proportions of the body and limbs there is a marked difference between the gorilla and man, which at once strikes the eye. The gorilla's brain-case is smaller, its trunk larger, its lower limbs shorter, its upper limbs longer in proportion than those of man. The differences between a gorilla's skull and a man's are truly immense. In the gorilla, the face, formed largely by the massive jaw-bones, predominates over the brain-case or cranium; in the man these proportions are reversed. In man, the occipital foramen, through which passes the spinal cord, is placed just behind the centre of the base of the skull, which is thus evenly balanced in the erect posture, whereas the gorilla, which goes habitually on all fours, and whose skull is inclined forward, in accordance with this posture, has the foramen further back. In man the surface of the skull is comparatively smooth, and the brow-ridges project but little, while in the gorilla, these ridges overhang the cavernous orbits like penthouse roofs. The absolute capacity of the cranium of the gorilla is far less than that of man; the smallest adult human cranium hardly measuring less than sixty-three cubic inches, while the largest gorilla cranium measured had a content of only thirty-four and a-half cubic inches. The large proportional size of the facial bones and the great projection of the jaws, confer on the gorilla's skull its small facial angle and brutal character, while its teeth differ from man's in relative size and number of fangs. Comparing the length of the extremities, it is seen that the gorilla's arm is of enormous length, in fact about one-sixth longer than the spine, whereas a man's arm is one-fifth shorter than the spine; both hand and foot are proportionally much longer in the gorilla than in man; the leg does not so much differ. The vertebral column of the gorilla differs from that of man in its curvature and other characters, as also the conformation of its narrow pelvis. The hand of the gorilla corresponds essentially as to bones and muscles with that of man, but is clumsier and heavier; its thumb is opposable like a human thumb, but is proportionately shorter than man's. The foot of the higher apes, though often spoken of as a hand, is anatomically not such, but a prehensile foot.'"

Adele.—"The conclusion, then, is that there exists an immense hiatus, a chasm between man and the highest type of apes as to their bodily structure adapted to their destination, that though there is a general design and similarity of structure in detail, every organ is differently constructed. Hence the difference which results and which can never make it plausible, in the eyes of any sane man, that one descends from the other. Well, I had made up my mind on the subject long ago when I saw specimens of the stuffed gorillas in the Museum of Natural History in Paris and in the British Museum. The face of those animals is so intensely and so horribly beastly, there is such an accumulation of every brutish trait in it, it exhibits such an unmitigated animal look that it sickens me to recall it, and I concluded then, as I do now, that the human face divine could never, never have developed from such beastly monsters."

Doctor.—"But to complete this part of the subject we must say a word about the supposed bridge, which our friends, the evolutionists, believe to have found between man and the ape. What is it, George?"

George.—"The microcephalus."

Adele.—"The what?"

George.—"The man with the small head is the literal signification of the word; but evolutionists indicate by it a class of men who are born idiots and imbeciles, and who look, in their outward form, more like monkeys than like men."

Adele.—"Well, and is it really a bridge between man and the ape?"

Doctor.—"No; the whole class of such imbeciles and idiots are merely a pathological phenomenon. I say the whole class, because there are microcephali—those that have a head and cranium much smaller than is ordinarily found in men; the dolicocephali—the longitudinal diameter of whose cranium is far larger than the transversal; the brachiocephali—those whose cranium is greater in length than in width. All these do not form a species or a constant permanent kind of beings, medium between man and the ape, but are simply an occasional and variable phenomenon, a defect or abnormal condition of the cranium of such beings, originating in some pathological reason, which accounts for such craniums being arrested in their development. But they prove nothing more. Let us then conclude with the words of Aeby: 'We deny, in the most emphatic manner, that there are found in any part of the actual creation, regular and normal forms, which may be considered as a passage and transition degree between man and the ape. Assuredly the microcephali seem in many respects to confound the human type with that of the ape. But the right to fill the normal series of forms with pathological ones, is but gratuitously assumed. ('Die Schädel Formen,' p. 88.)"

Adele.—"It is really a pity that when our poor friends, the transformists, seem to have hit something that presents a favorable side towards supporting their theory, lo and behold, when you investigate the thing somewhat more deeply, you find that our friends had been a little too sanguine, and as it is the case with such people, are very soon disappointed in their great expectation."

TWENTY-FIRST ARTICLE.

INTELLIGENCE AS THE EXCLUSIVE FACULTY OF MAN—FACULTIES COMMON TO MAN AND BRUTE ANIMALS—DIFFERENCE BETWEEN THE SENSE AND THE INTELLECT.

Doctor.—"In our last interview we laid down the immense difference existing between the physical nature of man and that of the lower animals. We will now pass to the absolutely decisive proof of man's infinite superiority over the whole animal kingdom. It lies in his possessing, to the exclusion of brute animals, an intellectual nature. Darwin himself freely admits the decisive character of such a proof: 'If no organic being, except man, possessed any mental power, or if his powers had been wholly of a different nature from those of the lower animals, we should never have been able to convince ourselves that any high faculties had been gradually developed. But it can be shown that there is no fundamental difference of this kind.' ('Descent,' page 35, Humboldt Ed.)"

Adele.—"Then we must prove that there *is* such fundamental difference?"

Doctor.—"Exactly, but we must, to attain our object, proceed very cautiously."

Adele.—"Why?"

Doctor.—"Because our friends, the evolutionists, know absolutely nothing of intellectual philosophy; hence, partly through ignorance and partly through anxiety to prop up their system they mix up and confound the very simplest notions of mankind. This renders necessary a wary, careful examination of everything they say; in their case one must proceed slowly, step by step, and never advance until the first step is proved and found to be absolutely safe and sound. Error lies in mist and darkness; truth delights in the unclouded brilliancy of the midday sun."

George.—"Then how shall we go about the matter?"

Doctor.—"There is but one method. This is: first to speak of those faculties common to man and the lower animals, and to carefully define each one of them as we go along; noting down their nature, their object, and the extension and limits of their operation; then, in the second place, to speak of those faculties and acts which are exclusively intellectual and belong to man alone, showing the difference between these and the former, and how such difference is in quality, in nature, in kind and not in quantity, as evolutionists pretend; and finally draw the conclusion that man is a creation apart—a kingdom by itself—infinitely superior to the animal brute."

George.—"That cannot but be highly satisfactory."

Adele.—"I am very anxious to enter upon this most decisive proof."

Doctor.—"Well, then, to begin, I premise that we are talking here of the highest form of animal life, that nearest to man. These animals, like man, are endowed with sensibility, and therefore with the power of being affected, modified, by perception of the external world. I presume, Adele, you understand what is meant by the power and faculty of sensibility or sensation?"

Adele.—"I believe it is that power by which an animal feels and perceives material objects—as, for instance, I am on the brow of a hill at an early hour before daybreak. The dawn appears in all the magnificence and variety of its beauty and charm; my eyes take in the whole scene, and a glow of delight overpowers me. Isn't that feeling and perceiving external objects?"

George.—"To be sure, and you have it to an exquisite degree."

Adele.—"In the same degree as your power of sarcasm."

Doctor.—"I want you to remark that the faculty of sensation implies the internal as well as the external senses. These are called so inasmuch as they are exercised upon those external objects which come in contact with them. The former are called internal, because they are exercised upon those sensible species which have come into the soul by means of the external senses."

Adele.—"I don't understand that."

Doctor.—"I will take your own example. You perceive and are delighted with the dawn on the morning you supposed. Well, that combination of colors, which we call the dawn, is far, far away from you, is it not?"

Adele.—"Certainly."

Doctor.—"And you will grant that the perception of the dawn is a kind of knowledge, and to obtain that knowledge you must come in contact with the object of it? In other words, the object must enter in some way or other into your soul for you to perceive it?"

Adele.—"I certainly may grant that much, that unless I come in contact with the object I want to know, unless I can get hold of it somehow, unless I can grasp it, I cannot by any means perceive it; because to perceive means something like grasping or apprehending, I presume?"

Doctor.—"But as you have conceded that the object is far away, you cannot surely grasp it, in the same manner as you would take hold with your hand any object within your reach. How, then, are you going to perceive or apprehend the dawn?"

Adele.—"I am sure I cannot say."

Doctor.—"Easily enough; the dawn makes an impression, a modification on your sense of sight, an impression which is a representation, an image of itself; for what else could it impress on you· but a likeness and an imprint of itself? That impression on your sense, representing the object which has struck it, and which, calling forth your vital activity is by the latter transmitted to your soul, and by means of which you are enabled to put yourself in contact with the object and to perceive it, is called sensible species or image. It is about this that the internal senses are exercised."

Adele.—"I see the whole thing now. An external object strikes my senses. Say a piece of music strikes my ear and produces an impression on it and a likeness of itself; this arouses my vital activity which transmits that impression or likeness to my soul; my soul is then put in contact with the object and is enabled to perceive it. That image of the object made and impressed on my senses upon which my internal activity or senses are exercised, is called sensible species or image."

Doctor.—"Excellently put. Now we must carefully note what is the real object of the senses. George, what do you say?"

George.—"I never heard that the senses perceive or can perceive anything else than external material objects, and I presume, of course, that such and no other must be their proper objects."

Adele.—"But why could not the senses perceive something higher than external objects?"

George.—"I believe, because the faculty of sensation is incorporated in, and depends upon, certain external instruments called organs, and cannot go beyond what can be apprehended in and through them. For instance, the sensation of sight is incorporated in and depends upon, the organ of the eye, and cannot go beyond what the eye can take in, that is, external material objects. This is so true that if the eye is wanting or destroyed no sensation of sight is any longer possible. Again, the sensation transmitted through one sense cannot be transmitted through another; the eye cannot give the sensation of sound nor the ear the sensation of smell, nor this the sensation of taste, nor all these the sensation of touch. The faculty then depends on, and is restricted to, what can be apprehended through the organs; and as these are confined to the particular and material, no other can be the objects of sensation."

Doctor.—"George is correct. That which depends on external material organs is necessarily restricted in its apprehension to that which can be transmitted by and through the external organs; and as nothing else but external material objects can affect the external organs, no others can be the object of sensation. These, as George has already remarked, are five—the eye, the ear, the smell, the taste and the touch. All animals then, man included, are provided with five senses and the power of sensation and perception. But this would not be adequate to the end for which animals were provided by the Creator with the senses. If the animal is able to be affected and modified by the external world and capable of perceiving it, this was given to him principally for the support, maintenance and development of his physical life; to know what may be conducive to all those ends and what may be injurious; to discern among the different sensations and perceptions what may be beneficial to his life and what may be hurtful; what may give him a sense of ease and well-being and what may affect him painfully, are the principal needs of the animal. These could not be supplied simply by the five distinct senses or organs of sensation with which the animal is endowed. For this a general internal sense is required by means of which the sensations transmitted by each sense could be perceived and apprehended as a whole, and the difference felt to exist between them. In this way the animal can discern and compare the different sensations and turn towards the beneficial and the pleasurable, and avoid those which are injurious or painful."

Adele.—"I am sure none can object to such a reasonable want of animal life."

Doctor.—"Besides this general sense, the animal is endowed with fancy and imagination."

Adele.—"What do you understand by that?"

Doctor.—"That faculty or power of the sentient principle which retains the images of objects perceived. It is evident that animals are endowed with such fancy or imagination from the dreams to which we observe them to be subject. Another faculty which enables them, among the various sensations, to discern which of them is beneficial to their well-being and which is injurious, and to adopt the one and to reject the other, is called the estimative faculty. Next comes the memory, which is the faculty of reproducing past sensations and perceptions, and of recognizing them. Finally, they are possessed of that faculty which is called appetite, or instinct."

"Adele.—"What is meant by that?"

Doctor.—"By appetite we mean that inclination or propension by which every being strives to attain that good or perfection which naturally becomes to it. Such appetite may be simply natural or spontaneous; the first is found in those creatures which are incapable of all kinds of knowledge and which seek after their good by a tendency impressed into them by the Creator; the second is that tendency after good and perfection proceeding in a being from a previous knowledge of its own. This spontaneous tendency may be sensitive and intellectual: if the spontaneous tendency inclines after the good just as it perceives it but knows not any reason why the thing or good is desirable, it is merely sensitive; if the tendency inclines after the good not simply as it perceives it but knows the reason why that thing is befitting and agreeable to it, it is an intellectual tendency. That spontaneous tendency by which an animal runs after a thing originating simply in its perception of it without any further knowledge of a reason why that good is agreeable to it, is called instinct."

Adele —"As when I show pussy some choice morsel she is fond of, she rushes after it. I suppose the instinct after the good things of this life is aroused in her by the perception of the attracting morsel."

Doctor.—"To conclude, we may take for granted that brute animals have in common with man the five senses with their respective organs to perceive external objects, the common and general sense to perceive the sum of its perceptions, the imagination to retain images, the estimative faculty to discern between the beneficial perceptions and those which are injurious, the memory to reproduce past images and to recognize them when so reproduced. They have also all the passions which proceed from the instinct after their own good and well-being; hence the passions of love and of aversion, of desire, of hatred, of hope, of courage, of fear, of admiration, of jealousy and vanity, etc. But here we must draw the line and insist that they can go no further in their knowledge and operations; that for real, true *bona fide*, intelligent operations they are absolutely unfit, for the simple reason that the principle which informs and animates their physical nature is simply a sentient but not a rational, intellectual and spiritual principle."

George.—"Then we ought to prove the difference between the sensitive and intellectual principles by clear, distinct, unmistakable mark."

Adele.—"To be sure, and are there such marks?"

Doctor.—"Undoubtedly, and clearly and easily pointed out. All we have to do is to inquire into the subject and the object of the sensitive and intellectual principle—in other words, what is it that feels? what is it which intelligences? what does it feel? what does it understand? There is, then, a subjective and objective difference between the sense and the intelligence, and when we have pointed it out we shall see the immense distance between the sentient principle and the intellectual. Now the subjective difference between the sense and the intellect consists in this, that the sense is an organic faculty, the intellect, on the contrary, is inorganic. The objective difference is that the sense can only apprehend the particular, the intellect the universal."

Adele.—"Will you please to explain both?"

Doctor.—"We will begin by the subjective. As matter is essentially necessary to form the animal, since the animal is composed of body and soul, so the corporal organ is essentially necessary to constitute the faculty of sensation, as sensation is the proper and exclusive operation of the animal as such, that is, a being composed of body and soul."

George.—"This is evident from the fact that when a particular organ is absent in an animal the corresponding sensation is impossible. A blind man cannot experience the sensation of sight; nor a deaf one experience that of hearing."

Doctor.—"But it is quite contrary as to the intellect. It originates exclusively in the soul, and not in the animal organism. Man is an intellectual being, not as an animal, but inasmuch as through the immateriality of his spirit he partakes of the angelic nature. The function of intelligence is not, like sensation, an act, the immediate and proximate cause of which is the material organ, invested and penetrated by the soul; but an act, the direct cause of which is the virtue and power of the soul alone, without any intrinsic concurrence or aid of the body."

Adele.—"How is that proven, uncle?"

Doctor.—"Because, if intelligence depended intrinsically on the organs of the body, it would be subject to all the laws concerning organic faculties. That is clear. Now every organic faculty must follow in every thing the alterations of the organism, so much so that its act is proportionate to the particular structure of the organ on one side, and on the other, to a degree of impression which is made upon it. It is thus with sensation. The more perfect is the organization, the more perfect is the power of sensation. The greater and the more intense the impression made upon it by external objects the greater and the more intense the feeling resulting therefrom."

Adele.—"These facts are certainly beyond dispute."

Doctor.—"Moreover, the organic faculty is weakened and wears out by use and exercise, because the organ upon which it depends is enfeebled and used up by continued action. So it is with the senses. Placed in atmosphere full of odors after a short while we no longer perceive the odors; a tune, if continued and monotonous, is no longer distinguishable, the touch becomes so accustomed to painful or pleasurable sensations as to end in becoming insensible to them; an excessive light dazzles the eye, and may be so strong as at once to destroy it; a viand, at first very tasteful, may, by frequent use, become indifferent and even disgustful."

Adele.—"I had never reflected upon such striking facts showing the dependence of the senses on the material organ."

Doctor.—"But there is much more proof of such dependence. The organic faculty cannot reflect upon itself nor raise itself above the wants of the organism, and much less act contrary to its tendencies. Mark well, Adele, I say in the first place, an organic faculty cannot reflect upon itself, because an organic faculty not being able to act without the concurrence of the organism, cannot bend over, so to speak, or return upon itself without the organ doing the same; and everybody knows this to be impossible."

Adele.—"Why?"

Doctor.—"Because that which is extended cannot return except upon an extended body different from itself. Suppose I bend a bar of iron; that part of the bar which I bend is different from the one upon which I bend it. Hence the reason why the eye cannot see its own vision, nor any other sense perceive the very act by which it perceives. I said, moreover, that the organic faculty cannot act beyond or contrary to the tendencies of the organism. The reason of this is that no faculty can go beyond or contrary to the subject of which it is an instrument."

George.—"How gloriously different it is with the intellect. Though it requires the senses properly disposed and arranged to draw ideas from them, yet, except that single condition, all the rest takes place in the inverse ratio of the organic process.

Adele.—"As for instance?"

George.—"If the sensation is in proportion to the impression made on the organs, the very opposite occurs in the acts of the intellect; its meditations are higher, more sublime, more profound, in proportion as we separate ourselves and keep away from external impression. In sensation the faculty is enfeebled and used up by the weakening and wearing out of the organ. The intellect, on the contrary, grows stronger and clearer and sharper and more sagacious as the organs are enfeebled by age. Continual and uniform use wears out the senses and oftentimes destroys them. The intellect expands, widens, grows more powerful, waxes deeper under a continual exercise and repetition of the acts, and instead of growing weary and disgusted like the senses, it derives greater pleasure, keener delight, more exquisite attraction as it continues to plunge deeper and deeper into the investigation of truth. The more it is exercised in the faculties of apprehension, of judgment, of reasoning, the more it feels capable to repeat these acts with rapidity and vigor. An idea strengthens it in proportion to its loftiness and sublimity, and the deeper it descends to grasp the very essence and nature of the object, and to sound its utmost depths the more vigorous it comes out of such abyss."

Doctor.—"Nor do we stop at that. The sense cannot reflect upon itself. The intellect, on the contrary, can easily turn upon itself, look over its own acts, and, as it were, penetrate into itself, going down to the very bottom of the being in which the act takes its rise. The intellect understands that; it understands that it can think over its own acts and attribute the action to itself."

Adele.—"I am delighted to perceive such grand and immense differences between the senses and the intellect."

Doctor.—"Let us now speak of the difference which exists between the senses and the intellect in regard of their respective objects. The senses, by the very fact of being organic faculties in their knowledge cannot go beyond the material order, and even in this cannot perceive but what is concrete and individual, capable to impress the senses, and to influence them in proportion to the amount of the impression. The eye cannot perceive but what is luminous, the ear cannot be affected but by sound, the smell by odors. The estimative faculty itself, though supreme among the internal faculties, is not exercised except upon concrete and individual things relative to the material wants of the sentient subject. Hence, the reason why the sense is called passive, not because it does not imply an action in the sensitive subject, otherwise sensation would no longer be a vital act, but because the action which it exercises is determined and measured by the impression of the object and the state of the organism. The difference in this regard between the intellect and the senses is immense. We may regard the intellect either as perceiving the first and highest truths or principles, or as reasoning upon them, or as reflecting upon itself by way of consciousness. In all these regards we find that no limits whatever are set to the order of its operations. Its adequate object is truth, as truth in all the extension of its boundless amplitude. In fact, the intellect, by means of reasoning, can exercise itself upon anything which presents the reason of being, and which may in some way be distinguished from nothing. Thus, it contemplates not only bodies but spirits, not only the objects of thought but the acts of the same, not only things which exist but those which are possible, not only the accidents but the substance, not only effects but causes, not only the finite but the infinite. Every thing, which is either real or ideal, objective or subjective, conditional or absolute, evident in itself, or proved to be so by reasoning, can be the object of the intellect. And if we consider intelligence not as a reasoning faculty, but inasmuch as it rests in the first conceptions or ideas of the mind, even in this respect the universality of its object reveals its intrinsic independence of the organs. Because it does not, as the sense, pause at the mere determinate, concrete fact, but apprehends the essence and nature of it, abstracting from it all material conditions of time, place and other individual adjuncts. The sense perceives an extended body, the intellect conceives the abstract reason of extension, the sense sees a plant, the intellect conceives life, the sense apprehends a new phenomenon, the intellect endeavors to grasp the reason of that novelty, and hence the necessity of a cause to account for that new existence."

Adele.—"I see very clearly the immense, impassable difference between the sense and the intellect. First, the subject of the sense: that which is sentient in an organic power, subject to and dependent upon the material organism and subject to all the laws, states, alterations and vicissitudes of the organism. The object of the sentient power is the material, the concrete and the particular. The subject, or the intellectual power, is inorganic and independent of the material organism, and therefore not only not subject to its laws, states, changes, alterations, or vicissitudes, but acting in a contrary sense. The object of the intellect is being truth universally considered in every sense and under every respect and every relation. The consequence is, therefore, that there is an insurmountable bridge between the sense and the intellect."

Doctor.—"We must say a word about the difference which arises from the tendency of the sentient beings and the intellectual. The apprehension of the former being confined to the material and individual, is also limited in its tendency, and craves and can crave but what is limited, concrete, particular, and hence is necessary, blind, uniform and unchangeable. The apprehension of the intellect being the truth in a universal sense, the infinite, the absolute, the tendency resulting from it is also boundless and unshackled in its aspiration and tendency, and no finite being or object can fix and determine it; hence it is free, variable, progressive, and the universal good and the infinite alone can tie it down or confine, or necessitate it."

Adele.—"Having seen what faculties brute animals have in common with man, and having fully discussed the differences which pass between the senses and the intellect, I am very anxious to find out whether brute animals have any kind of intellectual power, and if not, how is the absence of such power proved?"

Doctor.—"I am afraid you will have to restrain your curiosity till our next conversation. I see George here getting impatient, and I must myself own that we have long trespassed our usual limits."

TWENTY-SECOND ARTICLE.

ARE BRUTE ANIMALS ENDOWED WITH ANY SORT OF INTELLECT?

Adele.—"Well, I have restrained my impatience since our last conversation and I beg to again put the question: Are brute animals endowed with reason? For I am sure, what was said about the immense difference between the senses and the intellect was, by way of preamble to the real argument which follows from it, and which might be put as follows: there is an immense difference in nature between the senses and the intellect; hence a sentient principle and an intellectual principle are, in nature, widely different from each other. This will apply to brute animals if it is shown that they are simply sentient beings; and if, on the other hand, it is demonstrated, that man alone, in the whole animal kingdom, is gifted with reason and intellect. Hence, the question recurs—are brute animals endowed with any kind of reason? If they are, they differ from man only as to the quantity of their reasoning power. If they are *not*, of course they differ from man in nature and kind, and, therefore, the latter cannot have developed from them."

Doctor.—"You are right, Adele; the whole question, after having demonstrated the essential and radical difference between the senses and the intellect now hinges on the inquiry—are brute animals endowed with reason, or are they merely sentient beings and nothing more. What do you say, George?"

George.—"Evolutionists contend that brute animals are endowed with a certain amount of intellect and reasoning power. To prove this, they point to the great skill and masterly ability which is apparent in the actions and works of many animals. Not to speak, for instance, of the extraordinary art shown by bees and the previsions and precautions of ants, who can fail to discover a certain amount of intelligence in the animals nearer to man? Does not the dog exhibit great judgment in the services he renders his master? Does he not demonstrate his power of reasoning when, from external signs, he argues his master's anger, or his good will, his desire or his command?"

Adele.—"Take the case, for instance, of the dog belonging to the Parisian shoeblack, mentioned in *Chamber's Miscellany*, who used to cover himself with mud and lie in wait for the appearance of any gentleman with polished shoes, and manage to dirt them in order to make work for his master; or of the other, who followed for a whole day a gentleman who had put in his vest pocket a coin belonging to his master; having never lost sight of the gentleman till the latter had taken off his vest previously to his going to rest, he managed to steal both vest and coin, and ran back to his master with the booty."

Doctor.—"To avoid confusion we will take up all these things one after the other. And, in the first place, Catholic philosophy is not afraid to admit that brute animals have some kind of incipient, imperfect reflection; because as they are possessed of the general and common sense, they must be aware that they experience a certain sensation; for, as St. Augustine remarks, 'the animal would not move to seek for something or to avoid something else, if he did not know that he has sensations.' Again, Catholic philosophy may freely grant that brute animals may form judgments; because they are able, by means of their senses, to judge and to discern what object is proper to each sense, and, by means of the estimative faculty, to decide which things are beneficial and which injurious, and to run after the former and to shrink from the latter; but such judgments are not comparative, but simply instinctive and imprinted in them by the Creator."

Adele.—"What do you mean, uncle, that such judgments are not comparative but instinctive?"

Doctor.—"I mean that they are not formed after a previous

and clear knowledge and full apprehension and meaning of the terms of the judgment and the perception of their agreement or disagreement. For instance, you offer a dog a piece of decayed and putrid meat; he rushes towards, smells it, and goes away from it with signs of annoyance and disgust. There is a judgment. But is that judgment the effect of comparison ? Has the dog, after perceiving that decayed matter by means of his sense of smell, compared it with his welfare and the good of his health and pronounced it injurious? Certainly not; he has followed the tendency implanted in it by the Creator to run from certain things which his senses feel an aversion from."

George.—"Yes, but how is it proven that such judgments are the effect of instinct and not comparison ?"

Doctor.—"I was elucidating the terms for Adele. The proofs shall be given, and in abundance, that such judgments and other acts in brute animals are merely the result of their natural instinct."

Adele.—"You say, then, all these powers we have admitted in brute animals, such as an eminent and wonderful skill in their acts, reflection, judgment, reasoning, only proceed from instinct and not from the intellect ?"

Doctor.—"Certainly, and we shall be convinced of it by studying the real characters of such acts and powers. In the first place, the signs of the greatest and most wonderful skill and ingenuity are manifested by animals of the most inferior class, such as insects. The works of these tiny little beasts are often so fine and constructed with such skill and mastery, that if they proceeded from intelligence they would suppose an intelligence much superior to man's, and we would have to draw this consequence from their works, that insects are provided with an intellect far, far above that of man. Now what madman would entertain such an idea for a moment? In the second place, it should be observed that the animal shows itself industrious and skillful only in a given, definite and particular order of things, according to the species to which it belongs ; as to all other things, and to any different order of work or acts it is absolutely helpless, unfit and incapable. Now, how could skill and reason, good enough for one kind of actions, be absolutely and utterly good for nothing for all other kind and order of works. Thirdly, the very skillful works and the sagacity and expertness which animals employ on them, and which oftentimes imply and involve the most difficult calculation of mathematics, and the most profound acquaintance with natural laws are undertaken by them since the very first days of their existence, and are completed without failure. There is no apprenticeship with them ; there is no gradation or steps to be observed ; their youngest among them jump at once into those works and begin, prosecute and accomplish them with the same skill, confidence and unhesitating tact and dexterity as the oldest and the most experienced of their kind. This requires no proof; the youngest bee, no sooner is it formed, undertakes a piece of work as the most advanced and knowing bee in the aviary, and executes and terminates it with the same precision as the aged one. Say the same of castors, in the structure of their ingenious huts; of birds, in the admirable construction of their nests. Now, who can fail to see that if all this art, ingenuity, skill, dexterity and science were the product of reason and intelligence, it could not be possessed by animals at the dawn of life; they could only acquire it as man does, step by step, beginning from the lowest and the easiest, and advancing and progressing gradually, and not until a long time, and after many trials and numberless failures could they attain that unhesitating dexterity and perfection which they manifest so early? The consequence is evident, that what they do is the result and the effort of the unerring instinct planted into them by the Almighty. Again, if such operations were directed by reason, how is it that they are restricted to one definite and determinate thing, not only as to the subject and the object of them, but also as to the particular mode of performing them in spite of change of circumstances—in spite of the failure of the end for which they are intended, and for which they are undertaken? Thus the spider is as careful to use all the precautions to catch a fly when the latter can easily escape from it, as when, being wingless, it cannot move and is at its mercy; the spider, perfectly unconscious of the latter circumstance, sets its trap with as much cunning and wariness and waits for the result. The squirrel gathers and husbands its provisions, hiding the superfluous with the same care and industry in places where it may feel the want of them, as well as in places where abundance and plenty exclude all danger of famine. I might multiply examples, but it all comes to the same conclusion. All these operations are the effect of natural, blind instinct of animals, and not of reasoning and free choice. 'Animals, different from man,' says St. Thomas, 'have no intellect. This is clear from the fact that they perform, not different or contrary actions and works, as is the case of those who are endowed with intelligence; but perform, under the impulse of nature, certain definite actions uniform in all the individuals of the same species!'"

George.—"These proofs certainly cannot be gainsaid. If brute animals were intelligent, they would show that faculty not merely in one given, hackneyed kind of operation, no matter how skillfully performed, but in others of different kind. Their reason would not cease there and be good for nothing for all else. A man most skillful in one given art or science, gives evidence of his reason in other things. If brute animals were endowed with reason, like man, they would have to learn gradually, and not be able to perform the most difficult and perfect works without learning or training. If they possessed reason and intellect, they would, like man, accommodate themselves to circumstance of time and place, and would not go on blindly to perform exactly in the same manner, and with the same zeal, earnestness and vigor operations and acts become utterly useless because the end for which they were necessary had failed. They act then by instinct, that is, without reason, spontaneously, naturally, blindly and uniformly, without freedom or choice.

Adele.—"Very good, Mr. George. It is clear that you have the happy faculty of recapitulating as well as some one else."

Doctor.—"In the characters, so far described, of the actions and operations of brute animals, originates the most decisive and convincing argument of their want of reason and intellect. It is the absolute and total absence of progress in everything proceeding from, or concerning, them. Brutes are essentially stationary, either in their specific or individual capacity. One can foretell with absolute certainty that, for instance, the silk-worm will work out its thread a century hence, in the same manner as its fellow worms of the nineteenth century are doing now, in utter disregard of the accumulated experience of years or opportunity of improvements and perfection. Say the same of other animals. When one of them is born you can at once determine to what peculiar industry it will apply itself, and the degrees of perfection it will attain. Now, is this the manner of action among beings endowed with intellect? Let one compare a child of the human species with an adult and see the difference between them; let one bring face to face a barbarous nation with a civilized one, a nation at the dawn of its existence with the same fully developed and arrived at the summit of progress and advancement. In the brute, on the contrary, there is a perfect uniformity, nay, monotony. The same skill, the same dexterity, the same act in the new born as well as in the old; in the novice as well as in the most experienced; in the ancient generations as well as in modern ones. The evident consequence of which is that they are incapable of universal conception, and therefore wanting in intellect."

Adele.—"No matter, then, how singular and wonderful may appear the acts of certain animals; no matter how great may be the signs they give of reflection, of judgment, of reasoning, all these must be attributed to natural instinct; for the reason that they never go beyond a particular and restricted circle of things, are always uniform in the species and in individuals, and are ever exercised upon particular and concrete objects, and are devoid of the least imaginable progress and advancement."

Doctor.—"This conclusion becomes the more apparent from the

fact that brute animals are absolutely wanting in the power of abstraction and generalization."

George.—"I beg pardon, doctor. Darwin says they have, and attempts to prove it."

Doctor.—"Let us hear."

George.—"'If one may judge from the articles published lately great stress seems to be laid on the supposed entire absence in animals of the power of abstraction and of forming general concèpts. But when a dog sees another dog at a distance it is often clear that he perceives that it is a dog in the abstract; for when it gets nearer his whole manner suddenly changes if the other dog be a friend' ('Descent of Man,' p. 45)."

Doctor.—"And has Darwin no other proof to allege for the power of abstraction in animals?"

George.—"None other that I can find."

Doctor.—"Well, almost every word in the passage quoted is a most laughable absurdity and puts in the most unenviable light the colossal ignorance on the part of Darwin of the simplest and commonest notions of metaphysics. It would be impossible, if it did not stare one in the face, to imagine an educated man, a scientist who undertakes a comparison between man's intellectual powers and those of the brute creation, to be so utterly jeju e of true philosophy, so childishly idiotic as to spout out, without shame or compunction, without suspecting his supine ignorance, such absurd nonsense as your great Darwin. I remember that Huxley, in a certain essay on evolution, is highly indignant at Professor Flourens of the French Academy, because the latter handles Darwin's ignorance of metaphysical ideas with anything but gloved hands. Huxley waxes indignant, and, climbing a high horse, begs to tell M. Flourens that they, in England, are not accustomed to see their best scientists treated in such a cavalier manner. But when their best scientists give such evident proof of the sheerest and most astonishing ignorance of true philosophy and are by no means loath, in spite of such ignorance, to proclaim *ex cathedra* the most disgustful absurdities to deceive the simple, I beg to say that no amount of contempt or contumely can do justice to such unwarrantable, pitiful presumption. Let us come to the point now. 'When a dog,' he says, 'sees another dog at a distance, it is often clear that it is a dog in the abstract.' What is clear in the whole matter is that Darwin has not the remotest notion of what abstraction is. He thinks that abstraction means to perceive vaguely, indistinctly and confusedly. Blunder No. 1 : 'It is often clear that it is a dog in the abstract.' Blunder No. 2, much worse than the first. The poor man imagines that abstract things walk and disport themselves as he has done at the expense of his readers and worshippers in all his works, and confounds a fact and an individual existence with an idea."

Adele.—"But, uncle, please to explain to me as clearly as possible what is meant by the power of abstraction and generalization?"

Doctor.—"Well, please to follow me. An idea is a conception of a thing by our mind. It may be individual abstract and universal. An individual idea is the conception of a thing as it really exists in nature; hence the conception of a man, a horse, a tree, a pebble, is an individual idea, because it is the perception of objects just as they exist in nature."

Adele.—"I understand that very well."

Doctor.—"You understand also, I hope, that things as they exist in nature are composed of different elements, or parts, as we might call them for the sake of clearness; they are made up of essence and nature, of substance, of properties and qualities and modifications. Take, for instance, an oak tree. It must have the essence and nature of a tree, otherwise you could not classify it among trees; it has the substance of a tree, because it is a real something and truly existing; it has also certain peculiar properties which oblige you to classify it in the family of oaks and to distinguish it from other trees, and finally it has some individual qualities which distinguish that particular oak from all other oak trees, say, for instance, peculiar size and branches and age, etc."

Adele.—"I perceive all that perfectly."

Doctor.—"Very well, then, when you conceive or apprehend that oak tree just as it exists in nature, you have an individual idea. But suppose that in your mind you separate things; suppose that you want to fix your mind not on the whole tree, but on the nature and essence of that tree; suppose you want to conceive what is it that makes it a tree? What do you do then? You separate or abstract. You first eliminate from that oak tree before you all its individual qualities and peculiarities of size, branches, age, and so forth, that make it such and such an oak. When you take away and eliminate from it those properties that classify it among the family of oaks, what have you left now? Simply a tree. And what is a tree? A living being. You have then gone from abstraction to abstraction, and attained your object. You have abstracted or taken away from that individual oak, first, all those qualities that made it such an oak, and distinguished it from all other oaks; then you have abstracted from it all those properties which make it an oak, and distinguish it from all other trees, and finally you have arrived at the idea of a tree. Arrived there, you have asked what is a tree? and you have found that it is a living being. Step after step, and abstraction after abstraction, you have arrived at that which you sought, the nature and essence of a tree, which is to be simply *a living being*. An abstract idea, therefore, is the conception of the essence and nature of a thing stripped of individual conditions and peculiarities in which the thing appears in nature. The faculty of performing that elimination and stripping is called the faculty of abstraction."

Adele.—"I conceive very clearly what is the power of abstraction. But what is the power of generalization?".

Doctor.—"Suppose that besides the oak, you have before you the maple, the pine, the fir tree, and so forth. You strip each of all those peculiarities that make each a distinct tree among their own family, then take away those properties which make them such and such a family of trees, and you come to the idea of the nature and essence of a tree; and as you see that that conception applies to all of them, as trees, you discover that the idea, essence and nature of a thing is a general idea applicable to all such as exhibit that same nature and essenc . Hence the power of abstraction bends into that of generalization."

Adele.—"I see."

Doctor.—"Let us take another example of the power of abstraction and generalization. Suppose I say, Mr. So-and-So is a just man, what do you understand by that?"

Adele.—"I understand that he is careful to give every one his due."

Doctor.—"And to give every one his due is certainly a good and moral quality to have, is it not?"

Adele.—"Certainly."

Doctor.—"Well, consider that moral quality of giving every one his due, not as embodied and exercised in Mr. So-and-So, but in itself, separately from, and independently of him, and every other individual person, what would you call it?"

Adele.—"I presume you would call it justice, and the idea of justice would be the conception of giving every ene his due, not as realized in this or that individual, but in the abstract, and in itself."

Doctor.—"And would that conception be applicable to any act of man rendering every one his due?"

Adele.—"To be sure."

Doctor—"Or would that conception be subject to any change, or time and place, or of any other circumstance?"

Adele.—"Certainly not, justice would always mean the giving every one his due, and would be applicable to any one at all times and in all places."

Doctor.—"Then, that abstract idea is also universal and unchangeable in time and place."

Adele.—"Without doubt."

Doctor.—"Then, you have again the ideas of an example of abstraction and of generalization, and of the power of doing both."

Adele.—"I perceive the whole thing."

Doctor.—"George, passing over the nonsense of Mr. Darwin, do you know of any argument or proof alleged by any other scientist to show that brute animals have the power of abstraction and generalization, and consequently can form abstract and general ideas?"

George.—"As far as forming abstract ideas, I know nothing more than what is said by Darwin. With regard to the power of generalization and the forming of general ideas, Darwin attempts to prove it. When I say to my terrier in an eager voice: 'Hi, hi, where is it?' she at once takes it as a sign that something is to be hunted, and generally first looks quickly all around, and then rushes into the nearest thicket to scent for any game, but finding nothing she looks up into any neighboring tree for a squirrel. Now, do not these actions clearly show that she had in her mind a general idea or concèpt that some animal is to be discovered and hunted."

Doctor.—"Let me offer my best compliments to Darwin and to all his blind worshippers on this new discovery; that a particular statement, something to be done in a particular case, as that some animal is to be discovered and hunted—is a general idea or concèpt. If evolutionists have such a conception of a general idea it is no wonder that they identify man's intellect with the brute animal's instinct. Some animal is to be discovered and hunted—a general idea—a universal concèpt! The very same as the ideas of time, space, extension, existence, of life, of the finite, the infinite, the absolute, the relative, the idea of morality, of virtue, of vice, of justice and injustice, of righteousness and unrighteousness, of law, of order, and a hundred more like these? Let us conclude, for God's sake, and leave behind us such disgusting ignorance. Brute animals cannot exercise the power of abstraction and of generalization; they are not possessed of any abstract conceptions and universal ideas, therefore they have not the remotest trace of an intellect or reason, the property and privilege of man alone. It is this power which distances man infinitely from all lower animals, the faculty of abstraction and generalization, and the full patrimony of abstract and universal ideas. It is this power that has created all the prodigies of mechanical and fine arts, created the sciences, guided and ruled the greatest discoveries of the world; it is this power of an immense universal ideal, of the best and the greatest and the most perfect in everything which spurs man or stimulates him, leaves him unquiet and restless, and seeking always to advance in the way of progress, and after having attained a most wonderful development, to consider it as naught and begin a new journey forward. Is it not a shame even to compare this choice and wonderful creation of God with the brute beasts?"

TWENTY-THIRD ARTICLE.

THE EXCLUSIVE SIGN OF INTELLIGENCE.

Doctor.—"In our last conversation we proved that man alone is endowed with intelligence, that sublime faculty, which, according to the best and grandest among those who have cultivated philosophy, has been considered as infinitely superior to the senses; a faculty which has enabled man to produce his wonderful masterpieces in art and science, and which causes him to have nothing short than an infinite ideal as his beacon-light towards improvement and progress. We must, in this interview, consider the true, exclusive sign of this noble faculty—the language. 'What is it that man can do,' says a great authority in this matter, 'and of which we find no signs, no rudiments, in the whole brute world?' I answer, without hesitation: The one great barrier between the brute and man is *language*. Man speaks, and no brute has ever uttered a word. 'Language is our Rubicon and no brute will dare to cross it' (Max Müller, 'Science of Language'). Man, then, cannot descend from an animal because no brute can speak."

George.—"But, doctor, Darwin denies that: 'Nor, as we have seen, does the faculty of articulate speech in itself offer any insuperable objection to the belief that man has developed from some lower form' ('Descent')."

Doctor.—"I am quite aware that he says so, but I am confident that we shall be able to prove the contrary and to set off in the boldest and clearest light Darwin's supine ignorance and total unacquaintance with the commonest principles of logic and philosophy."

Adele.—"I expect to have a feast and a treat."

Doctor.—"George, how many kind of languages are there?"

George.—"Language being the external expression of sensations, feelings or thoughts, I should say, in general, that there are as many kinds of languages as there are ways of expressing those things."

Doctor.—"Very good. But restricting the word language to expressions which emanate from animals, how many kinds of languages would you admit?"

George.—"I would admit only two, the natural and the artificial."

Adele.—"Pray explain."

George.—"The natural language of animals consists in the simple emissions of sounds or cries, in their attitudes, in their looks and movement of the visage."

Adele.—"So the mewling of my cat, the raising of his paws—as the knights of old who put their lance in rest—to defend herself from the attacks of the dog, the sparkling of her eyes, and the contortions of her face is what you would call its natural language?"

George.—"Certainly."

Doctor.—"And such language is common to man and animals; but in the latter it is confined to a small number of signs, to manifest a feeling, a desire or an appeal."

George.—"'Man,' says Darwin, as a highly competent judge, Archbishop Whately remarks, 'is not the only animal that can make use of language to express what is passing in his mind, and can understand more or less what is so expressed by another' (*loc cit*)."

Doctor.—"Dear me, how puerile! how sickening! a very competent judge, no less than Archbishop Whatley, is called to account for—what? For that which the smallest child in all ages knows perfectly well."

Adele.—"Certainly, Mr. Darwin; we freely admit that both man and animals have certain common signs to express their sensations and feelings, and this is called natural language. For you to disturb for such a frivolity the shade of no less a personage than of His Grace himself is an unwarrantable liberty."

Doctor.—"This disposes in a lump of all the examples adduced by Darwin in support of his statement. Let us pass to artificial language. What do you mean by it, George?"

George.—"I mean by artificial language that which is formed of articulate sounds of the voice, and the signification of which is conventional; which articulate sounds, differently combined and arranged, are apt to express not only sensations or feelings, but thoughts and ideas infinitely distant from, and above, our senses and feelings."

Doctor.—"Do you understand, Adele?"

Adele.—"I would like to put some questions. What is meant by articulate sounds?"

Doctor.—"Suppose you hear a long, piercing shriek, you would call it one continued sound, would you not?"

Adele.—"Certainly."

Doctor.—"But suppose I make a number of distinct sounds and connect them together, so as to exhibit one perfect whole, like the joints or bones which, put together, form the human frame, what would you call that?"

Adele.—"I guess that is what you mean by articulate sounds, that is, the utterance of a number of distinct sounds put together; as, for instance, if I pronounce the word 'incontestible' I may consider every syllable of that word as so many distinct sounds, which, joined together, form that adjective."

Doctor.—"Articulate language, then, is a number of distinct

sounds put together to form a complete sign, to express what is wanted."

Adele.—"But why did George say, 'the signification of which is conventional or agreed upon?'"

Doctor.—"Because those sounds don't of their own nature express the object. If they do, it is only by an agreement, and not because there is an essential necessary relation between that sound and the object. You remember the well-known lines of Shakespeare:

"'What's in a name? That which we call a rose
By any other name would smell as sweet.'
· *Romeo and Juliet.*

What does the poet mean? That as there is no intrinsic necessary connection between the flower we wish to designate by that name and the sound *rose*, if we called that flower by any other name or sound, that change would not effect its nature and qualities, and therefore the rose would smell as sweet."

Adele.—"I understand now. But what did Mr. George mean or allude to by saying that artificial language, by combination and arrangement of words, could express not only sensations and feelings, but thoughts infinitely distinct from, and superior to, any sensation or feeling."

Doctor.—"He alluded to abstract and universal conceptions."

Adele.—"I would like to have those explained once more."

Doctor.—"According to the theory developed in our last interview, you will recollect, that to abstract is to draw, to dig the intelligible from the sensible, to get at the nature and essence of things, and that to generalize is the faculty of applying that idea to all such as represent and exhibit the same essence and nature. But it may not be amiss to give here another instance of those faculties of abstraction and generalization. Suppose a number of men pass before me. The first appears in all his individual peculiarities of body as to its form, its height, its size, its color, its vigor, its age, and so forth; similarly with his peculiarities of mind as to its powers; the second comes in sight also with his peculiar traits of body and mind; the third, and so on. Now, suppose that when they have all passed I begin to investigate what is common to all of them and what is special to each, and in trying to solve the problem I eliminate from all of them their individual differences of body and mind, and what have I left as a result? Evidently I have left the idea of what really makes a man, a body informed by a rational principle or mind; because after I have stripped each one of his peculiar traits, I find that, like all the rest, he has a body and a rational principle, and I conclude the real idea of man, of his true essence and nature, is that of a being composed of a body informed and vivified by a rational principle or substance. That is the abstract idea of man, that is, the conception by the mind of his real nature and essence stripped of all the peculiarities which accompany such and such a man. That idea is called abstract, from the Latin *abstruhere*, to strip off, to cut off from; because it is the conception of the real nature of a thing stripped of the peculiar traits of the individual objects in which it always appears, though clothed in each of them with peculiar modifications. That idea is called, also, universal, us we remarked, because representing and exhibiting the real nature of a thing it can be applied to all objects at all times and in all places which appear endowed with the same nature and essence."

Adele.—"I see, again, how true it is that thought is infinitely superior to any emotion and feeling."

Doctor.—"You understand, then, how articulate language can express thought and ideas. Coming, then, nearer to the point, we claim first, that articulate language is the exclusive property of man; second, that the power of connecting definite ideas with definite articulate sounds or words is al o the exclusive privilege of the human race, in which no lower animal can ever share; third, that far from receiving this gift by inheritance from a progenitor of lower form, or far from inventing and developing it of himself, man must have received it directly from the Creator. First, then, the power of emitting articulate sounds belong to man alone."

George.—"Darwin denies it, and says 'that it is not the mere articulation which is our distinguishing character,' because parrots and other birds possess this power."

Adele.—"Then it would be more logical to make us descend from parrots and not from the ape."

Doctor.—"And you would be right. But it requires the gigantic intellect of Darwin and its colossal logical powers to infer, from the few sounds which the parrot utters at random, and with reason and no reason—sounds which he has learned after long and repeated efforts, that the power of articulation is not the exclusive appendage of man. All the mammals which have organs better fitted than the parrot for articulation, have for thousands of years gone on emitting nothing but shrieks and cries, and cannot utter a single articulate sound, let alone a number of them. How is this accounted for? The ape, which imitates and mimics so well and so dexterously the actions of man, why does he fail to imitate him in his articulate language? How is it that no power of training can enable him to articulate a single word?"

George.—"But Mr. Darwin gives up this part of the argument in those. 'The habitual use of articulate language is, however, peculiar to man.'"

Adele.—"Which means—as a fact—the steady, constant, permanent use of articulate language is peculiar to man; and the rare, disconnected, occasional use, by fits and starts, belongs to animals. Much obliged for the concession. We don't require more to prove our statement."

Doctor.—"Let us pass to the second claim, that the power of connecting definite sounds with definite ideas is the sole and exclusive privilege of man."

George.—"'Not at all,' says Darwin; 'for it is certain that some parrots which have been taught to speak, connect, unerringly, words with things and persons with events.'"

Adele.—"What is the proof of such a grand assertion?"

George.—"Why, did not Admiral Sir J. Sullivan tell Mr. Darwin of an African parrot kept in his father's house, who said good morning to every one at breakfast, and good night to each as they left the room at night; and didn't this same parrot give a tremendous scolding to a dog which intruded into the house, and didn't this same long-headed and goody bird call another parrot, who was misbehaving—'you naughty polly?'"

Adele.—"To be sure; what else could you want? Animals of all kind connect definite sounds with definite ideas, and persons with events; because an African parrot learned to say good morning and good night, isn't that sufficient proof? Is not the argument according to all the rules of logic—I mean the logic that Mr. Darwin must have learned to draw a universal consequence from a particular fact in spite of and in opposition to all logic? But then, didn't the parrot scold poor doggy for his intrusion?. And what would you have more? I wonder if the canine intruder paid much heed to the scold; and I am curious to know if the naughty polly didn't retort in articulate language and tell her to mind her own business. That is what you scientists call reasoning, is it not?"

George.—"Do not get excited, Miss Adele, Darwin, as usual, takes it back. 'The lower animals differ from man solely *in his almost infinitely larger power* of associating together the most diversified sounds and ideas, and this obviously depends on the high development of his mental powers' (*loc. cit.* 50)."

Doctor.—"Though he fails to account for the cause of this high development of his mental powers, we will accept his difference, or rather distinction, without a difference, and pass on to the last question which resolves itself into three subordinate ones: Did man receive this articulate language from a lower progenitor? Did he invent it himself? Who gave it to him?"

Adele.—"How does Darwin answer the questions, Mr. George?"

George.—"By laying down two statements. The first is, 'that no philologist now supposes that any language has been deliberately invented; it has been slowly and unconsciously developed by many steps; second, that these steps were 'the imitation and modification of various natural sounds, the voices of other animals, and man's own instinctive cries, aided by signs and gestures,' and he concludes to show the plausibility of his theory by the words—'may not some unusually wise, ape-like animal have imitated the growl of a beast of prey, and thus told his fellow-monkeys the nature of the expected danger? This would have been the first step in the formation of language' (page 47)."

Adele.—"Very easily done, indeed!"

Doctor.—"To fling away all this silly trash at once, we will prove that language could not only not be invented by brute animals, but not even by man himself, and that if man speaks, it is owing to a beneficent gift of his Creator. Mark our statement contains two propositions: first, no brute animal could invent language; second, not even man himself could have done so."

Adele.—"How is the first part of the statement proven?"

Doctor.—"Easily enough. Language is made of abstract and universal ideas. But we have demonstrated that brute animals are not endowed with any faculties higher than sensibility and instinct, and hence are lacking in the faculty of abstraction and generalization. Therefore, it would be absolutely impossible for any of them to invent language, in spite of all the wise, ape-like animals of Darwin. George, please to give us the principal parts of speech?"

George.—"They are—articles, nouns, pronouns, adjectives, verbs, prepositions and interjections."

Adele.—"Why, he is reciting his grammar!"

Doctor.—"To be sure; and what is grammar but the art of speaking? Well, now, every one of those parts of speech implies an abstract and general idea. Let us go over a few of them. Take any of them. What is a noun? It is the name of anything which exists, or of which we have any notion, as New York, man, virtue, law, republic. It embraces concrete ideas as well as abstract and general. In the examples given New York is the only concrete idea, the others are abstract and general. The article, which is a word used before a noun in order to signify how far its signification extends, is in every language definite or indefinite, so *a* man implies any one man of the species, *the* man points out a certain particular man; and the first proposition as well as the second clearly indicates and implies both a general and a particular idea of man; an adjective, which is a word added to a noun to express a quality: as, an industrious man, a skillful artist, an excellent friend, is essentially an abstract idea. The examples given imply the abstract idea of industry, skill and moral excellence. I need not add that the pronoun in every language implies the idea of relation to subject. When I say—Lincoln was a very humane man; he emancipated the slaves—in uttering *he*, I intend to refer to Lincoln, and I must necessarily have and suppose the idea of relation. George, what is a verb?"

George.—"It is a word which signifies to be, to act, or to be acted upon: as, I am, I rule, I am ruled."

Doctor.—"Well, no form of speech better than the verb puts in a better light the necessity of abstract ideas for the formation of language. To *be* implies the abstract idea of existence; to *act* that of action and movement; to *be acted upon* the idea of passiveness. Then as existence, action and passiveness are modified by time they imply the idea of time. *I am reading* implies the abstract idea of present time; *I was reading* the idea of past time; *I shall* or *will read* the idea of future time. Then add the abstract ideas of possibility, condition and dependence, which oftentimes accompany verbs, and you will see that a multitude of abstract ideas accompany the principal ideas of existence, of action and passion which verbs represent. Shall I say anything about adverbs, which are to verbs what adjectives are to nouns? Is it necessary for me to mention that prepositions essentially imply a relation between two words, and consequently the abstract idea of relation, as much as conjunction imply connection of its abstract concèpt? We may then conclude that as language is necessarily and absolutely made up of abstract and general ideas, it follows that as animals are incapable of forming such ideas, they cannot, by any possible way, invent or form a language. Brute animals, therefore, can never speak."

Adele.—"Language, then, is simply and absolutely and exclusively man's privilege; and that gives the lie to the words of Darwin: 'Nor, as we have seen, does the faculty of articulate speech in itself offer any insuperable objection to the belief that man has been developed from some lower form.' By his leave we insist that as animals never did or could speak, there is a most insuperable objection to man being descended from a lower form; for, in that case, he would be as dumb as they are, and capable of nothing more than cries, shrieks, and howls."

Doctor.—"But let us pass to the other point, that men themselves could not invent language. Understand me; there are some writers who are of opinion that man cannot form abstract ideas or universal concèpts without the aid of language. But we will not enter into that question, as it would lead us much further than the limits appointed to our interviews would permit. Even allowing that man could think abstract and universal ideas without language, still we must contend that man could not and has not invented the language to express them."

Adele.—"You premise two things, uncle, that man could not, and that he has not, as a matter of fact, invented the language."

Doctor.—"Certainly; now for the proof of the first. Do you recollect how we defined the language?"

Adele.—"Yes, sir. Language is a number of articulate sounds the signification of which is arbitrary and conventional."

Doctor.—"Very good. Then, if the signification of sounds is arbitrary and conventional, when men wanted to invent a language they must have agreed upon the signification they would attach to certain sounds and the meaning they would attach to others."

Adele.—"I don't see how they could have done otherwise?"

Doctor.—"And do you not see that, in order to do all that, they must have spoken already; otherwise how could they communicate with each other in matters so extremely difficult and requiring the most exalted and the deepest knowledge of philosophy?"

Adele.—"I perceive, I overlooked a most important point. Every language supposes certain conventionalism because it implies a system of signs to which everyone attaches the same meaning. Now, the question is: Are these conventionalisms possible without a verbal communication? It was necessary to render this system of signs intelligible to all. But how to make it comprehensible without explanation and elucidations? And how to give such explanations without language?"

George.—"Therefore we must conclude with Rousseau that the language must have been of the highest necessity to invent language."

Doctor.—"In other words, the supporters of such opinion must continually revolve in a circle; they want man to invent the language and he must already speak a language to invent one. Whoever reflects for a moment what profound psychology is contained in language can fully convince himself of that truth. Language is a psychology in which every phenomenon of thought has its distinct form, its expression, its particular sign, where the whole nature is analyzed and taken in parts, wherein all the qualities of bodies as well as all the conceptions of the mind are abstracted and separated, one from the other, with a knowledge and skill such as to command the admiration of every reflecting mind. The ablest philosopher could not analyze the human mind with as much depth as the inventor of language would have been obliged to do. For there is not a shade of sentiment, an element of perception, or modification of being, a modification of faculties, of time, of place, of number, of person, of action, of passion —in a word there is not a state, an attitude, a relation of the human mind and life which has not its expression in language. And how could it be thought possible that the first inventors of language had such perfect knowledge of psychology all at once as to invent sounds for every one of those thoughts, ideas and sentiments? The thing is sheerly and utterly impossible."

Adele.—"But, uncle, you have said that, as a matter of fact, man has not invented the language. Will you be so kind as to prove it?"

Doctor.—"Certainly. All modern ethnographists are agreed on the following points: First, that there exists one mother-tongue from which all others have been derived; second, that the separation of idioms originated in a sudden and violent cause. Now, if language were man's invention we must suppose that every couple, or at least every family, would have composed a special one, and that, therefore, we should find no sort of analogy between any two such languages as is always the case with things depending on arbitrary and fortuitous events. But the fact is otherwise. There are in all languages affinities and relations which strike everyone who examines them, common terms which render all doubt of a common origin absolutely impossible. One person, then, and not a number of men or families, must have invented it. And who is that inventor? God or man? What proofs are alleged by our adversaries that man invented it? None. What reasons do they bring forward or what facts that man existed for some time without language? What proofs have they to show that both man and language were not contemporary? We conclude, then, with Alexander Humboldt, Merian, Klaproth, Fred. Schlegel, Herder, Turner Remusat, Niebuhr, Balbi, that man received his language from the Creator at the same time as his existence."

Adele.—"To sum up, then, we have seen that language, articulate and artificial, is spoken only by man, because man alone is endowed with intelligence, and that it is impossible that man could have inherited it from a lower ancestor, because neither brute animals nor man could have invented the language; the animals, because being wanting in the reasoning faculty, they are incapable of forming abstract and universal ideas; man, because to invent and adopt a conventional and arbitrary system of sounds, would already require a language fully complete and perfectly understood by those who would have to agree upon that system. God, then, must have given man his language."

George.—"The great conclusion of all our conversation then, may be expressed in the words of Max Müller: 'Through reason we not only stand a step above the brute creation, we belong to a different world!' ('Science of Language')."

Doctor.—Yes, sir, language is the exclusive sign of intelligence. Man alone speaks; therefore, he alone, in the whole animal creation, is endowed with intelligence, and consequently cannot owe his existence and origin to any lower form of life. He is a different world from all brute animals, a special creation of the Most High."

TWENTY-FOURTH ARTICLE.

IS IT A SAFE OPINION TO HOLD THAT MAN'S BODY WAS DEVELOPED FROM THE APE?

George.—"Doctor, I have heard that a Catholic could, without any trouble of conscience, hold the opinion that man's body was developed from the ape."

Adele.—"Why do you say man's body and not man?"

George.—"Because it is admitted by all, I believe, without exception, that the spiritual principle in man must be the result of a special action of God, and could never be developed from any lower form of animals."

Adele.—"Then the whole question is restricted to man's body, and you inquire, I believe, if it is safe and consistent with Catholic faith, to maintain that man's body could be developed from the ape?"

Doctor.—"An eminent Catholic scientist, Mivart, followed by some other writers, has maintained such opinion. After having given the theory that we may take the word creation in a twofold sense—first, creation from nothing, that is, that action of God which effects things from no preëxisting matter; and derivative creation, that is, that action of God which concurs with the natural forces in order to develop something from preëxisting materials, he concludes: 'Supposing the human soul to be directly and immediately created, yet each human body is evolved by the ordinary operation of natural physical laws' ('Genesis of Species,' p. 300, Appleton, '71)."

Adele.—"Let me try to understand this opinion. He maintains that there are two sorts of creation, the direct and immediate, that which effects things from nothing; man's soul is the immediate and direct effect of such creation. The other is a derivative creation, that is, when a thing is evolved from preëxisting materials according to, and in virtue of, the ordinary operation of physical laws. Man's body was the result of this derivative creation. But I don't see how the action of God has anything to do here, when the whole thing is the result of the operation of physical laws."

Doctor.—"According to our scientist, the action of God comes in here in the same manner as it concurs with every action of His creatures. You remember the doctrine explained in one of our conversations, that God's creative action may be considered under three different aspects: as strictly creative, that is, effecting finite substances from nothing; as conservative, inasmuch as it keeps in existence the substances it has created; and as concurrent, inasmuch as it incites created substances to action, aids them during the performance of action, and helps them to perfect it. It is in this manner that Saint George Mivart acknowledges the body of man to have been created by God, inasmuch as He concurred with the natural causes to develop it."

George.—"Then the creation of man's body presents no special features to distinguish it from any other natural event?"

Doctor.—"None whatever, according to Mivart."

Adele.—"And can we, as Catholics, safely maintain such opinion?"

Doctor.—"Assuredly not, either as Catholics or philosophers."

George.—"Why?"

Doctor.—"Because that opinion is not tenable, neither in theology nor philosophy. We will study the proofs together, but before we enter upon them we must premise a few remarks by way of explanation. First, in what sense do we maintain that man's body is a special creation of God? second, how are we to understand that God formed man's body out of the slime of the earth? With regard to the first question we hold: first, that man's body was *not* created from nothing; second, that it was not evolved from a preëxisting material, *according to the usual operation of physical forces and laws;* third, that God's infinite energy and power by an immediate, distinct, and *special act*, formed it out of the slime of the earth. Hence, we take the words of Genesis: 'The Lord God formed man of the slime of the earth' (Genesis, ch. 2), in their proper, obvious, natural, literal sense. This last statement will elucidate and explain how God formed man's body out of the clay of the earth. Some scientists, with that materialism which colors all their thoughts and ideas so peculiar to them, have imagined that when theologians affirm that God formed man's body from clay they represent Him as a downright, *bona fide* potter, mixing up and elaborating the soft earth to shape it into a statue exhibiting man's figure. I need not remark that such a monstrous idea never entered any other head except that of the scientists aforesaid. The formation of man's body from clay was the instantaneous effect and result of God's infinite will and energy; and theologians reject with scorn and contempt any such material and gross interpretation of their meaning and of that to be attached to the words of Genesis. And now, that we explained what is meant by man's body being a special creation of God, we may pass to the reasons which render Mivart's opinion unsafe and untenable. We will begin by theology. George, I suppose you are aware that there is a twofold set of doctrines of faith?"

George.—"Not that I am aware of. I am not very strong in the knowledge of our religion."

Adele.—"Nor I."

Doctor.—"It is a great pity. Nowadays every educated person ought to have a very respectable knowledge of his holy religion, so as to have all the principal difficulties which her enemies allege against her doctrine answered to the satisfaction of his own mind, and be able to solve the same difficulties for others. You ought to know, then, that there are two different sets of doctrines of faith: first, those that have been declared to be such by the Church, either in a General Council, or by the Pope alone speaking *ex cathedra*, that is to say, when he speaks and decides as the Doctor and Head of the Universal Church, and when he addresses the whole Church on a question of faith or morality. For instance, the Divinity of Our Lord is one of these doctrines, because declared to be so by the General Council of Nice. The doctrine of the Immaculate Conception is also one of the same class, because declared *ex cathedra* by Pius IX. There is another set of doctrines which have not been defined by any General Council or by any Pope speaking *ex cathedra*, but which are also part of the deposit of revealed truths, and are to be believed in the same manner as the first; and the reason is, because they have been held as doctrines of faith by the Church at all times and in all places, as it is evident by the unanimous testimony of the Fathers and Theologians, who have maintained and held them as such."

Adele.—"Uncle, who may the Fathers of the Church be?"

Doctor.—"They are men eminent for piety and knowledge of divine things, who, by their works, have defended, explained, elucidated the doctrines of the Church. They have lived almost in every century, and are preëminently the Doctors of the Church; and their united testimony on some points is of the greatest authority in ascertaining what was the faith of the Church, not only at their time, but previous to it, as they hold nothing but what was taught and handed down to them by their teachers and Fathers in the faith, who in their turn received it likewise."

Adele.—"And we are to believe that man's body, being the direct and immediate effect of a special act of God, is one of those truths of faith which has been held to be of faith and believed by the Church at all times and in all places, and this on the unanimous testimony of the Doctors and Theologians?"

Doctor.—"Certainly."

George.—"It will be highly interesting to hear such testimony."

Doctor.—"But I can give here only an abridgement of the combined testimony of the Fathers, as a long list of testimonies would tire Adele. I will except only a few, especially St. Augustine, St. Thomas, and Suarez, whose words I shall quote, because these three Doctors have been cited by Saint George Mivart as advocates of evolution. The Doctors of the Church as far back as St. Justin, who lived in the second century, down to our times, have not only taken the formation of the body of man and that of the woman, as related by Moses, in a literal, obvious and natural sense, but on the general theory and principle of St. Paul, they have seen in that narrative and its particulars the figure and the foreshadowing of some of the principal mysteries of the Christian dispensation. Thus, in the formation of man's body from the untilled virgin soil they have surmised the conception of Our Blessed Lord in the virginal cloister of His Blessed Mother. George, read the words of St. Irenæus which you will find marked."

George.—"'And as that first formed Adam received his substance from the *untilled and yet virgin earth*, and was fashioned by the hand of God (for all things were made by Him), and God took the slime of the earth and fashioned it into a man, likewise He (God) rightly accepted the Word recapitulating in Himself (Christ), Adam, and existing in Mary as yet Virgin, as the generation of Adam's recapitulation. For, if the first Adam had had a man as father, they (the heretics) would rightly say that the second Adam was engendered by Joseph. But if he (Adam) was taken from the earth and formed by the Word of God, it was necessary that the Word of God, taking upon Himself the recapitulation of Adam, should present a similitude of his generation' ('Against heretics,' book 3d, ch. 21, of God's Nativity from the Virgin)."

Doctor.—"It is evident from the text that the Fathers did not limit themselves to admitting, literally, the formation of Adam's body from the earth, but discovered in that formation the mystery of the conception of Christ from the Virgin."

Adele.—"I think the thought is very beautiful. God in creating and forming man was sketching out, as it were, the principal traits and the general lineaments of the second Adam, Our Blessed Lord. Hence, He formed Adam's body from the undisturbed, untilled virgin earth to shadow forth the conception of His Incarnate Son in the virgin cloister of Mary."

George.—"How swiftly a religious thought comes home to a woman's heart."

Doctor.—"Tertullian, a Doctor next to St. Irenæus, in the book on 'Christ's Flesh,' ch. 17 and 18, expresses the same thought: 'The earth was as yet virgin, not yet turned up by work, not yet submitted to the action of seeds, and we have been told that God made man from it into a living soul. Wherefore, if the first Adam was created from the earth, it rightly follows that the new Adam should, as the Apostle said, be brought forth into a vivifying spirit by God from the earth; that is, a flesh not yet touched by generation.' St. Basil, another great Doctor, who lived later on: 'Wherefore, as the first Adam did not come to light from the union of man and woman, but was formed out of the earth, so the new Adam, having to repair the corruption of the first, took a body formed in the virginal womb' ('Commentary on Isaias,' ch. 7, v. 201). Passing over St. Ambrose and other Doctors, we will come to St. Augustine, an evolutionist according to Mivart, a question which will be decided by the texts we shall quote. Read them, George, as I have put them down."

George.—" 'That the God of Majesty, incarnate in Mary, was not defiled by being born of a virgin, as He was not defiled by making man from the dust. Nor is it incredible that He should be born of a virgin who formed Adam from the virgin dust and woman from a rib.' ('Sermon on the Creed,' ch. 2) Again, 'Why do you not believe that He should have been fashioned in the womb of a virgin *whom you must believe* to have made man of the slime of the earth?' ('Sermon,' 243)."

Adele.—"That is contradicting evolution with a vengeance."

George.—"Again, 'So must you believe Christ to be the Son of God, that is, true God and one of the persons of the Trinity, as not to doubt of His Divinity, conceived as He was of the nature of the Father; and, likewise, so must you believe to be true man, as not to think his flesh to be of celestial origin or ærial, or of anything else, but the very same flesh as that of all men, that is to say, the very one which *God Himself formed from the earth for the first man*' ('On Faith to Peter'). Again, in the 'Sermon,' 109: 'Who shall say that the Word, by Whom all things were made, could not form unto Himself a flesh without a mother, as *He made the first man without father or mother?* But because He created both sexes, male and female; therefore, in being born, He wanted to honor both sexes.'"

Adele.—"It sounds almost profane here to remark that any supposition of St. Augustine having held the body of man to be the result of evolution become utterly absurd, when he affirms so clearly that God made the first man without father or mother. Surely, according to the hypothesis of evolution, the apish progenitors of man would have been his father and mother!"

Doctor.—"We will quote one more passage from St. Augustine, taken from p. 122, 'Sermon on the Nativity of Our Lord': 'If you contend to be contrary to nature that in the mystery of our redemption a Virgin is said to have conceived without the help of man, pray, according to what nature is it that the flesh of our parent was formed without flesh ? What kind of a reason is that, or, rather, what kind of blind contention to refuse to believe that God could form man from woman, when one already believes that He could form him from dust ? O, man! if you perceive such to be the will of the Omnipotent in this thing, why do you retract it as to the work ? And if you will earnestly investigate, besides the legitimate use of human conception, you will find that the Trinity has enacted three most wonderful species of birth. And truly the first is, *because Adam has been fashioned of the slime of the earth ;* the second, *that woman was formed of the male ;* the third, which is heavenly, is that Christ proceeded from a Virgin. Which of them is not novel? Which of them is not wonderful? Which of them can be comprehended by human inquiry unless we adhere to faith ?' "

George.—"Nothing can be clearer than that St. Augustine held the body of the first man to have been created immediately and directly by the will of the Almighty."

Doctor.—"Well, let us pass to the other two Doctors quoted by Mivart, St. Thomas and Suarez."

Adele.—"Who is St. Thomas, uncle ?"

Doctor.—"Perhaps the greatest intellect which God has ever created. He was born in 1225 of noble parents, in a small town called Aquinas, in the southern part of Italy, hence he is called St. Thomas of Aquinas. For purity of doctrine, for depth and sublimity of mind, for clearness, precision, and order in treating every possible theological and philosophical question with an ease and felicity of language absolutely matchless, he stands preëminently among the colossal intellects of mankind. He died at the early age of 51, and during that short span of life he contrived to write twenty-three volumes, in folio, besides spending most of his time in teaching and in the works of the ministry. When the question of miracles came up for his canonization Pope John XXII. exclaimed that it was not necessary to look for miracles in his case, as every article of the 'Theological Summa' or abridgment (his best work) was a miracle. The authority of St. Thomas' teaching in the Church is immense, and our present Holy Father has, with perfect consciousness of the wants of the Church at the present time, urged all to the study of that prince among the master minds of mankind."

Adele.—"After such a testimony of the grandeur of St. Thomas' intellect, I am anxious to hear his opinion."

Doctor.—" 'It is to be held,' says St. Thomas, in his 'Summa,' first part, question 19, article 2d, 'that the formation of man's body could not be effected by any created agency, but immediately by God.' See article 4, question 92. I quote the last: 'It is to be maintained that the natural generation of any kind of a species is from certain definite matter. Now, the matter from which man is naturally generated is the human semen. Therefore an individual of the human species cannot be naturally engendered from any other matter. Now, God alone, as the Creator of nature, can produce things beyond the order of nature. Hence God alone could form man from the slime of the earth. and woman from man.' Again, in the 'Commentary' on the four books, so called, of the sayings of Peter Lombard, Distinction 18, question 1, article 1, he says: 'I answer by saying that among Catholics there can be no doubt as to the fact of the woman having been formed from man's rib, whatever fables the Jews may spout about this; because it is no more against reason or the Divine power to suppose that the woman should be made from man's body, than that the body of man should be formed from the slime of the earth, as both things are entirely above the power of nature.'"

George.—"Then the question of man's body being created directly by God is again settled, so far as St. Thomas is concerned. Let us come to the other theologian on whom Mivart relies so much."

Doctor.—"Suarez is one of the greatest theologians of the seventeenth century. He was born in Grenada and joined early the Society of Jesus and honored it by his immense labors and sublimity and depth of intellect. The testimony of this theologian is so strong against the theory that I cannot imagine how Saint George could have invoked Suarez in favor of his theory. Here are the words of Suarez: 'It is to be maintained that man's body was produced immediately by God.' Now, mark what follows: 'The above statement is a truth of Catholic faith, and is taught by St. Thomas *with whom agree all other Fathers and theologians*' ('De Opere sex Dierum,' Lib. 3; 'De Hominis Creatione,' Edition Vives)."

Adele.—"Suarez is rather hard on Saint George."

Doctor.—"All modern theologians maintain the same. It suffices to consult Contenson, Thommasinus, Billuart, Perrone, Palmieri, Cercia, Mazzella, Schebeen, Hurter, Schouppe, Youngman, Zigliara, Ubaldi, etc., etc. George, please to read the words of Doctor Schebeen of Cologne, which I have marked in his 'Katholische Dogmatik,' vol. 2, Freiburg, 1878, p. 144."

George.—"'Relatively, to the first constituent part of man—the body—revelation accords with the dogma of the Church through its teaching about man's origin, and which indirectly embraces all men springing from the first; a doctrine which is authenticated and authorized by the natural consciousness, and partly by the sensible instinct that the body has taken its component material form respectively to its material element from the earth; that it has received its definite organization as man's body, not through the blind, accidental operation of physical force, but according to a special and definite divine idea, *either immediately from God, as in the case of the first man*, or mediately through the plastic force of a principle realizing the same nature. It is, *therefore, a heresy to pretend that man, as to his body, has descended from the ape* in consequence of progressive changes come over the forms, even if one should suppose that upon the complete evolution of the form God simultaneously created the soul.'"

Adele.—"Who is the other author whom I see marked, uncle?"

Doctor,—"It is another modern theologian's work, Schouppe's ('Course of Sacred Scripture'). His testimony will be the last we shall allege. In raising the question, what things in the narrative of Genesis about the creation of the world and of man are dogmatically certain, and what are free and disputed, he answers: 'are dogmatically certain, and of faith the following points: first, God in the beginning of time created the whole universe from nothing; second, God created the first man after His own image and likeness from whom the whole of mankind takes its origin' (Paris ed., vol. 1, part second, p. 145)."

Adele.—"It is evident to me now that a Catholic cannot maintain the opinion of Saint George Mivart, that the body of man may be supposed to have descended from an apish couple, and that, when once born from those animals, God put into it a spiritual principle. The belief of the Church at all times and in all places, as attested by the Fathers, Doctors and theologians in the direct immediate creation of the body of man by God, utterly excludes and repudiates such supposition."

George.—"Besides, I reckon philosophy would have a great deal to say against such supposition, as we said in the beginning."

Doctor.—"Certainly it has, and as you have suggested it, you will please to give us your thoughts on the subject at our next meeting."

Adele.—"But, uncle, before we pass to the philosophy of the thing, I am anxious to know what mysteries of the Christian dispensation did the fathers of the Christian Church see in the creation of woman from man's rib?"

Doctor.—"I am glad you mentioned it, Adele, for I should not have liked to omit that explanation. I will give you the explanation of St. Augustine and St. John Chrysostom, who are followed by all the rest of the Fathers. The first in explaining the words of St. John the Evangelist, relating the Passion of Our Lord: 'One of the soldiers with a spear opened His (Our Lord's) side, and immediately there came out blood and water,' says, 'Of a set purpose did the Evangelist use the word *opened*, and did not say *struck* or *wounded*, or something else, but *opened*, in order that the door of life might somewhat be thrown open, from whence originated the sacraments of the Church, without which none can enter into that which is true life. . . . In view of this was the first woman formed from the side of the sleeping man, and called life and the mother of the living. For she presaged great good before the great evil of prevarication. This second Adam, having bowed His head, slept on the Cross that a spouse might hence be formed to Him which should emanate from the side of a sleeping one.' 'O, death by which the dead return to life!' What can be purer than that blood? What more salutary than that wound?"

Adele.—Beautiful, indeed, uncle! I seem to see it. Adam is sleeping, and from his breast, which God has opened, and from one of his ribs, woman is formed, the life and mother of all living. Our dearest Lord, the second Adam, sleeps the sleep of death on the cross; His sacred side is opened in order that the Church, His beloved spouse, might be formed out of the blood and water which issued from that side, because the Church is made up principally of the sacraments, the chief of which are baptism represented by the water, and the Holy Eucharist represented by the blood; and thus the Church was formed out of the side of her Divine spouse, and became the life and the mother of all the living."

George.—"Excellently said, Miss Adele."

Doctor.—"The other is St. John Chrysostom in the sermon explaining the same text: 'I have said that that blood and that water represented baptism and the Holy Eucharist. For on these is founded the Church, on the laver of regeneration and renovation of the Holy Spirit. I say on baptism and the holy mysteries which appear to have issued from the side. Hence Christ from His side constructed the Church, as from the side of Adam was formed Eve. For which reason St. Paul testifies, saying, 'we are of His body and of His bones meaning to signify that side. Because as from Adam's side God caused the woman to be produced, so from Christ's own side water and blood emanated, by means of which the Church might be redeemed.'"

Adele.—"I see the same beautiful thought; and the mystery of the institution of God's Church, the bride of Christ, seen by all the Fathers in the formation of woman from Adam's rib."

Doctor.—"And mark well, both of you, that on Saint Mivart's supposition not only the whole mysterious significance and prophetic presaging of the peculiar formation of woman is swept away, but the narration of Genesis loses every possible meaning, because on Mivart's supposition woman must have descended, naturally, in the course of natural laws, from an apish couple like man, and if so, what possible sense can we attach to Moses' narrative? It becomes a legend, a myth, a pious fairy sketch and imagination of the sacred writer. Now, the latter supposition is utterly untenable, and among all theologians one only has ever been found to indulge in it, L. was followed by none, and concemned by all who considered it as a sheer extravagance."

TWENTY-FIFTH ARTICLE.

HAS MIVART'S OPINION ANY THEOLOGICAL GROUNDS IN ITS SUPPORT?

Doctor.—"If you paid strict attention to what we said at our last meeting you will have observed that Saint George's opinion contradicts in about five or six different ways the ordinary infallible teaching of the Church as to the origin of man's body."

George.—"It would be well to point them out separately, that one may easily perceive and remember them."

Doctor.—"That opinion, in the first place, assumes that man's body was not created immediately and directly by a distinct special act of God's infinite will, and the daily ordinary teaching of the Church affirms the contrary, that is, that God did immediately and directly form man's body, and that of the woman. Secondly, the opinion of Saint George takes for granted that there was nothing extraordinary or surprising about the formation of both, whereas the ordinary teaching of God's Church is that the whole thing was entirely out of all ordinary course, and quite extraordinary and wonderful. Thirdly, the opinion of Mivart implies that man's body must have come from the natural sexual union of two lower animals, male and female, who would naturally be called its parents, and the Fathers, Doctors and Theologians of the Church utterly reject any such supposition, and insist that Adam had no parents."

Adele.—"I see clearly all the different aspects in which that opinion is opposed to what the Fathers have taught."

Doctor.—"Fourthly, that opinion supposes that man's body would have sprung from the slime of the earth, only mediately and in a far-off way in the sense that the flesh which man would have inherited from his apish progenitors, when it started the first step on its way to evolution, was indeed slime, but in no other sense, whilst the Church, by her ordinary teaching, proclaims from the house tops that Adam was formed from the untilled, uncut, undisturbed earth, not submitted to the action of seeds, or plough. Finally, the opinion of Saint George removes and destroys all possible analogy between the creation and formation of man and woman, and the conception of Our Blessed Lord in the virgin cloister of Mary, and the formation of the Church Christ's holy bride from this wounded side, as Eve was formed from man's side; an analogy insisted upon by all the Fathers, and which is founded on the philosophy of faith as proclaimed by St. Paul."

George.—"But, doctor, Professor Mivart claims that the doctrine of evolution was held by three of the greatest Doctors of the Church,

St. Augustine, St. Thomas, and Suarez, and he brings forward testimonies from the works of those three to make good his claim."

Adele.—"But did we not read the testimony of those three Doctors, proving in a manner which can admit no possible doubt or hesitation that they held the body of man to have been formed immediately and directly by a special act of Omnipotence by God Himself?"

George.—"Certainly we did."

Adele.—"Then how can they hold evolution? Can we imagine that they contradict themselves?"

Doctor.—"It is not necessary to go so far as that, Adele. Suppose that the testimonies alleged from those three Doctors really proved that they maintained the opinion of evolution in general, it would by no means follow that they applied that opinion to man also, as the texts we brought forward to the contrary clearly and incontestably prove. We said in one of our conversations that the opinion maintaining evolution, as far as animal brutes is concerned, is an open question. Consequently. St. Augustine, St. Thomas, and Suarez might have held evolution and yet not apply it to man. So Mivart and all those Catholics who have a leaning for evolution as applying to all beings, man included, and try to support their opinion by some few words of those three Doctors seeming to teach evolution in general, labor under a very grave mistake, and fail to perceive that, even supposing those Doctors to have expressed views favoring evolution, in the texts they allege, all that would not prove that they applied the same views to man. They should prove by clear, distinct testimonies bearing immediately and directly on the subject matter, that man's body was descended from some brute animal. Until they have done that the authorities they cite avail them not a jot."

Adele.—"But did those three Doctors really express views favoring evolution in general?"

Doctor.—"Yes, as much as you and I. But to the satisfaction of everyone we will examine the texts quoted by Mivart and see what they really teach. Now, George, let us have the texts from St. Augustine, but try to be as plain in your statements as you possibly can, otherwise Adele will not be able to follow us and may be bored to death."

George.—"As far as I can understand the texts given by Saint George in testimony of St Augustine favoring evolution, amount to this: That God created all things together, inasmuch as He, in the matter which He created from nothing, implanted the power, the seed of all things, which would in the course of time be evolved and developed into anything. I need only quote the following words: 'Certain hidden seeds of all things, which are corporally and visibly born, are hid in the physical elements of this world. '*Omnium quippe rerum quae corporaliter visibiliterque nascuntur occu'ti quaedam semina in istis corporeis mundi hujus elementis latent.*' ('De Genesi ad Literam,' Lib. v. ch. 5.) And he goes on to say: 'As in the grain are invisibly contained all those things which gradually develop into a tree, so this world is to be thought, as God created all things together, to have had at once all those things which in it and with it were made when the day was made, not only the heavens, with the sun, and the moon, and the stars, but also all those things which the water and the earth potentially and causatively produced before they appeared in the course of time.' ('De Generi ad Lit.,' Lib. v., ch. 22.)"

Adele.—"So it is clear, from these texts, that St. Augustine teaches three things: first, that God created all things together; second, in the sense that in creating matter He implanted in it the power or the germ of developing into anything; third, that all things which appeared in the course of time were the product and the development of those seeds and germs hidden in the primitive elements. All that seems to be evolution with a vengeance, I must confess."

Doctor.—"And yet St. Augustine is not an evolutionist."

George.—"How, then, do you explain St. Augustine?"

Doctor.—"It is not necessary for me to explain anything. Saint Thomas, whom Saint George and compeers would place on their side, has explained it for me with that decisive glance and lucidity which is peculiar to himself. The question hinges on this: What did St. Augustine mean by matter or the primitive elements which God created, having received by the Creator the power, the germ, the seed of being developed into anything? If St. Augustine meant by that that matter had received the active force to develop itself into anything without the aid of anybody, and without any other act of the Creator, then Saint George and Company are right, St. Augustine is an evolutionist. If, on the other hand, the holy Doctor, by saying that matter received the capacity, the germ, the seed of being developed into anything, meant it in a passive sense, that is, understood it in the sense that it was so made by its natural constitution as to present no obstacle to be moulded into anything, and that not by a native force, but by God's action, then St. Augustine is not an evolutionist, and Saint George and Company are mistaken in their understanding of his teachings. Now, St. Thomas interprets St. Augustine in the latter sense. In the 'Summa Theologica,' Part First, question 91, article 2, where he maintains that man's body was created immediately by God, he proposes to himself the following objection: 'According to St. Augustine, man, as to his body, was made first among the works of the six days, according to causative reasons which God implanted in every material creature, and afterward it was actually formed. But that which preëxists in some corporal creature, according to causal reason, can be produced by some corporal agency. Hence the human body has been the product of a created agency and not the immediate effect of God. How does St. Thomas answer? Listen: 'A thing is said to preëxist in a creature according to productive or causal reasons in two ways. In the first way, according to a capacity both active and passive, that is, not only that some thing can be produced from preëxisting matter, but that some preëxisting creature can produce it. In the second way, after a passive capacity only, in the case that a thing can be produced by God from preëxisting matter; and in this sense, according to St. Augustine, man's body was preëxisting in the works already made according to causal reasons.' (*Ad Quartum.*)"

Adele.—"Then when we hear that causative reasons or germs were implanted by the Creator in the first elements, we must understand that God made matter so as to be able, under His action, to receive any form or change, but not to do so by itself without the special act of God?"

Doctor.—"Certainly. St. Thomas, in the 3rd article of the 92d question, where he proves the formation of woman from Adam's body, raises the same question from St. Augustine, and answers in the same way. 'The woman's body preëxisted in conformity with causal reasons in the first works, not in an active capacity, but in a passive capacity only, that is, relatively to the active power of the Creator. (*Ad Secundum.*)"

George.—"Well, it is clear that St. Thomas interprets St. Augustine's theory, that all things preëxisted germinally and potentially in the first created elements in a passive sense, inasmuch as matter was so made as, under the action of God to be capable of being moulded into any thing. But what then? The question is: does St. Thomas interpret him rightly?"

Doctor.—"St. Thomas interprets St. Augustine as the latter interprets himself, since in other places St. Augustine flatly maintains the special actual creation of each species."

Adele.—"Is it possible?"

Doctor.—"Nothing more true. George, please take that volume of the holy Doctor and read the passages marked."

George.—"'We must believe God to be the Author and Maker of all things which are originated, visible and invisible; not as to vices which are against nature, but as to the natures themselves, and *that there is not a creature, which has not received from Him the beginning and perfection of its kind and substance*' ('De Genesi ad Literam' says, ch. 4, part 18). Again: 'It has not been said that God made darkness, *because God created the species themselves*, not privations which appertain to nothing.' (The same work, ch. 5, part 25.) Again, in the same work:

'God both makes and arranges certain things; others he merely puts in order. Thus *He both makes and arranges the species and natures themselves.* He does not effect the privations of species or the defects of natures, but only regulates them'—'Quaedam et facit Deus et ordinat, quaedam vero tantum ordinat. *Ita species naturisque ipsas et facit et ordinat;* privationes autem specierum defectusque naturarum non facit sed ordinat tantum."

Doctor.—"Now, if St. Augustine holds that God Himself created every species, how could He maintain that they were evolved by the germinal and potential capacity of matter taken in an active sense? In the interpretation of St. Thomas everything goes on smoothly. St. Augustine is right when he teaches that God endowed matter with potential and germinal capacity to be moulded into anything, and he is also right when he teaches that God Himself creates the species and nature of things, because it is under God's special action that matter yields whatever God wishes to produce from it."

Adele.—"I think the matter is disposed of as far as St. Augustine is concerned. Nor is Mivart right with regard to St. Thomas."

Doctor.—"Well, George, what does Mivart allege to make St. Thomas an evolutionist?"

George.—"He cites the saying of St. Thomas, that 'in the first institution of nature we do not look for miracles but for the laws of nature.' (1 part, qu. 67, art. 4, ad 3.) Hence, he concludes that, as the holding of a special creation for each species would be a miracle, and not a result of the laws of nature, St. Thomas maintains the spontaneous natural evolution of species."

Adele.—"Well, uncle, what is the answer to that?"

Doctor.—"The answer is, that St. Thomas, from the principle quoted, holds the very opposite of what Saint George wishes to make out, and I think that Saint George was in duty bound to understand in what sense St. Thomas holds that principle before drawing his conclusion, and to be extremely lenient with Saint George, we have a right to accuse him of unworthy precipitancy in jumping to a conclusion not at all warranted, and the very contrary to that which St. Thomas draws from the principle. In his commentary on the book of sentences, 1 Dict. 18, quest. 1, art. 1, ad 5, the holy Doctor explains the saying of St. Augustine as follows: 'The institution of natural things may be considered in two different ways with regard to the manner of creating, and in respect to those which are consequent on the things created. The mode of creating could not be natural, as no certain natural principle had preceded, the activity and passiveness of which could have been sufficient to naturally produce those effects, and therefore it required a supernatural agency to produce the first principle of species as that the body of man should be formed from the earth and woman's body from the rib, and the like. But the properties appertaining to the created natures must not be attributed to a miracle, as that waters should miraculously remain in the sky. The creation of things does require a supernatural agency, and the saying of St. Augustine that in the first institution of nature we should not have recourse to miracles but to the natural laws, applies only to the properties of the nature created and the laws by which they are regulated, and by no means to the mode of creating these natures, which always is and must be beyond and above any natural agency."

Adele.—"Dear me, how you men can mix up things when you want to. All that St. Augustine meant by that saying, is that the creation of all things is always by an activity above nature, that is, G d. That there are certain properties attached to each nature which naturally flow from it, and which must be always attributed to the nature as a necessary consequence, and not to a miracle. For instance, take matter; how does it exist? There is no principle in nature to cause it. God therefore must create it. Take some properties of matter—say, inertia, divisibility, attraction, and so on; these properties, if found in it, must be attributed to the nature of matter, and not to a miracle or extraordinary action."

George.—"Very good indeed."

Doctor.—"If Saint George and Company had taken the trouble to understand the sense in which St. Thomas explained that saying of St. Augustine in the place he quotes, he would have found that the saying will not help a jot as proving evolution, because in that place St. Thomas is remarking on a theory of St. Basil, intended to account for light and darkness of the first day by the emission or contracting of light of the luminous body. St. Thomas remarks that the theory cannot hold, because it is contrary to the nature of a luminous body to withdraw its light; that can only be done by a miracle and in the first institution of nature; we do not seek for miracles, but for what the natures of things are capable of."

Adele.—"Well, let us pass to the other great theologian whom Saint George invokes in his favor. Mr. George, what is this testimony?"

George.—"Mivart does not give any text of Suarez, but says that he 'has a separate section in opposition to those who maintain the distinct creation of the various kinds or substantial forms of organic life' ('The Genesis of Species,' Introd., page 31. Appleton, 1871.)"

Doctor.—"Saint George is misrepresenting Suarez, either through his great anxiety to find supporters for his strange theory, or through precipitation and haste in not caring to go deeper into the matter and to ascertain the real opinion of that great theologian. (The text Saint George quotes is from the fifteenth Disputation of the first volume of 'Metaphysics', section 2, numbers 2, 9, 18, 15.) You are to understand, Adele, that the schoolmen called all principle animating matter, such as the active principle in plants, and sensitive principle in animals, substantial forms. Now Suarez teaches in the section cited by Saint George that the substantial forms of plants and animals are not produced by creation, but are evolved from matter itself, according to natural agents. In force of this he all at once ranks poor Suarez among evolutionists, but the acute scientist failed or did not care to perceive that Suarez was speaking of the substantial forms considered after all species are produced; but with regard to the latter he maintains that their forms were evolved from matter indeed, but by a special action of God."

George.—"But how can we ascertain that such is the interpretation of Suarez's theory ?"

Doctor.—"By other passages and works. Surely an author cannot say everything at the same time and place on subjects which have a great variety and difference of aspects and relations. Besides, the real opinion of an author, as Saint George too well knows, must be gathered from what he says and maintains when he is treating of the subject professedly and directly. Now Suarez clearly and distinctly maintains, in the work on the 'Creation of the Six Days,' that plants and animals were immediately and directly produced by God from matter, therefore they cannot have been produced by evolution. In the second book of that work, chapter seventh, after having given the opinion of those who held that plants had been gradually evolved from matter by the natural forces, he says. 'The contrary opinion is to be held, that is, that God produced on this day herbs, trees and other vegetables actually in their own species and nature. This is the common opinion of the Fathers St. Basil, St. Ambrose, St. Chrysostom, St. John Damascene, Theodoretus, St. Cyril, Beda. The same is held by St. Thomas. . . . But there is a special reason with regard to animals, because they cannot be produced from their seed; since the seed must be separated from the animal, nor can it naturally be preserved apart from the animal or produce its operation. *Hence it was necessary that all animal species should at first be immediately created by the Author of nature in one or some individuals.* (N. 2.) *Ideo necessarium fuit species singulas eorum immediate ab auctore naturæ in aliquo, vel in aliquibus individuis primo fieri.*"

George.—"But, Doctor, there is Father Harper, in his 'Metaphysics of the Schools,' who proves that all the Fathers and schoolmen admitted evolution."

Adele.—"What kind of evolution?"

George.—"Evolution in its universal sense and application."

Doctor.—"Well, how badly are poor authors, who work so hard in writing books and in endeavoring to make things clear, treated by a genus of superficial ignoramuses, who run over such works just to find a phrase, a word, a colon or semicolon which they can twist and distort into their own opinion, utterly reckless of the rest. Adele, take Father Harper's Second Volume, page 743, and read the words marked.

Adele.—"'Evidently there must have been a beginning to each higher family of living things. There must have been a first plant, a first fish, a first bird, a first quadruped. Hereditary propagation must have been established subsequently to the production of the first pair in each family of life. That these primitive pairs then should have been evolved out of the potentiality of matter without parentage, in other words, that the matter (in itself utterly incapable of the task) should have been proximately disposed for such evolution, belongs to a special Divine Administration: In other words, God must have been the sole efficient cause of the organisation requisite, and therefore, in the strictest sense, is said to have formed such pairs, and in particular the human body, out of the preëxistent matter.'"

George.—"Then in what sense do the Fathers and schoolmen hold evolution?"

Doctor.—"First, in the sense that plants and animals were not created from nothing, but evolved by God from matter. Secondly, they hold evolution within the species as we explained in one of our interviews.

Adele.—"But, uncle, I have heard somebody say that Father Secchi was an evolutionist?"

Doctor.—"Well, you may as well read his words also, and with them we will put an end to this long conversation."

Adele.—"'The idea of successive transformation understood with proper prudence and moderation is not inconsistent either with reason or religion. In fact, if we do not pretend that everything was produced by means of pure inborn native forces of brute matter, but admit that such forces were imparted to it by the First Cause, which created matter, and gave power to produce certain effects, there is no obstacle to believing that, so long as no new force is called into play, various organisms may be developed in one way rather than in another, and thus give rise to different beings. But when from a series of such beings we pass to another which contains a new principle, the question altogether changes. From the vegetable without sensibility we cannot pass to the animal, which has sensations without a new power which cannot spring from the organization alone or matter. And the same may be said, only with stronger reason, when from the brute animal we wish to travel to man, who reasons, reflects, and has consciousness.* A new principle then must be associated to the physical force of matter to obtain such results' ('Discourse on the Grandeur of Creation')."

TWENTY-SIXTH ARTICLE.

IS MIVART'S OPINION SCIENTIFICALLY AND PHILOSOPHICALLY TENABLE?

George.—"It is with great curiosity and interest, Doctor, that I shall hear your remarks on Sir George's theory with regard to the origin of man's body. I believe you said that that question is not tenable, either scientifically or philosophically. Now I presume to think that it will be very hard to prove that."

Adele.—"Why?"

George.—"On account of the standing and rank which Mivart enjoys among the scientists of to day."

Adele.—"That is a very poor reason to my mind, Mr. George. Why, Sir George cannot hold a higher rank among the scientists of the present time than Darwin, Huxley, Haeckel, Wallace, Grant and the whole galaxy of respectable, highly-to-be-honored, evolutionists; and yet, if I must judge from the various specimens I have had in the course of our conversations, they are anything but a model of reasoning of accurate observation, of serious, earnest, sound judgment. On the contrary, they have appeared to me as a set of men highly and blindly prejudiced in favor of a preconceived pet theory, as a mother is predisposed in favor of a child, no matter how plain, how distorted, how monstrous nature may have made it; that under the possession of such prejudice they shut their eyes to every clear, well ascertained fact which may militate against it, build a grand and imposing structure on any stray fact which may have the least and the remotest resemblance in their favor, and, above all, drawing most liberally and largely on the heedlessness and credulity of their readers, take peculiar care to assert themselves loudly and confidently, and to look with utter disdain and supreme superciliousness on any one who dares to dissent from them. Such is the character of your scientists as I have gathered it in the course of our interviews. Why should your Saint George be wholly exempt from the common and general characteristics of those of his class?"

Doctor.—"The fact that in refuting Darwin's theory he has substituted none to support evolution, except some unknown and mysterious law of nature; the fact that in endeavoring to prop up his opinion with the authority of St. Augustine, St. Thomas and Suarez he has acted with such precipitation and carelessness as not to ascertain the real meaning of the words he quoted when, as in the case of St. Thomas and Suarez, the authors themselves explain in what sense the words on which Saint George relies so much to strengthen his position, ought to be taken the fact that Saint George, instead of looking for the opinion of those Doctors in works and places where they discuss the subject *ex professo*, has gone out of his way to look for it when they are treating of different subjects and merely alluding to the other in a very limited, restricted sense, all this proves clearly that he is not exempt from the general failing of scientists, of exaggerating to any extent the apparent strength of their proofs, and of supposing all their readers superficial and careless, incapable of weighing those proofs and of rating them at their just value. And now for the proofs that Saint George's opinion is neither scientific nor philosophical. In the first place, for what reason has Saint George invented his hypothesis? To account for the origin of man's body by means of evolution. Man's body is the outcome, the offspring of an apish couple. Why? Because the natural law of evolution must have its play; because man's body can easily be effected by the exercise of natural forces. Very well, then. And why do you stop at man's body and not make the whole man, both body and soul, the result of the same natural laws? If the body can be produced by the law of evolution, why not the soul?"

George.—"Mivart replies, because nature cannot evolve a spiritual substance; that must be effected by God Himself."

Doctor.—"I know Mivart's assertion that a spiritual principle cannot be evolved by the natural force of evolution. But how does he prove that? On what ground does he limit the power of evolution? Surely, in a system in which the whole living universe, vegetable and animal, is made to issue forth from a primitive cell, who can, with scientific consistency, say that so far it can go and no further? What does science know about a spiritual substance requiring an independent and special creation? On what scientific ground is the power of evolution limited? From a primitive cell it was powerful enough to evolve a multicellular system, and from that to develop into the highest and most elaborated living plants. Then, from a living principle, from a simple internal movement, such as is found in plants, it was powerful enough to develop into a sentient principle, at first very imperfect, and then from the imperfect to the more perfect, until it reaches the highest animal organization and the exquisite sensibility of the best form of animals, as far as to arrive at man's body. All other evolutionists go further and say the whole man, body and soul, such as we see him, has developed from the natural law of evolution, and these are logical and consistent. Saint George, after agreeing with all these evolutionists, as far as to man's body, suddenly and arbitrarily stops and tells us man's soul cannot be the result of evolution."

Adele.—"It certainly seems to be illogical."

George.—"But Saint George stops at that because, as I have said a while ago, it is beyond and above the power of nature to produce a spiritual substance. 'Physical science,' he says, 'as such, has nothing at all to do with the soul of man, which is hyperphysical.' (Page 303.)"

Doctor.—"But how does Saint George prove, scientifically, that man's soul is hyperphysical? All evolutionists have a right to say, so far as science is concerned: all we know is that we observe man to be just as he is; you say he is made of body and soul; that the latter is a spiritual principle; that evolution could only produce and bring forth his body but could not affect his soul; that such a soul must have come directly from the hands of the Creator; we know nothing about your distinctions, hence can take no cognizance of such distinctions; you admit that man's body is the result of evolution, therefore you must, as a scientist, admit that the whole man, just as he appears, is the product of natural laws."

Adele.—"Then the opinion of Saint George and his adherents rests on no logical, consistent scientific basis? It admits man's body to have come in the natural course of evolution, and then without a scientific reason in the world, it stops at the body, confines therein the whole power of natural laws, and calls for an intervention of the Creator to account for man's soul."

Doctor.—"Besides, the theory we are examining is scientifically faulty for another reason. If man's body, according to Saint George, has descended from the ape, how is the immense difference existing between the body of the former and that of the latter accounted for? We have pointed out in one of our conversations that man's body differs from the ape's in such manner as to render all possible hypothesis of the one descending from the other absolutely absurd. But allow the supposition for a moment, to please Professor Mivart, how is the immense difference between the one and the other accounted for? Mr. George, what has Mivart to answer to such a question?"

George.—"I am not aware that he even takes it under consideration."

Doctor.—"Well, three suppositions can be made to account for such difference. The first is that the differences in man's body were gradually and insensibly developed in the course of evolution. The second is that they were caused by the spiritual substance which came to animate it. The third that they were caused by God Himself when He evolved it from the clay. Now let us examine each supposition. Can we admit the first, George?"

George.—"Certainly not."

Adele.—"Why?"

George.—"Because if the differences and peculiar features and traits of man's body had arisen gradually and insensibly in the course of evolution, it would have taken a long, long time to arrive at those distinct decisive properties, and that only after many and many trials and rudimental imperfect sketches. The consequence of this is that we should find specimens and traces of such intermediate forms and sketches of the human frame. But where are such vestiges or traces? Nowhere. Wherever man's remains have been found they appear identical with man's present frame, and there is not a single instance to the contrary."

Adele.—"Then the first supposition must be rejected?"

Doctor.—"The second is much worse. It supposes that the spiritual substance which comes to animate the apish offspring, which is to be turned into man, itself produces all those distinctive differences in order to adapt that animal frame and body to its own use."

Adele.—"It seems rather plausible."

Doctor.—"It is much worse I say than the first supposition. Because it supposes a power in the soul which is contradicted by all experience we have now. That the spiritual principle which is within us has some mysterious influence over the body to which it is united, and which it actualizes as its substantial form, is known to everyone; that such influence reaches, to a very great extent, over the whole body and its functions so as to affect it as to its locomotive, vegetative, and sensitive functions, is also apparent; but that it should have such power and energy over all the different parts of the bodily frame as to change their shape and form, upset their old destination and give them another direction and aim, join them anew in a different way and transform, as it were, the whole general constitution of man's bodily frame, that is, a power which none has ever dreamt of attributing to the spiritual principle we call the soul. And such a power would have been necessary in order to make good the supposition that the differences between man's body and the ape's were caused by the spiritual principle which came to animate it. It should have had the power to change every bone and every joint and the whole framework of the skeleton, and fill it up with organs almost new in every particular as we have pointed out. Now such a supposition is impossible."

Adele.—"Why?"

Doctor.—"Because what has been done once by a certain cause, the cause remaining the same, may be done over again. If the spiritual principle had the energy to change the whole structure in whole and in part of an ape's body, to change itself into a man's frame, why cannot the same principle change, remodel man's frame now, or renew it when decayed? Besides, granting that supposition for a moment, we have a few questions to ask of Saint George. First, had the spiritual principle already taken possession of the fortunate ape's body as its substantial form, before it began to work the change spoken of, or did it cause the changes before actually taking possession of it? If the first, will Saint George please to explain how it is possible to suppose that a spiritual principle could take possession of a body not suited to it by nature or construction, as its substantial form or acts? Or could it start operations in a body not at all convenient to its act? If the second, will Saint George explain how the spiritual substance, acting outwardly, and at the distance from the apish construction could affect it so as to produce all the changes necessary to make it a fit abode for itself?"

Adele.—"I am not sure I follow you. You say, uncle, that if we suppose the spiritual principle to have caused the differences we observe in man's body; when it came to animate it, we should account for the following: First, how is it possible that a spiritual principle could be united to a body and organism not adapted to its nature and actions? And how could it be supposed to begin operations in and through organs unfit and incompetent for it? Next, supposing it to have caused the changes before it was actually united to or took possession of it, how are we to account for such an extraordinary power as to cause all those changes at a distance? Is that what you mean?

Doctor.—"Certainly. And, as these difficulties cannot be explained away it follows that the supposition is absurd and untenable?"

George.—"And that we must fall back on the special and immediate creation of man's body."

Doctor.- "But we are not as yet through with Professor Saint George's hypothesis. It supposes that the bodies of the first man and woman each descended from an apish couple, in the natural course of sexual union, and that God Almighty breathed into each one of those bodies the breath of life; that is, placed in each a spiritual substance, by Himself directly created. Now we may ask: Were those bodies the ape's descendants at the moment God placed the spiritual principle in them quick and alive, or were they dead? If they were alive, they must have been animated by the sensitive principle or soul; if they were dead, they must have been nothing but dead matter. In both suppositions, in order to keep up and maintain the course of natural laws, and to avoid the interference of the Creator, as scientists are pleased to express it, we are forced to increase such interference, to multiply the instances of its exercise."

Adele.—"How?"

Doctor.—"Thus: Say we suppose that when God placed the spiritual principle in the ape's descendants, they were already animated by a sentient principle such as vivifies all animals, it follows that the Creator must first have banished, destroyed, annihilated the sentient principle from those bodies to make room for the spiritual principle. Now this is certainly a supernatural interference. And it was necessary; for how could we suppose God to have put the human soul in the body of an animal already in possession of a sentient principle? God then, by an immediate and direct action, must have eliminated the sentient principle from those bodies and supplied it with the spiritual principle. Mark three acts of supernatural interference: first, the removal of the sentient principle; second, its annihilation, or its maintenance outside of its own natural body; third, the insertion of a spiritual substance. Three acts of supernatural interference to allow one effect to result from natural causes."

Adele.—"I understand easily how, instead of avoiding the supernatural interference, Saint George's hypothesis multiplies it."

Doctor.—"Take the second supposition, that those two bodies were dead before the human soul came to animate them. Here again we have the same objection, that of increasing the demand for supernatural interference."

George.—"How?"

Doctor.—"Because to infuse a spiritual substance into the dead body of an ape is beyond the course of natural laws, and is, therefore, a supernatural and miraculous intervention, besides the other wonderful interventions spoken above."

Adele.—"I don't fully understand you."

Doctor.—"Is it within the province of any natural agency or cause to put a spiritual substance into the dead body of an animal? Certainly not. It is a much greater miracle than to restore a dead man to life. Now, in the hypothesis we are examining, to place a spiritual substance into the dead body of an ape to make a man of both, would absolutely require such a miraculous intervention. Hence the miraculous interventions are multiplied, and it would be much more simple to admit the special and immediate creation of man both as to his body and to his soul. Now, Adele, please to give me a resumé of all the reasons which make Saint George's hypothesis unscientific and unphilosophical before we come to the end of our conversation."

Adele.—"If I recollect aright I think the first reason given why Mr. Mivart's hypothesis should be considered unscientific, is that, whereas it admits evolution in general, in consequence of some special law which he does not explain, it stops at man's souls without alleging any reason whatever for putting a limit to the fecundity and fertility or capabilities of evolution."

George.—"Very good, indeed!"

Adele.—"The second reason is, that Mivart cannot, on his hypothesis, account for the immense difference existing in the details of man's body and that of the ape. And we proved that such difference cannot be accounted for by such a gradual, insensible change and transformation which might have occurred in man's ancestors, to slowly make way for him, because no traces have ever been found of such intermediate stages. We proved also that such change could not be effected by the spiritual principle infused into it, neither before the infusion nor after. Not before the infusion, because in that case the spiritual substance must be supposed to have been endowed with such a power as to cause those changes at a distance; nor after, because the very infusion of the spiritual principle into a body totally unfit for its occupation and animation, must be first accounted for before we suppose it to be able to act and to cause the changes. In fact, such union were impossible, as the spiritual principle could not be joined except to a body adapted to its nature and its action. Finally, we have proved that, to suppose man's body to have developed from an ape and to have afterwards received the spiritual principle immediately from God, demands more acts of supernatural interference and miraculous intervention than the supposition of a special immediate creation by God, of both the body and the soul of man."

George.—"Very well; I am convinced now that Saint George's hypothesis is absolutely groundless, not only in theology, but also in science and philosophy. But I am sure that the illustrious professor's intention was good and excellent, that of demonstrating that, even supposing the evolution of species to be proven, no possible conflict would result between it and revelation; as the Christian Revelation does not condemn the system of evolution and transformation of species, either by natural selection or by some other hidden law of nature."

Doctor.—"We have proved that evolution cannot be held as sound and safe opinion if applied to man, either with regard to his body or to his soul, and therefore the good intention of Saint George comes to nought. But I must say I deplore this too great anxiety on the part of Christians and Catholics to yield to the pretensions of scientists, in most cases false and groundless, in too many cases ridiculous and absurd, so far as even to forget the rights of Revelation. We gain nothing by such liberality for revealed truths, and by no manner of means satisfy the scientist whose appetite is as boundless as it is unreasonable, and I wish to conclude with the immortal words of Doctor Brownson on exactly the same subject and about the same good intention praised by George here. 'We think,' says Brownson, 'the writers aim questionable. The theories in question (evolution in general and the origin of man's body by evolution) may contain some truth, as does every error into which the human mind can fall, for all error consists in the misapprehension, misapplication or perversion of truth; but, as theories, *both are false, irredeemably false*, and are to be as unqualifiedly condemned as any erroneous theories ever broached. We in our efforts to conciliate the professional scientists are likely to be successful only in weakening the cause of truth, of obscuring the very truth we would have them adopt. If we are Catholics let us be Catholics, and be careful to make no compromises and seek no alien alliances. The spirit, as the tendency of the age, is at enmity with God, and must be fought, not coaxed. No concord between Christ and Belial is possible.' ('True and False Science,' vol. 9, page 528.)"

TWENTY-SEVENTH ARTICLE.

IS MAN AS OLD AS A CERTAIN SCIENCE WOULD MAKE HIM OUT TO BE?

Doctor.—"The question to be taken up, next to man's origin, is his age. How long has man existed upon the earth? Is he of comparatively recent origin, or does he count his years by hundreds of thousands?"

Adele.—"And what matters it whether man has existed six or eight thousand years, or whether he has lived upon earth for a hundred thousand?"

Doctor.—"Scientists being under the impression that Revelation teaches, and that Christians are bound to maintain that man is of comparatively recent origin, say a few thousand years, do their utmost to prove the great antiquity of man in order to give the lie to Revelation."

George.—"And is it not true, Doctor, that Moses teaches man to have existed only about a few thousand years?"

Doctor.—"We will discuss that question by and by. Let us first examine, one by one, the arguments by which scientists endeavor to prove the great antiquity of man. George, can you give these arguments?"

George.—"I will do my best. In the first place, there is the proof drawn from tools and utensils. In excavating into the stratas of the earth there have been found in different places implements and tools made by man, such as ploughs, arrows, and such like, some of which are made of stone, some of scoria or flint, and others from iron. Now such tools are not found mixed up all together in every strata, but in the recent and superior stratas we meet with those made of iron, in the lower and more ancient stratas those made of scoria or flint, and farther down in the very lowest ones those made of stone. From which fact, it is evident, that mankind must have passed through three successive epochs, the first and the most ancient one, that during which men made use of stones to fashion arms, tools, implements, or utensils for domestic purposes, and such epoch is called the Stone Age. The next is that during which men began to make use of scoria or copper, and that is called the Flint Age. The last and the more recent, when men learned the use of iron, and which is called the Iron Age."

Adele.—"Well, then, what has all that to do with the Age of Man? What signifies that he at one time made use of stones to make arms or tools, and later on used any kind of rude metal, that which I suppose is meant by flint or scoria, and that finally he learned the great use he could make of iron?"

George.—"It signifies a great deal. In the first place it is clear from those facts that man must be much older than Moses makes him out to be. Because each of those epochs must necessarily have lasted a long time, several thousands of years. For if man once was in such a barbarous state as to ignore the use of metals for self-defence or for the maintenance of life, it must have taken him a long, long time to get out of such state of infancy, so to call it, and to learn how to make use of those metals most easily extracted from the earth, and afterwards to learn the value and the use of harder metals and those which require more skill and more ability to handle, until he reached the more recent and historical epoch where he shows himself fully equipped with knowledge of all sciences and arts, not only mechanical but liberal. Hence some scientists of the highest reputation date the apparition of man in the world very far back. Some, as Vogt, Wallace, Buckner, say that he has been on the earth over a hundred thousand years. Others, like Canestrini, raise the number to two hundred thousand."

Adele.—"I see their aim; from the nature and roughness of their tools they argue man's uncivilized state and infer the length of centuries he must have gone through to become civilized. Well, what is the next argument?"

George.—"The next proof is derived from the remains of human bones which have been found in several caves in Belgium and in France. Such fossils have been found together with the bones of animals belonging to species which have long, long disappeared."

Adele —"And because those human fossils have been found with those of animals belonging to species long perished, I presume your scientists infer that man's age must be the same as that of the lost animal species?"

George.—"Exactly. The next proof is drawn from the ruins of various human habitations appertaining to prehistorical ages. Such are tombs made of clay or rough stones for the burying of the dead; many of which have been found in Italy, in Greece and in the northern parts of Europe. To the same class belong those rustic huts, called lacustral, built on meadows on artificial soil made of earth and stones and kept together by poles and stakes. They are found principally in Switzerland and Denmark, and are supposed to date at least ten thousand years before all historical times. Add to these those large masses of shells, which are found on the littoral of Denmark, mixed up with remains of fishes and implements of flint and looking like tombs."

Adele.—"Why, the proofs of man's prehistoric age seem to be very abundant. Are there any more?"

George.—"Certainly; there are other proofs, founded on astronomy."

Adele.—"Let us have them."

George.—"We know from Diodorus Siculus that the Chaldeans had made astronomical observations embracing a period of at least 472,000 years. In 1798, in the expedition of the French to Egypt under Napoleon the Great, some French scientists, who accompanied it, found two pictures of a Zodiac, one in a temple at Dendèrah, the other also in a temple of Esné. In these the state of the heavens was represented as it should have been according to well known rules of astronomy twelve thousand years before our time."

Adele.—"Well, are there any more proofs?"

George.—"To be sure, and they are taken from the annals and histories of nations, by which it is easily shown that many people are much older than Adam is represented to be. The Egyptians, for example, according to Herodotus, count as many dynasties of kings as to require a great many thousands of years. Diodorus Siculus testifies that the Egyptian priests from the beginning of their rule down to Alexander the Great had gone through twenty-three thousand years. The same may be said of the Chaldeans, Chinese, etc."

Doctor.—"You have well condensed the chief proofs alleged by scientists for the pretended antiquity of man."

Adele.—"And is man as ancient as they pretend to make him?"

Doctor.—"We shall see. In the first place, I want to remark that we, Christians, are at perfect liberty to hold whatever opinion is found to be well supported by science as to the antiquity of man. We are not tied down to any system or tenet of faith. The chronology of Moses is by no means certain. Because the different versions, as, for instance, the Hebrew, the Samaritan, and the Greek of the Septuagint do not agree upon the point. The Samaritan text makes the Age of Man shorter than the Hebrew, this makes it medium; the Greek makes it longer than the other two. The Church, far from deciding the question, uses indifferently those different texts. In the Latin version, called the Vulgate, approved by the Council of Trent, the Hebrew text has been followed, which counts 4,000 before Christ. In the Roman Martyrology, the Greek text is followed, which raises it to 5.300 years. Hence it is evident that no Catholic is tied down to the chronology of the Hebrew text and may adopt others which bring the Age of Man up to 8,000 years or more. To come now to the three epochs of stone, flint and iron, I must say that all which is said about them is but uncertain and arbitrary. To draw a conclusion from the use of stone implements and arms to prove the enormous an-.iquity of man a hundred, two hundred thousand, scientists ought to prove two things: First, that the use of such implements was general, simultaneous and uniform in every part of the world for some time, and then, that it was succeeded in the same manner, that is, simultaneously and uniformly in all places by the use of flint, and copper, and iron. Second, they should determine the duration of each distinctive epoch, so that we could get an accurate idea of that space of time called prehistoric, from the total reckoning of all those epochs. But the friends of man's great antiquity neither attempt, nor can succeed, to demonstrate either."

George.—"It is clear that they cannot show the use of stony implements to have been common, simultaneous and uniform among all peoples at the same time. Because, in spite of their great confidence in affirmation, it is absolutely certain that the use of stone, of iron and of bronze prevailed at the same time among different nations, for the reason that not all nations alike had the same beginning, development and grade of civilization. So, that, whilst among one nation prevailed the use of stony implements, arms and tools, in consequence of their ignoring how to extract and work metal; among other nations and people better advanced in culture, we find at the same time the use of flint, and even iron."

Doctor.—"For instance, whilst the Greeks and the Romans were exceedingly skillful in the working of every kind of metal, at the same epoch and time we find at the extremity of Europe, among the Scythians beyond the Black Sea and in the interior of Germany and other regions the use of stony implements. Even now among the indigenous population of Africa, Australia and North America are found rude implements, arms made of sharpened stones, of bones of animals and fishes, whilst people who have emigrated to those regions from Europe are at the height of civilization and culture. Who would not then laugh to scorn that modern geologist who, from the fact of having found buried in the earth any of those rude instruments used by the indigenous population of the countries just mentioned, should conclude that it must have been worked thousands of centuries ago?"

George.—"Mr. Wright, Secretary of the London Ethnological Society, asserts that the stone epoch cannot be really determined, because not only flint, but also iron implements are found to have been in use at the same time and among the same people; the stone implements being used by the poor, the others by the rich. (Lubbock, page 63.)"

Doctor.—"But suppose it was demonstrated that the use of stone implements prevailed in some country for a time before that of metals, what would that prove? They ought to show how long that period lasted before flint or iron began to be used. But all that is absolutely uncertain, and is determined by some on sheer conjectures and guesses, with a prodigious quantity of fancy and imagination. This is admitted even by such men as Lubbock, Vogt, Buckner, Lyell, Stoppani and others."

George.—"Then, again, it is assumed for certain that all the so-called implements or arms found in the earth of stone, or flint have been made by man; whereas nothing is more doubtful than that; because in the very rude state in which they are discovered it is more than probable that they may have been formed accidentally by nature. As Professor Stoppani says, ("Course of Geology," vol. ch. 31. Milan, '73), speaking of the excavations of the Janiculus in Rome: 'What wonder that among millions of splinters of flint we should find a pair of them very much resembling the rude beginning of human art, for instance, pieces like the points of a spear?'"

Adele.—"Let us hear something now of the human remains. What have you got to say about them, Mr. George; do they prove your great antiquity?"

George.—"Such as the cranium, for instance, of Engis on the Meuse, that of Arezeo, and the famous jaw and other human bones found in Abbeville. Well, to draw a scientific conclusion from these bones three things ought to be proved: first, that these remains are found in layers belonging to epochs much more ancient than the Quaternary; second, that they have been found in a virgin soil which has never been disturbed by the hand of man, or by some upheaval or cataclysm of nature; third, that the fact of its origination has never been altered or modified by any falsification or systematic interpretation."

Doctor.—"With regard to the famous jaw of Abbeville and other human bones, they are discarded now as a most solemn fraud and imposture, since the gelatine in those bones was discovered to be quite fresh, which proves that those remains had been buried at an epoch quite recent. But I will say no more about human remains, as I intend that we should devote a whole conversation to the discussion of every one of the pretended discoveries of human remains which are supposed to prove man's great antiquity."

Adele.—"Then let us turn to the lacustrian huts, or cabins, or cities."

George.—"With regard to lacustrian habitations, or constructions on piles, so numerous on the lakes of Switzerland, and in which were found utensils in horn or stone, and almost all the furniture of ancient inhabitants, we must remark that it is quite impossible to determine their age; and that neither Keller, nor Desor, nor Van Baer, nor Lyell, nor any of the antiquarians have felt authorized to venture any hypothesis."

Doctor.—'On the other hand, the most ancient craniums therein discovered are perfectly similiar to those of the Swiss of the present day; the plants and animals are the same as are seen now all over Switzerland."

George.—"Hence the most renowned geologists are of opinion that they are not as ancient as they have been thought by those who are bent on seeing great antiquity where it does not exist."

Doctor.—"Hochstetter thinks it highly probable that the lacustrian cities do not reach beyond ten centuries before the Christian Era. And Franz Maurer places their date between the fifth and eighth century before the Christian age; whereas Hustler places the most recent in the third century before Christ."

George.—"And with regard to the strata of rough sand with which it is covered, and which Morlot required centuries upon centuries for its formation, Wagner stakes his scientific reputation that it could be formed in as many minutes."

Adele.—"I am satisfied, from the disagreement of so many scientists you gentlemen have quoted, and who differ, one from another, that no certain argument can be drawn from your lacustrian cities. But what about the accumulations of vegetable matter which are call turfpits?"

George.—"According to the observations made in Eastern Frisia, two hundred years are sufficient to form a layer of turfpit, thirty feet in depth, whereas, according to the theory of Boucher de Perthes, it would require three thousand years."

Adele.—"I begin to see the usual disagreement."

George.—Burmeister, on his part, affirms that it has been observed how turfpits, perfectly exhausted, have been refilled to thickness of five feet in the space of thirty years."

Doctor.—"With regard to the objects which are found buried in turfpits we cannot come to any certain conclusion as far as the depth at which they lie is considered, because, on the one hand, every one is aware that such objects fall deeper in proportion as the pit is of recent date, and therefore not as yet hardened; and, on the other hand, if we were to adopt the calculations of some geologists with regard to the length of time which is necessary to form such pits, the objects formed in them should have been in existence before the flood. Now, coins, hatchets, kitchen utensils found in them are all of Roman origin. Hence the whole system of those geologists falls to the ground like a house of cards."

Adele.—"And what about the great historical antiquity claimed by so many nations?"

Doctor.—"Why, it is laughed at by all real historians, who admit, unanimously, that a childish pride has made those nations imagine and invent their fabulous antiquity."

Adele.—"But, uncle, what about the Zodiacs of Dendérah and Esné?"

Doctor.—"The discovery of these two Zodiacs filled the infidel scientists who accompanied the expedition with delight, because they pretended that those Zodiacs proved the human race to be much more ancient than Moses has made it. As it was an unhoped-for opportunity to prove the sacred historian in error, the scientists raised a great clamor about such discovery. But serious and grave astronomers and archæologists did not fail soon to pull down such flimsy structure, and to make the matter worse for the scientists, Champollion, after having ascertained and proved by the distinctive marks and character of their structure that the temples in which these Zodiacs were found could not ascend any higher than the time of Trajan and the Antonines, in 1830, he succeeded in deciphering the symbols and inscriptions of such monuments. And what do you think these were found to be?"

Adele.—"What?"

Doctor.—"But a very poor specimen of sculpture of the Roman period. 'The Zodiac of Dendérah,' says the Viscount de Rongé, 'has become celebrated in consequence of the very learned discussions it has given rise to; but it is well known now with certainty that it cannot be more ancient than the Ptolomees.'"

Adele.—"As usual, the best proofs alleged by scientists to sustain their point, the most plausible argument, nay, the most clinching argument, apparently in the end, turns out to be the feeblest and the flimsiest. I wonder if scientists will ever learn a lesson from so many defeats to which they have been subject, and which are brought about by their unseemly eagerness and anxiety to pounce upon anything which could, by any possibility, be tormented and pressed into a testimony against Christianity. Let them have a feather, a straw, an infinitesimal shadow, and they grow jubilant; they run wild with delight and hug it with the transport of a passionate lover, exaggerate it, magnify its proportions, till, in their sight, it grows and swells into a giant, a mountain, a huge monster, and then they proclaim, in the market-place, from the house tops, that it is all over with Revelation. By and by, other scientists having become sobered down, and not being possessed by that satanic malevolence against Revelation, as the others examine it coolly and dispassionately, and find out, and come to the conclusion that the whole thing was a bubble, and Revelation remains as it ever was, unassailable and invulnerable."

TWENTY-EIGHTH ARTICLE.

IS THERE SUCH A THING AS THE FOSSIL REMAINS OF MAN?

Doctor.—"As we have seen in our last interview, to show the great antiquity of man, scientists of the evolutionist school have endeavored to find out the fossil remains of man wherever they could before the Quaternary epoch. But to their great chagrin all their efforts have proved vain and useless; not as much as a vestige of man's bones has ever been found which could be truly and really traced to any older period. In the present interview we will go over every one of those so-called proofs alleged by the evolutionists with the view of establishing that great antiquity. George, you are at home here, and I expect you will give us, one after the other, the alleged facts.'

George.—"I am ready."

Adele.—"Please to express yourself in plain, lucid, unprofessional, unsophisticated language."

George.—"I shall be proud to follow your directions. If I understand the doctor correctly he wishes to examine and to put to a thorough discussion all those human skeletons which have been found here and there at different times, and which have been held up as testimony and evidence of the man fossil."

Doctor.—"Exactly."

George.—"Well, the first one is the cranium of Neanderthal. It was found by Dr. Fuhlrott, near Düsseldorf, in the interior of a small cave, under a layer of clay, a yard and a half in thickness, without any protecting envelope of stalagmite. The bones had in great part preserved their organic substance; there were no traces of antediluvian animal bones; the cranium did not differ in the least from the average type of the Germanic race, and had no resemblance whatever to the Simian type. They have pretended that its singular form indicated an epoch very far back, and that by its inferior organization it belongs to that race which has ever been found as most ancient in Europe."

Adele.—"Well, uncle, is it as venerably old as it is said to be?"

Doctor.—"No. Pruner Bey, a very careful scientist, had already affirmed the identity of the cranium of Neanderthal with one of the Celtic type, when Professors Quatrefages and Hamy found it to belong to a type already existing, so that Lyell, convinced by the evidence, wrote the following remarkable words: 'With regard to the remarkable cranium of Neanderthal, it is, so far, a case too much isolated, too exceptional, and too uncertain in its origin to warrant us to base any theory on its abnormal characters.' ('Antiquity of Man,' page 307.) And Huxley says: 'In no sense can the Neanderthal bones be regarded as the remains of a human being intermediate between men and apes.' ('Man's Place in Nature,' page 253.)"

Adele.—"Cranium No. 1 thrown out of court."

George.—"Cranium No. 2 is that of Engbis. It was found among the debris and remains of bones of mammoths, rhinoceros, hyenas, wolves and horses. Pruner Bey thought it to be that of a Celtic woman. Schmerling, of that of a negress. But Huxley deemed it to be the cranium of a European woman, and adds that by its characters, both of superiority and inferiority, it must either have belonged to a philosopher or held the brain of a savage. 'It is, in fact, a fair average human skull, which might have belonged to a philosopher, or might have contained the thoughtless brains of a savage.' ('Man's Place in Nature,' p. 253.)"

Adele.— 'It must have been the progenitor skull of all the future scientists, who are a fair specimen of the reasoning powers of a philosopher or of a savage."

Doctor.—"You will have much more reason to say so when you hear the conclusion which Huxley draws from the total absence of fact as to the great antiquity of man. Go on, George."

George.—"Next come the skulls from the tumuli at Borreby, in Denmark. These tumuli or tombs are probably those inhabited by man in the Stone age, and the skulls found in them resemble, according to Huxley, 'the Neanderthal form more closely than any of the Australian skulls do.' (*Ib.*)"

Adele.—"Therefore they prove nothing more about man's great antiquity than the Neanderthal skull. Exit No. 3 skull as valueless."

Doctor.—"You may place between these last two the skull of Eguisheim, according to Huxley's opinions."

Adele.—"Then exit skull, No. 4. What is the next, Mr. George?"

George.—"The next are no less than whole human skeletons

found in Stoderthelze in Sweden. But the anatomical characters of such skulls differ very little from those of the craniums of modern times gathered in Western Europe by anthropologists. They are, then, no proof of the pretended antiquity of man. The next one is the Californian skull, found in 1866, in a well to the depth of three hundred and thirty feet."

Doctor.—"Mr. Whitney discovered in this skull the type of the skulls of Indians who live at the present on the declivities of Sierra Nevada, and stated that the facial angle does not reveal any inferiority of development. ('Comptes rendus du Congress de Bruxelles,' page 542.)"

George.—"Comes now the skeleton of Brüx, in Bohemia. It was found in 1873, in the alluvian sand to the depth of four feet and a half. Two feet above the skeleton was found a hatchet worked in stone."

Adele.—"Well, what about both the skeleton and the hatchet?"

George.—"Professor Rositanski declared the cranium to belong to a type inferior to that of Neanderthal. But Professor Schaaffhausen affirms to have discovered that the cranium and the other parts of the skeleton bear the traces of a profound pathological alteration. The bones of the head, and especially the parietal bones, seemed to have been softened and corroded by festering. ('Comptes rendus,' etc., p. 544.)"

Doctor.—"Tell us now something about the man fossil of Denise."

George.—"These bones were found at a small depth in a layer of ashes certainly handled since historical times."

Doctor.—"You must remark, George, that it has been suspected by a great many that this group of bones has been fabricated by a forger. In any case the tofus, or deposit of calcareous matter which contains the bones, is the product of the last volcanic eruption, which is accounted in geology almost as pertaining to modern times. Then it has another character, which excluded very long antiquity."

Adele.—"And what is it?"

Doctor.—"The skull belongs to the ordinary Caucasian type."

Adele.—"So it has the honor of belonging to our race, then!"

George.—"Next appears the skull in the chambers of Cro-Magnon, France."

Adele.—"Pray, what do you mean by chambers?"

George.—"I mean a kind of tunnels formed by incessant lowering of tender layers of calcareous rock due to atmospheric agents. They have oftentimes been utilized as habitations and rendezvous of hunters. They are hid sometimes by slopes of crumbling debris. Now, at the bottom of a yellow layer containing some pieces of flint mixed up with broken bones of elephants, bears, horses, etc.; also some whole bones of foxes have been found, three whole skulls, with a number of bones and limbs, one of these heads, that of an old man, exhibits the exaggeration of those traits which distinguish the type of man from the anthropomorphous. (Hamy, 'Precis,' p. 276.) Broca calls it an exceptional indiv·dual.' One may well inquire if chance has not brought about that the first face of man of the race called troglodytes, should be that of an individual presenting excessive anatomical characters.' (Bulletin de la Société Anthropologique, Second Series, vol. 3, p. 477.)"

Adele.—"What may you mean by troglodytes, Mr. George?"

Doctor.—"He means cave-dwellers, and you must forgive him if he uses words in vogue among scientists."

Adele.—"Do these prove the great antiquity of man?"

Doctor.—"Nothing beyond the age which separates us from the Quarternary epoch. At the sitting of the French Academy, March 30th, 1874, the celebrated Quatrefages and Hamy have presented the second delivery of their work 'Crania Ethnica'—'The Skulls of the Human Races.' This second delivery is entirely taken up with the race, so called, Cro-Magnon. They attach to the men—Cro-Magnon, those of Magdalen, of the Basse Langerie, of Bruniquel, Aurignac, Menton, Cantalupo, Solutrè, Grenelle, Goyat, and go on to say: 'The Cro-Magnon man has travelled the ages which separate us from the Quaternary epoch; he is found at different prehistorical epochs; he is preserved in transitory state till our present time, and is even now represented by a certain number of isolated individuals. He has been found in Chauny in a Gallic cemetery of the Iron epoch in Paris in the excavations of the Hotel-Dieu. But it is principally in Africa where we must look for the representatives of this race in the tombs of Roknar among the Kabiles of Beni-Menasser and Djurjura.' It is evident from such testimony that the race Cro-Magnon belongs to the epoch between us and the Quaternary, and hence eliminates all idea of great antiquity."

Adele.—"Well, we have disposed of the skulls of Cro-Magnon, who or what comes next?"

George.—"The skeleton of *Laugerie Basse*. It was discovered in 1873 by Carthailhac Massenat and Lalande, in a thick layer containing various objects in a bed of burned earth and coal. They wanted to prove that it represented the skeleton of man of great antiquity who had been buried by an accidental caving in of the ground."

Doctor.—"Other scientists have proved from all the circumstances in which the skeleton was found, that it was buried there by men or friends at no very remote period. Professor F. Hement, in a letter written to the Academy of Sciences, did not hesitate to say: 'The skeleton found by Massenat was certainly buried there and not hid by a caving in of the ground.'"

Adele.—"I am afraid you are digging up a whole cemetery, Mr. George. Are there any other fossil remains of man ?"

George.—"I am sorry to say that there are. To pass over a few less important, there is the Pliocene man of Savona who next demands our attention."

Adele.—"You mean a fossil man supposed to belong to the Pliocene epoch ?"

George.—"Exactly."

Adele.—"Tell us about it, then."

George.—"Some years ago, in a trench dug out on the ridge of a promontory called Calle del Vento, working men discovered at the depth of about nine feet, first a skull, then the different parts of a whole skeleton. The ground seemed really to belong to the Pliocene period, because one-half of the shells found in it belonged to a species already extinct. It was soon inferred that the remains of the man must have been as old as the deposit which contained it. Broca pretended to see in it anatomical characters of great value."

Doctor.—"But facts gathered a little later have deprived this skeleton of all the importance given to it. Because it has been shown that nothing in the physical state of the bones marks any difference between them and those of any ligurian of the historical times. Professor Hamy did not hesitate to write in his 'Precis de Paleontologie Humaine,' p. 67: "The pretended man fossil of the Pliocene period of Savona seems to have been buried in a deposit at a date much more recent than that of its formation, to which some naturalists have attached so much importance."

Adele.—"Then the conclusion about this man fossil of Savona is that the deposit in which it was found was really of the Pliocene epoch, but it is not demonstrated that the man was buried there at the same epoch of the formation of the deposit, and therefore this skeleton of Savona proves nothing as to the great age of man."

Doctor.—"Precisely."

George.—"The next in order are the skeletons of the cave so-called, of the Dead Man."

Adele.—"Do tell us about them, it is so charming to handle such pleasant subjects!"

George.—"This cave is situated near Lozere, in France. It was visited and explored by Professor Broca. It is principally a burying grotto, wherein have been discovered bodkins made of bones, points of spear, remnants of feasts, ashes, relics of coal, seven fire-places, with knives and scrapers of flint. At the one side of the cave, there is a kind of dwelling, capable of sheltering a whole tribe. In that dwelling were found the skulls of seven men, six women and three children, remarkable, as Broca says, by the expression of gentleness in their traits, and the purity of their outlines."

Doctor.—"Well, by acknowledgment of the Professor himself, it is conceded now that such remains do not claim a time much farther back than that of the Phœnicians; whom every one knows to be historical people, and therefore proves nothing as to the great antiquity of man."

Adele.—"Shall we never leave caves, and sepulchres, and damp, gloomy tombs, and get in the open air?"

Doctor.—"Have patience yet a while till we dispose of all the discoveries in that line. Go on, George."

George.—"The next one is the man-fossil of the grottoes of Menton. These are situated alongside the seashore, in the province of Porto Maurizio, in the commune of Ventimiglia, Italy, at a little distance from the French frontier. They are natural cracks of the mountain known by the name of the Mountain of the Red Rocks. Riviere, after having found a great number of utensils in flint and bones, sea and land shells, and remains of animals, discovered in the cave called Carillon, a human skeleton lying on the left side in the longitudinal bed of the grotto. The head, somewhat more elevated than the rest of the body, was lightly bent, and it rested on the soil by the lateral part of the skull and of the face."

Adele.—"And what is to be concluded from such discovery?"

Doctor.—"M. Riviere himself has declared that the man of Menton could not by any manner of means be called the fossil man, and that it presented no traits, whatever, of anything that might approach the ape; and in the last meeting of the delegates of the scientific societies, April, 1874, he protested honestly and strongly against those who had qualified his discovery as that of fossil man."

George.—"And here end all the discoveries so far made."

Adele.—"Many thanks, indeed, for the news."

Doctor.—"But before winding up this subject I want to call your attention to something much more interesting and amusing. The great professor, Huxley, after having examined all the remains, discovered and appreciated them at their proper value with a simplicity which has no parallel, with a naiveness truly enchanting, with an absolute trust in the enormous gullibility of his readers, concludes that some way or other the primeval man, wanted by evolution, must be found somewhere (otherwise what would become of evolution?), that time will show him if one has only faith and patience."

Adele.—"That is charming, indeed."

Doctor.—"George, please to read the words marked."

George.—"'In conclusion,' says Huxley, 'I may say that the fossil remains of man hitherto discovered do not seem to me to take us appreciably nearer to that lower pithecoid form by the modification of which he has probably become what he is."

Doctor.—"Pithecoid, that is, some kind of being between the ape and man."

George.—"Where, then, must we look for primeval man? Was the oldest Homo sapiens pliocene, or miocene, or yet more ancient? In still older strata do the fossilized bones of an ape, more anthrophoid, or a man more pithecoid than any yet known, await the researches of some unborn paleontologist? Time will show."

Doctor.—"Which is as much as to say there is not the slightest fact to show the existence of a man-ape, nor of its great antiquity. Some future paleontologist may find and discover such facts. In the meantime, what is the conclusion that Huxley draws from his honest admission? Does he grant that the absence of such facts must shake from the foundation the whole system of evolution? Quite the contrary. Read on, George."

George.—"'But, in the meanwhile, if any form of the doctrine of progressive development is correct, we must extend by long epochs.'"

Adele.—"In spite of facts to the contrary. Excuse me for the interruption."

George.—"'We must extend by long epochs the most liberal estimate that has yet been made of the antiquity of man.' ('Man's Place in Nature,' 253 and 254)"

Doctor.—"Admire the colossal logical structure of your modern science. It proves evolution by the supposed facts, and the supposed facts by evolution. But the exquisiteness of the joke on the part of scientists is their appearing to be serious, and in being fully confident that not one of their readers can see as far as his own nose to discover the absurdity and the inconsistency of their reasoning. They know they can draw on the heedless superstition and credulity of modern infidel reader to an unlimited extent."

Adele.—"I see now that Mr. Huxley must have been describing his own skull and brain when qualifying the skull of Enghis as something uncertain and doubtful, a skull that might have belonged to a philosopher as well as to a savage; in the opinion of Huxley, I presume, there being not much difference between the skull of a philosopher and that of a savage."

TWENTY-NINTH ARTICLE.
IS CIVILIZED MAN THE NATURAL PRODUCT OF THE SAVAGE?

Doctor.—"Next to the great antiquity of man must be placed the question of his primitive condition. Was the early condition of man the savage state or was it not? Evolutionists can have but one answer to the problem, and that is that man appeared at first in the most abject and savage condition as it is possible to imagine; because as he is, according to evolution, the lineal descendant of the ape, it follows that he cannot have inherited any but the animal condition of his ancestors and repectable sires, that is, just the animal state and the very minimum of intelligence, possibly a grain more or less higher than that possessed by his simian parents."

George.—"Of course, that is the evident consequence of evolution."

Adele.—"And as we have proved the system of evolution to be false, the consequence must share the fate of the premises."

Doctor.—"Certainly, but, for our own satisfaction, I intend to discuss the subject thoroughly and prove two distinct statements which I make. The first is that true science emphatically repudiates and rejects all such supposition of man's primitive state to have been savage, by proving that as a fact man from his first appearance shows himself to be furnished and equipped with all the elements of civilization. The second statement is that if man had appeared in his early stage in the condition of a savage, he could never by himself and natural development have become civilized. And now for the proof. George, do you know of any decisive proof which puts beyond all dispute the fact that man's primeval state was not the savage but the civilized?"

George.—"I do. Language."

Adele.—"How does language prove that man's primeval condition is the civilized and not the savage?"

Doctor.—"Certainly; when we have considered the full import and the deep significance of language, you will see the truth of that statement. George, what truths are to-day put beyond dispute by real, competent judges with regard to language?"

George.—"The first is that man could not invent the language for the reasons we gave in another conversation, and for many more which could be added. This is admitted by Darwin himself when he says that 'no philologist now supposes that any language has been deliberately invented.' ('Descent of Man,' p. 47, Humb. ed.) He contends, however, that it has been slowly and unconsciously developed by many steps, and proposes the bow-wow theory and the imitations of the sounds of nature, or the pooh-pooh theory."

Adele.—"What is the bow-wow theory?"

George.—"That which holds that language has been invented by imitating the cries of animals."

Adele.—"And what is the other?"

George.—"The other is the theory which maintains language to have originated in the imitation of the sounds of nature, as buzz, rattle, etc. Now, Max Müller has refuted both theories with the skill and the authority of a master."

Adele.—"I would like to hear his reasons refuting both."

George.—"Well, I will give you some idea of them. And first, as to the bow-wow theory: 'It is supposed, then,' says Müller, 'that man being as yet mute, heard the voices of birds and dogs and cows, the thunder of the clouds, the roaring of the sea, the rustling of the forest, the murmurs of the brook and the whisper of the breeze. He tried to imitate these sounds, and finding his mimicking cries useful as signs of the object from which they proceeded, he followed up the idea and elaborated the language.' ('Science of Language,' vol. I., p. 359.)"

Adele.—"And what is to be said to that?"

George.—"Professor Müller answers that 'though there are names in every language formed by mere imitation of sound, yet these constitute a very small proportion of our dictionary. They are the playthings, not the tools of language, and any attempt to reduce the most common and necessary words to imitative roots ends in complete failure. Herder himself, after having most strenuously defended this theory, and having gained a prize, which the Berlin Academy had offered for the best essay on the origin of language, renounced it openly towards the latter years of his life, and threw himself in despair into the arms of those who looked upon languages as miraculously revealed. We cannot deny the possibility that a language might have been formed on the principle of imitation. All we say is, that as yet no language has been discovered that was so formed.' And after having demonstrated that many words, seemingly invented on the imitation theory, have a different root, he concludes: 'The number of names which are really formed by an imitation of sound dwindle down to a very small quotum, if cross-examined by the comparative philologist, and we are left in the end with the conviction, that though a language might have been made out of the roaring, fizzing, hissing, gobbling, twittering, cracking, banging, slamming and rattling sounds of nature, the tongues, with which we are acquainted, point to a different origin.' And so we find many philosophers, and among them Condillac, protesting against a theory which would place man even below the animal. Why should man be supposed, they say, to have taken a lesson from birds and beasts? Does he not utter cries and sobs and shouts himself, according as he is affected by fear, pain or joy? These cries or interjections were represented as natural and real beginnings of the human language."

Adele.—"I supose this leads us into the other theory."

George.—"Which Max Müller calls the pooh-pooh theory, which supposes that human language was elaborated after the model of man's natural cries and expression. It is also called Interjectional theory."

Adele.—"And what must one think of it?"

George.—"'Our answer,' says Müller 'to this theory is the same as to the former. There are, no doubt, in every language interjections, and some of them become traditional and enter into the composition of words. But these interjections are only the outskirts of real language. Language begins where interjections end. There is as much difference between a real word, such as 'to laugh,' and the interjection, 'ha, ha!' between 'I suffer' and 'oh!' as there is between the involuntary act and noise of sneezing and the verb 'to sneeze.' An excellent answer to the interjectional theory has been given by Horne Tooke: 'The dominion of speech,' he says, 'is erected upon the downfall of interjections. Without the artful contrivances of language mankind would have had nothing but interjections with which to communicate orally any of their feelings. The neighing of a horse, the lowing of a cow, the barking of a dog, the purring of a cat, sneezing, coughing, groaning, shrieking, and every other involuntary convulsion with oral sound have almost as good a title to be called parts of speech as interjections have. Voluntary interjections are only employed where the suddenness and vehemence of some affection or passion returns man to their natural state and makes them for a moment forget the use of speech, or when from some circumstance the shortness of time will not permit them to exercise it."

Doctor.—"The conclusion of all this is, therefore, that man neither deliberately, nor insensibly, and step by step, can have invented the language, and that the language must have been taught by the Creator. But, George, can we maintain that the Creator gave man the faculty of speech and taught him the language with which to exercise that faculty without giving him the ideas to understand the meaning of what he should utter in speech?"

George.—"Certainly not. To have a language, and to be able to use it, one must have knowledge, and the sense of the word must precede, or at least be simultaneous with the word. How, then, could the Creator give man the faculty of language without revealing to him, in some way, the ideas and principles it is fitted to express, and without expressing which it cannot be language?"

Adele.—"But, gentlemen, I cannot see what all this has got to do with one attempting to prove that man's primeval state was not the savage?"

Doctor.—"Don't you see, Adele, that if the primitive man was taught language by the Creator, and if together with language, ideas and principles were taught him which language is calculated to express, it follows that man began as civilized, and not as a savage?"

Adele.—"I see, now; the first man spoke, he understood what he uttered, therefore he began with knowledge adequate to the language, and hence the first moments of his existence are not those of savage but of civilized being. But, uncle, they may urge the objection that even savages have a language, and that does not prevent them from being savages; why, then, is language in the primeval man a sign of knowledge and culture, and not in the savage?"

Doctor.—"Savages have a language, to be sure, and yet they remain savages because that very language gives indisputable proof and evidence that they have degenerated from a primitive, perfect state; because their language shows a degree of intelligence and culture which is in full contradiction with their present state. Take for instance those savage American tribes who speak the Maya and the Betoy, and you will find that they make use of two forms of verbs, one which indicates the time, and the other simply points out the relation existing between the attribute and the subject. Now, who can have taught those rude men such a fine logical distinction? It is evident that their language points out to a primitive state of culture and refinement from which they have degenerated. We have, therefore, a perfect right to assume that, owing to the fact of man being provided with language and using it for all purposes for which it is intended, he appeared at first in a civilized and not in a barbarous or savage state."

George.—"To this must be added the fact that all philologists admit, without a dissenting voice, that all languages are derived from one primitive, perfect language."

Doctor.—"Certainly, they all agree as to that, though they cannot tell what language was the primitive one. Perhaps that language is lost, perhaps it was altered at the time of the confusion of tongues, in consequence of the attempt to build the Tower of Babel. What is absolutely certain is that all known languages prove, to demonstration, that they have all originated from one single language."

Adele.—"And is that another proof of the fact that man's primeval state was that of culture and not savageism?"

Doctor.—"Of course, a man speaking a perfect language and understanding its terms is a cultured and not a savage being, a being endowed with all the knowledge necessary to his welfare and well-being. Now, George, before we pass to the other statement which I have made, do you know of any other argument to prove the fact of man's primeval cultured state?"

George.—"The other argument is that man appears since the cradle of history as a social being. There is no instance in history showing that man has ever appeared in any other state but the social. Now, society means communication and interchange of ideas, feelings, mutual help, and services, both morally and physically, and therefore implies a certain amount of culture and civilization."

Adele.—"Well, I am perfectly satisfied that man's primitive state was not the savage, but the cultivated and civilized. The fact of man being furnished with a language and being in a social state fully and amply proving it. Now, I am anxious to know the proof of the other statement, that if man's primitive state had been the savage, he could never by himself have freed himself from it and passed to the state of civilization."

Doctor.—"Why, the proof is twofold: first, reason, and second, facts. The reason is very simple—'You cannot give yourself what you haven't got,' is the saying of the schoolmen, and applies perfectly to our subject. What is meant by a savage? Mark well, I don't mean savage as we find him now, with a language, a certain amount of social state, even a certain organized government, and so forth. I mean the savage as implied by the hypothesis; that is, a human being, perfectly destitute of all knowledge of language, in the lowest possible state of ignorance just next to the animal. Such a being must gradually pass from the state of absolute ignorance to that of partial knowledge, of absolute brutish manners, customs and habits to those of partial cultivation, of absolute helplessness to that of finding means for food, shelter, and finally, of comfort and elegance. How can he do so? What means has he got? Nothing but his absolute ignorance and entire helplessness. Then the theory we are refuting, as Dr. Brownson puts it, 'asserts effects without causes, that nothing can make itself something or, what is the same thing, that the stream can rise higher than its fountain, the effect surpass the cause, the man in and of himself can make himself more than he is. All growth is by accretion and assimilation from without. The germ of the oak containing the law of its development, is in the acorn but without air, light, heat and moisture derived from without, the acorn will not germinate and grow into the oak. The law is universal. The human body grows and attains its maturity only under proper external conditions, and by assimilating its appropriate food. The soul can grow or advance only by assimilating spiritual instruction and oral truth, or elevate itself to a higher condition without assimilating a grace from a course above itself. So, if man had begun in the savage state, he could never by his own indigenous and unassisted efforts have risen above it.' ('The Primeval Man Not a Savage,' vol. 9, p. 468.)"

George.—"The fact proves your reason, Doctor. In no instance has a savage nation or people become civilized by their own unaided, unassisted efforts; and, again, if man had, or could have risen from the savage state, the experiment could be tried, and the possibility of such a thing ascertained. But in every case it has been found that a man left to himself, to his own pure unassisted nature, can never come out of such a state. Take two children, a male and female, separate them from all social surroundings, and place them in an absolute isolation, leave them to the free, untrammeled, uncontrolled development of nature and what is the result? They will be as ignorant as the lowest brutes, and infinitely more helpless than the lowest animals. Take the instance of the young savage of Aveyron."

Adele.—"What is that, Mr. George?"

George.—"Three gentlemen were hunting in a wood at Aveyron, France, when they saw a young man about twelve years of age, perfectly naked, gathering roots and glands through the forest. When he perceived the hunters, he ran away and climbed upon a tree to avoid their pursuit. The hunters finally succeeded in capturing him and brought him to Rodez, in the Hospice in St. Affrique, and then to the Institute of the Deaf and Dumb in Paris. Doctor Pinel, one of the most celebrated alienist doctors of France, describes him in very interesting words: 'His senses,' he says, 'are reduced to such inertia as to be in that respect much inferior to those of some of our domestic animals. The eyes, without any fixedness, without expression, wander vaguely from one object to the other without ever resting on any; and they were so poorly developed and exercised as not to be able to distinguish objects in relief from those only painted. The organ of the hearing was equally insensible to the most powerful sounds as well as to the sweetest music. That of the speech was reduced to the state of perfect dumbness, and did not let out but a uniform guttural sound. The organ of smell was so poorly cultivated as to render it quite indifferent for him to breathe the most exquisite perfumes as well as the most fetid exhalations. Finally, the touch was confined to the merest mechanical function of grasping and clutching bodies. He was incapable of attention, of judging and of imitating—so confined was he, and restricted in ideas, even those relative to his natural wants that, after several months, he had not succeeded in learning how to open a door, or to climb upon a chair to reach the food raised to the level of his hands. Deprived of all means of communication, he attached no expression or intention to the movements of his body, passed with rapidity and without reason from a most apathetic sadness to roars of laughter, the most immoderate. Insensible to every kind of moral affections, his discernment did not go beyond a calculation of gluttony, all his pleasures, beyond some agreeable sensation of the taste, all his intelligence confined within the range of a very few ideas relative to his wants; in a word, his whole existence was purely animal.'"

Doctor.—"Now, in my opinion and conviction, this portrait of the young savage of Aveyron is and will always be to the end of the chapter, the portrait of primeval man, such as he would have been if created and placed in the world in the state of pure nature without any other aid of language, instruction, or society."

George.—"Pinel declared the young savage an idiot. Itard, the celebrated doctor and director of the Institute of Deaf and Dumb, believed, on the contrary, in the integrity of the intellectual faculties of the same, but only in the state of complete apathy and inaction, and undertook to revive them. After the most extraordinary and persevering efforts he succeeded but very imperfectly, owing to the long inaction of the intellectual and affective faculties of the young savage, and of the frightful numbness of the organs of speech and of hearing."

Doctor.—"We may conclude, then, in the words of the same great and humane scientist, Itard, in the page 95 of his report: 'Man in the state of pure nature is inferior to a great number of animals. He terrifies, by his nullity and his barbarism, the moral superiority which is supposed to be natural to man, is not assured to him except by means of society and civilization.'"

George—"And he adds these solemn words: 'I have no doubt that if two children of both sexes were isolated since their early infancy, and the same were done with two quadrupeds of a species the less intelligent, these last would turn out to be much superior to the first, with regard to the means of providing for their wants and of watching, either on their preservation or that of their young ones.'"

Adele.—"We may conclude, then, that if man had appeared in the state of barbarism and total ignorance of language and instruction, he would have remained in the same state forever, and would very soon have become extinct."

Doctor.—"Certainly. Science, then, and philosophy bring in their verdict in favor of the teaching of the Christian Revelation, that the first man was created by God perfect in body and soul, and that his mind was filled with instruction and knowledge necessary, not only for his welfare and that of his family, but necessary in order that he might be the head of the race, not only physically, but morally and socially."

George.—"How do we, then, account for the evident signs of ignorance and barbarism in the Stone age?"

Doctor.—"We have proved at what value those ages ought to be estimated. At the same time, whatever of ignorance and barbarism is recorded in history, it is easily explained by the dogma of the fall of man, the consequence of which was a darkening of his mind and a weakening of his will, and the loss of harmony in man's powers and faculties, and the prevalence which his passions obtained over his will and his mind. Still, men did not lose all necessary and useful knowledge, especially those who remained in Asia, the cradle of mankind. The ignorance and barbarism which are inferred from the few general facts, which science can really prove, are easily accounted for by a portion of mankind, after the confusion of tongues, having emigrated to the cold regions of Europe, thus being cut off from all traditions and the society of others, and who gradually lost all knowledge of things and gave rise to the men of the caves and of the Stone age."

Adele.—"I can easily understand how, after the dispersion of those who built the Tower of Babel, some of them gradually and insensibly fell lower and lower into ignorance, until some of their descendants present the phenomenon of the men of those ages, called barbarous. And what to my mind proves this most triumphantly is that all records of barbarism and ignorance are found only in Europe, and none whatever in Asia, where the true religion flourished, at least among one nation, and the others more or less retained some truths of the old religion."

Doctor.—"Bravo, Adele; and with your happy remark we will close this part of the subject."

THIRTIETH ARTICLE.

MAN'S PLACE IN THE UNIVERSE—ARE OTHER WORLDS THAN OURS INHABITED?

Doctor.—"The next question which we should treat is the unity of the human species. But as we have said enough in our conversation to prove such a truth, I think it will be better for us to pass to other subjects."

George.—"I was going to make the same remark. We have seen —speaking of evolution—the truth of that great principle that if two individuals—no matter to what race they may belong—be capable of sexual union, and if such union be fruitful and fertile, it is an evident sign that they belong to the same species. Now all the known races of mankind can unite together, and their union is not only fertile, but the offspring emanating from them are in their turn indefinitely fruitful; therefore, all the human races belong to a single species. Besides the unity of the primitive language, which is evidenced by the fact that all known languages to day have been demonstrated to have originated in a single primitive one, emphasizes the same truth as the unity of the human species."

Adele.—"Well, then, we will pass to the question next in order."

George.—"Which, I think, is the place which man holds in the universe."

Doctor.—"Exactly. But under these questions others are involved which we must discuss, and foremost among them is the question whether other worlds besides our earth are filled with life, and especially with intelligent substances united to some kind of a body."

Adele.—"I don't understand anything at all."

Doctor.—"What is it you don't understand?"

Adele.—"First, I see no connection between the question of man's place in the universe and that which inquires if other worlds than our earth contain life and intelligent beings."

Doctor.—"Don't you see, Adele, that we could not determine or define man's place in the universe unless we could ascertain whether other intelligent substances, inferior or superior to man, whatever they may be, are living in other worlds? How could we locate him, so to speak, unless we knew whether he is the only intelligent substance created, or whether there are others?"

Adele.—"But what did you mean when you said whether there are other intelligent substances united to some kind of a body? Did you mean whether there be other men in the worlds above us?"

Doctor.—"I meant two things in putting the question: whether there be in other planets or stars intelligent substances incorporated into some kind of a body; first, I did not mean to speak of angels, because we know by Revelation that they' are pure spiritual substances, neither united actually, nor intended to be united to a body; but I meant spiritual substances, more or less like man, united to a body; second, when I said united to some kind of a body I meant to imply that such a body need not necessarily be the same as man's body; but such as could be adapted to the peculiar conditions of each heavenly body in which it might happen to reside."

Adele.—"I think I perceive now. We inquire if there be other intelligent beings in the heavenly bodies, in order to be able to assign man his own place. And when we seek if there be other intelligent indwellers in those worlds, we do not mean angels, but intellectual substances united to a body, so formed and constructed as to be adapted to the peculiar conditions and circumstances of each heavenly body in which they might chance to dwell."

George.—"Very clearly summed up, indeed."

Doctor.—"Tell us, George, what do your scientists accuse Christianity of in respect to the question we are discussing?"

George.—"They accuse Revelation of two great errors, the geocentric error and the anthropocentric error."

Adele.—"Dear me, that is dreadful! and what may they mean by the geocentric and the anthropocentric errors?"

George.—"I will give the words of Buckner: 'The first consists in considering the earth as the centre, the capital point of the world; in admitting that the whole universe has been made solely and exclusively for this infinitesimally small point of space. The second is that which considers man as the centre and the end of the inorganic and organic world, of which he is at the same time the master and the king.' The first of these two errors, adds Buckner, has been removed and rooted out by Copernicus, Kepler, Galileo and Newton. The second has been done away with by Lamarck, Goethe, Lyell and Darwin."

Doctor.—"And these great men would deserve our heartfelt thanks and our eternal gratitude if the things were true, if the errors were really held by Revelation as taught by Christianity. But such errors are only in the brain of scientists."

Adele.—"What! does not Christianity teach that the earth is the centre of the universe, and that man is the centre and the end of all inferior creatures and the king and master of creation?"

Doctor.—"Revelation never taught any such thing that the earth is the centre of the universe, or that it was immovable in space, and that the sun and the stars moved around it. Such opinion was held by the scientists of those days, and the Fathers and Doctors of the Church followed it, as the Doctors of the present time follow the most commonly received opinions of the scientific world, neither more nor less. With regard to man, if by considering him as the centre and aim of all other mundane creatures, we intend to signify that he is the centre of the universe and the king and master of all life which may be contained therein, Revelation never taught, nor obliges any one to hold, such a thing. If by that assertion we mean to convey the truth that man is the centre of all life, vegetable or animal, on this earth, and that he is the king of all creatures inferior to him, none can object to such a statement as being a consequence deduced from the essential relation of things, and consequently a metaphysical truth. But we shall understand all these things clearly and distinctly when we have discussed the following questions: first, can we, as Catholics, maintain that besides man, the greatest creation of God visible on earth, there may be in the other planets, in our sun, in the millions and tens of thousand millions of stars, other intelligent substances united to a body adapted to the conditions of those worlds, intellectual substances like, or even superior to, man? second question, can such opinion be demonstrated by any scientific or philosophical arguments, and what can be the value of the same? third question, how is such opinion of the plurality of worlds reconciled with the dogmas of Christianity?"

Adele.—"I am very anxious to enter into such an interesting and attractive discussion."

Doctor.—"We will quote four authorities in confirmation of the statement, that it is free to every Catholic to maintain the plurality of worlds, in the sense we have explained; that is, the existence in other worlds, not only of organic and animal life but also of intellectual substances, united to some kind of a body adapted to the conditions of those worlds. George, please to read from the 'Conferences' of Father Felix, the words I have marked."

George.—"'You wish absolutely to discover in the moon, you want to find in the stars and in the suns, brethren in intelligence and liberty, and, as certain geniuses who pretend to have the intuitive vision of all the worlds, you desire to salute across space societies and astronomical civilizations. So be it. If you have no other reasons to dissent from us there is nothing which will prevent us to hold out to you the hand of fellowship, nor you to grasp ours. Put in the sidereal worlds as many populations as you please, under such form and at such degree of temperature, material and moral, as you list to imagine, the Catholic dogma possesses a tolerance which will astonish you. . . . Is it absolutely desired that the planets, the suns, the stars, be filled with inhabitants, capable, like us, to know, to love, to glorify the Creator? I am loath to proclaim it again, the dogma has no repugnance to it; it does neither deny nor affirm anything on that hypothesis.' ('Conference de Notre Dame de Paris, 1863—Le Mystère de la Creation et la Science des Mondes.')"

Adele.—"That is a clear testimony."

Doctor.—"And receives value from the fact that it was preached before an immense audience not only of lay persons, but of ecclesiastics of every rank and dignity. George, read the second testimony, that of Father Gratry."

Adele.—"Who is Father Gratry, uncle?"

Doctor.—"A very remarkable writer of philosophy, well known all through the modern Catholic world, and especially France. He was a member of the French Oratorians. In his 'Letters on Religion,' explaining the words of Our Lord: 'And other sheep I have which are not of this fold; them also I must bring, and there shall be one fold and one shepherd' he says the words which George is going to read."

George.—"'I cannot think of the inhabitants of other worlds without at once feeling my reason and my faith become enlivened and invigorated. I see those wonderful brethren, and in such multitude are very likely to be found, some much greater, much more beautiful, and much more advanced than men, much more capable of an indomitable and creative faith. How many noble and splendid beauties are to be found already upon our earth, thanks be to God, visible angels sent by God to speak to our souls and to open our hearts. What, then, must those beauties be, so much more noble and so much more sublime!' ('Lettres sur la Religion,' Paris, 1869.)"

Adele.—"I admire very much the enthusiasm of Father Gratry."

Doctor.—"Let us now take the testimony of one of the greatest astronomers of our day, Father Secchi. He has no doubt whatever about the plurality of worlds, and it is not necessary for us to remark that if such opinions were at variance with any tenet of the Catholic faith, Father Secchi, who was as great a Catholic as he was a scientist, would not have held it for a moment. Read the words, George."

George.—"'Life fills the universe, and with life is associated intelligence, and as creatures inferior to us abound, so there may exist in different external conditions creatures much more capable than men. Between the feeble light which shines in our frail compound, by means of which we can know so many wonderful things, and the Wisdom of the Creator of all things, there lies an infinite distance, which may be filled by an infinite number of grades of creatures for which the theorems, which in us are the fruit of hard studies, may be only simple intuitions.' ('Le Stelle,' Milano, 1877, p. 339.)"

Doctor.—"The other testimony which is much more important is that of Abbé Moigno. Before you ask, Adele, I will tell you who is the Abbé Moigno. He is a French ecclesiastic, a scientist of very great value. He was the founder of a magazine called the *Cosmos*, and has published several scientific and theological works, among which the work called 'The Splendors of Faith.' In this last work he affirms that he was authorized by the Congregation of the Roman Index, that is, that Congregation of Cardinals and theologians who examine books to find out whether there be any doctrine in them opposed to faith or morals, to apprise M. Flammarion that the plurality of worlds was not opposed to any Catholic doctrine."

Adele.—"Who is Flammarion?"

Doctor.—"A French astronomer who, among other works, has written a book on the 'Plurality of Worlds.' In this book he asserted that such an opinion could not be reconciled with the Catholic doctrine of the Creation and Redemption. The Abbé Moigno wrote to the Commission of the Index about the matter, and was by them authorized to tell the author of the book that he was mistaken in his assertion that the plurality of worlds did in no way conflict with the doctrines of the Creation, Incarnation and Redemption as taught by the Catholic Church."

George.—"I presume the Commission of the Roman Index ought to know what is and what is not opposed to Catholic doctrine, and we may, therefore, rest assured that the opinion can safely be held by any one who has reasons sufficient to incline him towards it."

Doctor.—"It follows also that no Catholic doctrine obliges any one to hold or maintain that the earth is the centre of the universe in any sense opposed to science; and that the boast of Buckner, that Copernicus, Galileo, etc., had done away with that error is futile.

If there was an error it was a scientific one of which Catholic doctrine is not responsible. Nor, again, are we bound by any doctrine to maintain that man is the end and aim of the universe and the king of the same. Because, as we can maintain that there may be nobler, greater, loftier created intelligences united to a body, it is evident that man cannot be the end of these and the king over them. One remark I want both of you to keep steadily in view, and it is this, that, so far as real facts are concerned, man is the only incorporated intelligence in the universe. There may be other intelligences, as we have said, greater or nobler, but we are not, and cannot be, certain of it. The plurality of the worlds of intelligences is an hypothesis, a conjecture, a wish, a desideratum, but nothing more. Science can go no further than that. No incorporated intelligence other than man has been observed in the planets, stars, suns, or otherwise. Consequently, so far as real science, which means certain knowledge, is concerned, we know only of that incorporated, spiritual, intelligent, substance called man, and no more."

Adele.—"That is plain enough, and I cannot see, uncle, why you insist so much on it."

Doctor.—"I insist so much on it on account of the consequence which flows from the same."

George.—"And that is?"

Doctor.—"That, so far as real science is concerned, the earth as being the indwelling place of the only really ascertained, incorporated intelligence, is infinitely superior to all other worlds wherein intelligences are supposed, but are not ascertained, to exist."

George.—"I see."

Doctor.—"To wind up our present conversation, I want you to read a passage from the greatest astonomer of our times which fully develops my last remark. It is that of Francis Arago, the brightest scientific glory of France."

George.—"'Since by the measurements in which the evidence of the method keeps equal steps with the precision of the results, the volume of the earth has been reduced to less than a millionth part of the volume of the sun, the fact that the sun itself, carried as it were into the starry regions, must occupy a very modest place amid the milliards of stars which the telescope has signaled; the fact that the over ninety-one millions of miles which separate the earth from the sun have become, in consequence of their comparative littleness, a base absolutely unfit to the researches of the dimensions of the visible world; since the velocity of the luminous rays, two hundred thousand miles a second, hardly suffices to the valuations of science; since, finally, by a chain of proofs perfectly irresistible, it has been ascertained that certain stars are so far from us that their light could not reach us in less than a million of years, we remain, as it were, crushed before such immensity. In giving man and the planet in which he lives such a small place in the material world, astronomy seems to have made such progress only in order to humble us. But in looking at the question from another point of view, if one reflects on the extreme weakness of the natural means by the help of which such great problems have been approached and resolved, if one consider that to catch and to measure the greatest part of those quantities forming to-day the basis of astronomical calculations, man has been obliged to perfect very much the most fine and delicate organ and to add immensely to the power of his eye; if one will observe that it has been equally necessary to invent proper methods to measure long intervals of time, to struggle against the most microscopic effects which the continual variations of temperature produce in metals, and, for that matter, on all instruments; to guard himself against the illusions without number which is caused on the route of the luminous rays by the atmosphere—now cold, now warm, then dry or damp, now tranquil and then agitated—across which all observation must inevitably be made, then the weak being reacquires all his advantages. Alongside of such wonderful works of the mind what signify the weakness and fragility of our body? What matters it that the dimensions of the planets in which it has fallen to our lot to appear, but for a few instants, are as a grain of sand?' ('Notices Historiques,' vol. 2, p. 278.)"

Doctor.—"And mark, both you, that Arago only notices the works of human genius in one department of science—that of astronomy. How much more could be said if we cast a glance at the whole encyclopedia of natural sciences? How much more could we add if from natural sciences we arise to metaphysical sciences, and from these to the miracles of human genius in all and every one of the fine arts in which, especially, man truly deserves the appellation of creator? Supposing, then, that the worlds above us were lifeless and uninhabited, their extraordinary and prodigious material dimensions were as no thing compared with the almost infinite capabilities of the human mind, the human will, and therefore the earth, the abode of the latter, would be vastly superior in worth and dignity to the countless suns and stars which dot the firmament."

THIRTY-FIRST ARTICLE.

SCIENTIFIC AND PHILOSOPHICAL REASONS FOR THE PLURALITY OF WORLDS.

Doctor.—"George, what is the value of the scientific argument in favor of the plurality of worlds? Are there any real facts which have been observed by astronomers indicating that there is in the worlds beyond and above us life in all its variety and stages, from the purely organic and vegetable to the highest intellectual substances incorporated in a body?"

George.—"I regret to say there are no facts proving such a conclusion. No actual observation has ever been made demonstrating the existence of life in any of the worlds above us."

Adele.—"What, then, is this scientific argument in favor of our opinion? What is its value? I wish we had a perfect demonstration of such a thing; for I am charmed with the idea of peopling those great and enormous regions with life and energy in every shape."

George.—"Scientists and astronomers can go as far as this; that they can, by actual observation, prove the habitability, so to speak, of other worlds besides our planet, and the fact that our earth is in no way distinguished from others in that respect; from that they not only answer the objection raised against our hypothesis with regard to the conditions necessary for life, but prove, furthermore, the possibility of the existence of life in those regions."

Doctor.—"Yes, sir, astronomy can go no further than the limits just mentioned. Yet it is a giant step toward the demonstration of the hypothesis. If ever the discovery of better instruments, magnifying to an unlimited extent the power of our present telescopes shall be made, or some other means shall be found, in the course of centuries, of approaching nearer and nearer other planets or other suns, mankind may yet be able to actually observe life, and, mayhap, enter into communication with the inhabitants of those worlds."

George.—"The last hypothesis of mankind ever being able to be placed in communication with the inhabitants of other worlds seems rather an extravagant thought, doctor, if you will allow me to say so, and might expose one who should dream of such a thing to laughter and ridicule."

Doctor.—"No danger of such thing, George, in the judgment of true serious thinkers. Why, the universe—the work of infinite power, wisdom and goodness, the expression of the infinite perfections of the same abyss of excellence and being—is as yet almost a *sealed book* to us. We know but little of all which it can reveal of the treasures which have been lavished on it with such bountiful hands. We may compare it to a panorama of the most magnificent and glorious beauties, covered by an immense and thick curtain. Only an infinitesimal corner of that curtain is lifted to enable us to catch a glimpse of the unutterable beauties of those superb realms. From time to time, when God, in His infinite providence deems it fit, He lifts a little more of that corner, and the vision of new and more important, and yet more exquisite beauties bursts before some chosen genius, and a new revelation is made to mankind. This is the history of all discoveries, George; and where is the serious thinker who shall limit God's providence from lifting that curtain and that veil, more and more, in the course of ages? Or, shall any one say that the revelation is exhausted; that the universe can tell us no more of the unutterable grandeur of its bountiful Creator than the little—the very little—we know?"

George.—"I take it back, doctor. I see I spoke in folly."

Adele.—"I am glad of your frank acknowledgment."

Doctor.—"Well, let us go on. Please to state, for the sake of Adele, here, what are the conditions necessary for the habitability of life, and what is the importance of each."

George.—"The first necessary condition is the atmosphere on the surface of planets and its influence upon life. On the earth the atmosphere is a mixture of 79 parts of azote and 21 of oxygen; from the fish to man, all animals owe to this mixture, more or less modified, their life and its maintenance. The same must be said of vegetables, which in day time breathe in a manner the very reverse of ours, and at night in a manner similar to ours. Air, therefore, is the first and the indispensable aliment of all terrestrial life. Every living being is dependent on the atmosphere, because every living being carries in itself a mechanical and chemical apparatus of respiration, constructed according to the interior nature of the atmosphere. Besides these properties relative to the indispensable respiration for the life of the globe, the atmospheric fluid possesses others no less remarkable. If, for the internal functions of the body, the pulmonary apparatus is so organized as to transform, incessantly, the blood of the veins into arterial blood, and thus ever to renew the principles of our life, for the external functions, the senses, and especially those of sight and hearing, are constructed with a view of receiving and of transmitting to the brain all the external influences of which the atmosphere is the medium."

Adele.—"I know, of course, that the mechanism of the organs of speech impress on the atmosphere those vibrations which constitute sound and which carry the voice to the mechanism of the ear; on the other hand, the mechanism of the ear, constructed after a correlative susceptibility, receives those vibrations and transmits them to the brain and the internal senses."

Doctor.—"And what is the consequence of the agency of the air as to our organs of speech and hearing?"

Adele.—"The consequence is so important that, even supposing we could live without the atmosphere, without it we should become deaf and dumb and an eternal silence would reign in the universe."

George.—"What we have said of the senses of hearing and speaking must be said also of the organs of sight. Everyone knows that the diffusion of light is due to the atmospheric mass, and that, without it, no objects would be visible except those which are directly exposed to the solar light, no shadow or *chiaro oscuro;* either the dazzling light of the sun or the complete obscurity of the night—neither dawn nor twilight. Nor is that all; without atmosphere no clouds; a monotonous and wearisome light uniformly poured down by the sun without the least variety of appearance in the sky. In fact, there would be no longer a sky. That limpid and pure azure which charms our eyes would be substituted by an immensity, sombre and dark. Those splendid combinations of light in our sky at daybreak and at night; those enchanting golden rays of the dawn upon our landscapes; the red clouds, the glories of the twilight upon our mountains; those phantastic creations of thousand shades of color succeeding each other around us, all such wonders would be unknown if the earth were deprived of the atmosphere; it would be a lugubrious, mournful empire such as Dante imagined in the silent regions of Purgatory where he met the spirits of Limbo."

Adele.—"I would never have given you credit, Mr. George, for so much practical fancy as you are displaying."

George.—"Thanks for nothing. Let us go further. The atmosphere envelops our globe like a reservoir which preserves both the solar and the terrestrial heat. Without it, the heat would be sent up into the higher regions of space, and our earth would be reduced to the lot, pretty much like that of the high altitudes of the Andes and the Himalayas or Alpine peaks, where the atmosphere, being highly rarefied, there reigns but a desert of snow and the sombre silence of death."

Doctor.—"Pass on to the influence of the atmosphere upon water, George."

George.—"It is well known that water constitutes the principal element of all liquids in action, in the terrestrial disposition of things, either in the vessels of animals or in the tissues of plants, that such element, moreover, is most indispensable for the function of life, and that without it no organic transformations could take place, either in the animal or vegetable kingdom. Now, the existence of the atmosphere is a necessary condition to the existence of water or of any other liquid on the surface of a planet. Its absence implies, by the very fact, the absence of all liquids."

Adele.—"Why?"

George.—"Because all liquid mass or collection, to be formed and to be maintained and preserved, necessitates some kind of atmospheric pressure. All worlds, therefore, which should be without atmosphere, by that very fact, would be deprived of all kind of liquids."

Adele.—"Well, I am more than convinced that the atmosphere is the first necessary condition upon our planet to make life possible or agreeable. Are there any other?"

George.—"Certainly. The next condition is that there must be a certain amount of heat and light to render life possible. I suppose it is not necessary for me to go into any lengthy discussion to prove that absolute condition for life. No organic or animal being can live in the absence of the necessary heat; without it, it freezes and dies. A plant without light also withers and perishes."

Adele.—"I understand that perfectly."

Doctor.—"Now, the conclusion is that, perhaps, with the exception of the moon, we find in all the other planets of our system these or similar conditions of life to be verified."

Adele.—"You don't say, uncle?"

Doctor.—"To be sure. And to start from heat and light, I may mention the calculations of astronomers about the quantity of heat and light which the planetary worlds receive from the sun. Taking the earth as a starting point of comparison, we find that Mercury receives seven times more light and heat than our globe, Venus twice the amount, Mars one-half less, the telescopic planets seven times less, Jupiter twenty-seven times less, Saturn ninety times less, Uranus three hundred and ninety times less, and finally, Neptune nine hundred times less."

Adele.—"Uncle, what do you mean by telescopic planets?"

Doctor.—"Those which have been discovered through the telescope. Those respective distances of the planets from the solar focus, among which the Earth exhibits no particular privilege, determines a gradual diminution in the temperature of their surfaces from Mercury to Neptune, and those distances must be taken as the fundamental basis in the investigation of their temperature, because it has been demonstrated that the central fire of each planet has but a very trifling influence upon the heat on its surface."

Adele.—"Then, how could life be possible, uncle, on the planet Mercury which receives seven times more heat and light from the Sun; the inhabitants there, I am afraid, would be roasted to a cinder, and, on the other hand, on the planets Jupiter, Saturn, Uranus and Neptune, they would be frozen to death?"

Doctor.—"What we have demonstrated is that on these planets there is heat and light. Now, God Almighty may have adapted the conditions of the inhabitants of each of those planets to the peculiar conditions of each, and where man, or the animals and plants of our globe would be burned or frozen, other beings with a different body and organs may live in comfort."

Adele.—"I see, the objection would only hold for the living beings with organism such as we are acquainted with."

George.—"Even in certain parts of our globe animals and plants live and flourish when others would perish through too much heat or cold."

Doctor.—"Let us pass to the atmosphere. George, is there any atmosphere on the surface of the planets?"

George.—"To answer your question, I must remark that when we speak of the atmosphere on the planets others than our globe, we do not intend to affirm that the air and the water of those planets are the same which we breathe and drink. Nothing goes to prove that in all cases the liquids and gases of the planets are of the same chemical composition as those of the earth. I said in all cases, because there are some notable exceptions to the statements just made. Spectral analysis has demonstrated that in Mars and Venus the water is chemically the same as ours. But there is, on the contrary, a remarkable difference between the liquids and the gases of Jupiter and Saturn and those of our globe.".

Adele.—"Pray, what do you mean by spectral analysis, and how does that demonstrate that the water in Mars and Venus is the same as ours?"

George.—"I presume you know what is meant by the solar spectrum?"

Adele.—"I have an idea, but I would like to have it explained by yourself, who can do it so happily and with such lucidity of style and language."

George.—"You are getting rather profuse in compliments, Miss Adele. Well, let us take a prism—that is, a piece of crystal having three angles; let a ray of the sun's light pass through it, and what is the consequence? The light, which is composed of seven principal colors, is divided and a belt appears behind the prism, consisting of seven colors, in the following order: violet, indigo blue, green, yellow, orange and red. The colors divided themselves, each one according to its characteristic traits; the more glowing, the red, does not allow itself to deviate from its straight path and crosses the prism in a straight line; the orange undergoes a little the influence of the prism and bents a little and comes to place itself next to the red; the yellow feels that influence more and places itself next; the green and then the blue are yet more pliable and feeble, and come next in order, followed by the indigo and the violet. This little colored flag has the name of solar spectrum."

Adele.—"Many thanks for your explanation, but what has that to with our subject?"

George.—"Excuse me for a moment till I get to it. The length of the spectrum represents nothing but light, that is, the solar rays sensible to the retina of our eye. Our eye begins to see when the ethereal vibrations reach the number of four hundred and fifty trillions, and ends when they exceed seven hundred trillions, purple violet; but beyond that nature always acts without our perceiving it. Certain chemical substances, for instance the plate of the photograph, see much farther than purple violet. Our ears hear the aerial vibration from 32 a second (bass) to 36,000 (sharp), beyond that we hear no more. Thus are our senses limited, but not the facts of nature. The colors are like the notes of the gamut—effects of numbers; in music as well as in painting, they are notes."

Adele.—"Exceedingly obliged for so much information, but can see no drift yet."

George.—"Patience yet awhile. It is in the molecular arrangement of transparent substance that the different reflections of light, that is, colors, originate. That rose which opens its calyx in the middle of flower-beds receives the same light as the lily, the violet, the geranium, etc.; and yet it is so different from the others. What is the cause? The molecular reflection produces the whole difference, and one may say, without exaggeration, that objects are of all colors except of those in which they appear to be decked. Why is that meadow so green? Because it absorbs all other colors except the green of which it will have none, and casts away from it. White is formed by the reflecting nature of the object which absorbs nothing and sends back everything; black, by a surface which absorbs everything and returns nothing."

Adele.—"Pass on, Mr. George."

George.—"Did you ever hear of the microscopic lines of the spectrum?"

Adele —"No, sir."

George.—"In 1815 Fraunhofer, a Bavarian optician, was studying the solar spectrum, in order to find in it some fixed points which might be independent of the nature of the prism used to produce the spectrum, when he met with a happy discovery. He observed that by giving the prism a certain special position one could see suddenly to appear in the spectral image, certain obscure rays cutting transversally the seven colors of the spectrum. These are called microscopic lines, and Fraunhofer counted six hundred of them in the spectrum, later on Brewster counted two thousand, now they have reached the number of five thousand. These rays of the solar spectrum are constant and invariable whenever the spectrum which is observed is the effect of solar light. They are found in the light of the day, in that of the clouds and of all terrestrial objects. This discovery of the microscopic lines was followed by another yet more important. It was discovered that by observing across a prism a ray of light coming from some terrestrial luminous object, for instance, a jet of gas, not only a spectrum was produced similar to that of the sun's light, but that such spectrum is also traversed by lines, and that the distribution and arrangement of these lines differ according to the nature of the light to be examined, and that they present a constant and invariable order characteristic of each one. This has given rise to what is called spectral analysis and to the spectroscope."

Adele.—"How ?"

George.—"Do you not see that if every substance seen through a prism reflects lines so arranged as to point out its own particular nature, it follows that from the particular arrangement of the lines reflected in the spectroscope, an instrument invented purposely to analyze those lines, we can tell the nature of the substance ?"

Adele.—"I see, now, from the spectrum of each luminous object, and from the particular arrangement of the dark lines seen on the spectrum, we can tell the nature of the substance to be observed. And, I presume, that is the way you can tell whether the water in Venus is of the same nature as ours."

Doctor.—"Yes, and a great many more things. In fact this has been one of the most useful and most beautiful discoveries of modern times. By it we can tell with as much certainty and accuracy what is the nature of the substances and objects, lying far, far away from us, millions and millions of miles, just as if we were looking at them with our naked eye and touching them with our hands. Let us now wind up our scientific argument in favor of the plurality of worlds. We have seen that the planets, and the sun even, present very little difficulties in the way of their being inhabited, that the essential requisites for life are substantially to be found in worlds other than our globe, and that with little variation in the organization of them to adapt them to their peculiar abodes, there is no insurmountable difficulty against those worlds being peopled with myriads of living beings. The philosophical arguments will put this probability in a much better and stronger light."

THIRTY-SECOND ARTICLE.

PHILOSOPHICAL PROOFS FOR THE PLURALITY OF WORLDS.

Doctor.—"Before we come to all those philosophical probabilities or proofs, if we may so call them in a certain sense, for the plurality of worlds, it will be very useful to recall some of the facts of astronomy upon the grandeur and immensity of those worlds which roll in space. The knowledge of such facts will not only facilitate the understanding of the proofs we are going to allege, but also set them in a stronger and more luminous point of view. To start from the lowest and the most insignificant facts, we will describe the immensity of our own solar system."

Adele.—"Mr. George, I suspect your services are on demand now?"

Doctor.—"Yes, tell us about our own solar and planetary system."

George.—"I will begin by the Sun. According to the most recent observation, it seems to be demonstrated that the Sun is entirely in a state of temperature so high that it must be entirely liquid if not vaporous. It seems, according to the expression of Kepler, a gigantic magnet upholding, by the simple laws of reciprocal attraction, all the other worlds of the group which it governs, a permanent focus or repository of electricity, setting in motion on all these worlds, that imponderable agent which plays such great part among the forces in action of our system."

Adele.—"I suppose you mean ether?"

George.—"Certainly. The globe of the Sun is one million three hundred thousand times larger than our Earth. Its specific weight is three hundred and twenty-four thousand times greater than that of the Earth and seven hundred times greater than that of all the planets and their satellites put together. Spectral analysis has proved that the solar globe is surrounded by an atmosphere impregnated with vapors of the same materials as the Sun, vapors in which predominate those of iron, calcium, magnesia, and hydrogen. It has a movement of rotation around its axis, which it accomplishes in twenty-five of our days, but such movement does not produce on the surface of the Sun, as on that of the planets, the alternations of day and night. It is not known by what mysterious agent are the solar light and heat engendered. We may safely affirm that, in spite of the enormous quantity of both which it sends out in space, we cannot observe any diminution in its disc. A mysterious force, which has been named universal gravitation, causes the heavenly bodies of our system to hang and revolve around the Sun; planets, satellites, asteroids, comets, meteors, embracing under one law and government all the beings which the Sun illuminates. The first planet which we meet, on starting from the centre of the system to the periphery, is Mercury. It is distant from the Sun about forty-two millions six hundred and sixty-nine thousand miles. It is smaller than our Earth; its diameter not exceeding six hundred and sixty-nine thousand miles; whereas, that of the Earth, exceeds nine thousand five hundred and sixty-nine miles. The next is Venus, that beautiful planet which precedes the morning dawn and the night. It is in its mean distance sixty-six millions one hundred and forty thousand miles from the Sun. The third in order is the Earth, which is ninety-one millions four hundred and thirty thousand miles from the Sun. Sixty millions of miles further is seen Mars. About one hundred millions of miles further appears a kind of zone or belt in which have been discovered seventy fragments of planets. Beyond that zone gravitates the colossal globe of Jupiter, four hundred and ninety-eight millions six hundred and thirty-nine thousand miles at its greatest distance from the Sun. Next appears Saturn, the mean distance of which is eight hundred and seventy-two millions and thirty-seven thousand miles. Uranus comes next, which at its greatest distance is one thousand eight hundred millions five hundred and sixty-five thousand miles from the Sun. The last, lately discovered, is Neptune, three milliards three hundred millions distant from the centre of the system. The year of Neptune is equivalent to one hundred and sixty-four years of our own."

Adele.—"Pass on to the satellites, Mr. George."

George.—"I am not making up a compendium of astronomy. I merely alluded to our own solar system in order to pave the way to the description of the immensity of the heavens. It appears, then, that our own planetary system, as I have pointed it out, is terminated by the planet Neptune, which measures twenty-one milliards of miles in circumference. Still, the empire of the Sun is not limited by such narrow and puny limits. Besides the possibility of the existence of other planets revolving beyond its orbit, innumerable comets, subject to solar attraction, furrow on every side and in every sense the plains of the heavens, and return from time to time and at definite epochs to quench their thirst at the solar source, a perennial focus and fountain of light and electricity. I shall say nothing of the number of these comets, of their nature or of the distance which they travel. It will suffice to mention that the great comet of 1811 employed three thousand years to accomplish its revolution, and that it places in its travels between it and the Sun no less than forty milliards nine hundred and fifty millions of miles of distance."

Doctor.—"But whatever may be the extension and the immensity of the solar dominion, the preceding magnitudes and figures which appear so enormous can hardly be compared, owing to their insignificance, to the magnitudes observed in stellar astronomy. In the latter science we no longer count by miles but by thousands of miles. Each star in heaven is a sun brilliant of its own light. They have measured the luminous intensity of the stars nearest to us, and it has been found that some of them, like Sirius, which is called the Giant Sun, are now lightsome and more voluminous than our Sun, that the latter placed at the distance of Sirius would only appear to us as a little star of third magnitude. These vast and brilliant suns are centres of magnificent systems, some of which may be like to ours, some may be inferior, and the great majority of them much superior in extent and in planetary circles to our system. These stars or suns are innumerable, and fill space at a distance one from another perfectly amazing. The star nearest to us, for instance, is twenty-four trillions of miles distant from our Sun. The others, like Cygnus, Sirius, Vega, the Polar Star, Capella, count the distance from the Sun at hundreds and thousands of trillions. But these are the nearest stars; as to the millions and millions of others which people the immensity of space, it is naturally impossible to reckon their distance."

George.—"Astronomers have tried to give an idea of such distance by taking as basis and measure the velocity of light."

Adele.—"Do let us have some of these calculations!"

George.—"According to the latest and most accurate measure, we know that light travels at the rate of two hundred thousand mile a second, or twelve millions a minute. And yet it employs three years and six months to reach us from the star nearest to us in the Constellation of Centaur. It travels 14 years to reach us from Sirius and 21 years from Vega. The luminous rays sent us by the Polar Star arrive after fifty years. Those sent us by the Goat travel seventy-two years before reaching us. But beyond these stars near to us the distance is much greater. The light of the last stars, seen through a telescope, nine feet in diameter, employs one thousand years, and that of the last stars seen through a telescope, eighteen feet, requires two thousand seven hundred years to reach us, and finally, it is well known that the light of some of them requires five thousand, ten thousand, and one hundred thousand years to strike the earth."

Adele.—"How great is God in the heavens! Truly may He be called the God of the heavenly armies."

Doctor.—"To realize such wonders, let us suppose that the magnificent Sirius should become extinct to-day by some catastrophe, as the light which emanates from it requires fourteen years to reach us we should yet see it after fourteen years in the same place in the heavens, whence, in reality, it had long disappeared. If the stars were all annihilated to-day they would, nevertheless, shine for years, for centuries, for thousands of years and centuries. If, from describing the magnitude and distance of the starry heavens, we pass to the number of them here, new realms of wonder are opened before us. George, give us some idea of it?"

George.—"It is well known that, in order to facilitate the pointing out of the light of the stars, they have been classified according to the order of size and magnitude, from the point of view of the same light and brilliancy. It is also well known that the denomination of magnitude does not apply to the real dimensions of the stars which are unknown to us except by their apparent splendor; the stars which appear to us the smallest, being considered as the most distant. Now, we count in both hemispheres, eighteen stars of the first magnitude, sixty of the second, two hundred of the third, five hundred of the fourth, one thousand four hundred of the fifth, four thousand of the sixth. Here winds up the number of the stars viewed with the naked eye. But the progression continues in the same ratio beyond that limit, and increases in the same manner according as we consider the smallest magnitudes. This augmentation will be the more easily understood the more we reflect that stars appear the smallest in proportion as their distance from the earth is the greatest. Beyond, then, the sixth, we count the stars visible by the telescope; and to give an idea of the numerical increase of these stars, we say that the eighth magnitude contains forty thousand, the ninth one hundred and twenty thousand, the tenth three hundred and sixty thousand. The progression continues: Arago counted nine million five hundred and sixty-six thousand stars of the thirteenth magnitude, twenty-eight million six hundred and ninety-seven thousand of the fourteenth, and valued at forty-three millions, the whole number of stars visible to the fourteenth. For the sixteenth magnitute the number arises to seventy-five millions of stars visible through the telescope. To this, we must add, that a great number of stars which appeared single to the naked eye, were found to be double when seen through the telescopes of Herschel, Struve and Lord Rosse. Let us remark, now, that the greatest part of the stars seen in the heaven, and particularly those belonging to the *Milky Way*, form a group called in astronomy, a Nebula. Now, if it be asked how many suns are found in the Milky Way, we answer that, through the aid of his powerful telescope, William Herschel, in a quarter of an hour, on the restricted plane of fifteen minutes of diameter, saw the prodigious number of one hundred and sixteen thousand stars pass before his eye; and applying that calculation to the plane of the Milky Way, he found no less than eighteen millions of suns. Of course, this is one Nebula. Who could count the number of suns which are found in other nebulæ? Who could number the latter in the far, far distant depths of space? Such calculations are absolutely beyond the power of any human intellect."

Doctor.—"Let us sum up, in a few words, the few facts we have given of astronomical science, and afterwards draw the conclusion which naturally springs from them. First, the stars are so many Suns similar to ours, and shining with native light; second, these systems, which may be ranked in the first order, and which are similar to our own system, are governed by the same law of gravitation, and to the same laws discovered by Kepler as regulating the planets which gravitate around our Sun; third, the Milky Way is a belt, formed by an enormous grouping of complicated masses of stars, each one of which may be regarded as implying innumerable systems of superior order; fourth, besides the stars, we find in the heavens very many masses of luminous matter shining with their own native light, not as yet concreted in definite bodies, but in gaseous state, which form the nebulæ. They form systems apart, and in spite of their gaseous state they have forms perceptibly constant; fifth, all these float in space at most enormous distances; sixth, but immense as this space is supposed to be, yet it does not constitute the real and true boundaries of creation, because the very best and greatest instruments, such as the colossal telescopes of Lord Rosse Russel, Melbourne, in Australia, Washington, Paris, cannot penetrate through the firmament, which is truly unfathomable."

Adele.—"Then the conclusion you wish to draw, uncle, is the immense and boundless grandeur of the universe, the unutterable magnitude of the masses of worlds which roll in space, and the comparative littleness and insignificance of the planet on which we live."

Doctor.—"Certainly I do. And this simply with a view of formulating the arguments which philosophy discovers in favor of the plurality of worlds. Now, listen to the first one. Why did God create the universe, Adele?"

Adele.—"Why, to manifest and to make known His own infinite perfections by means of the very slight expression and copy which He could effect in the world He created."

Doctor.—"But to whom was this manifestation to be made? We may consider all the beings of creation as so many tongues proclaiming loudly the glories of the Creator and the unparalleled and infinite beauties of their pattern. But to whom should these eloquent tongues speak? Whom should they address?"

Adele.—"Surely to man, or some one like man, who could both see and perceive those beauties and praise and glorify the Creator."

Doctor.—"Right. And suppose all those myriads of millions of worlds of realms of unutterable grandeur, suppose that immense and colossal galaxy of beauties, such as astronomy has manifested to have been for innumerable centuries without any intelligent spectator, without any enraptured admirer, do you not see that in such supposition we find something wanting in the design of the Creator; it would seem to us as if all these worlds were existing for so long without accomplishing the end for which they were made? On the other hand, fill these immense worlds with intelligent spectators, and what is the consequence? Why, that at every epoch of time, and in all points of space, a canticle of glory, a hymn of praise, a song of admiration, a jubilee of complacency and delight, would be rising up to the great Creator from myriads and tens of thousands of millions of worlds and realms filled up, and teeming with inhabitants endowed, perhaps, with an intelligence more noble, more sublime and lofty, soaring in the highest regions of truth, intelligences vaster, more profound, more appreciative than ours, and therefore intelligences which could understand and admire much better than mankind the grandeur and immensity of the Creator."

Adele.—"Certainly; it seems to me that the end for which the world was made would have been better attained in this hypothesis than in the other."

Doctor.—"And hence is it that the greatest geniuses of mankind have leaned towards the plurality of the worlds. They have delighted in thinking that the immense realms of the universe were filled with spectators of the great panorama of Creation, and were charmed in offering to Him from the very depths of their hearts the song and canticle of praise and thanksgiving. But there are other arguments which we will consider at our next interview."

THIRTY-THIRD ARTICLE.

PHILOSOPHICAL ARGUMENT FOR THE PLURALITY OF WORLDS.

Adele.—"The first argument proving the plurality of worlds has taken a very strong hold on my mind. It charms me to think that in numberless worlds there are intelligent inhabitants who sing the praises of the Creator and exalt His infinite grandeur and excellence, as manifested in the works which they see and admire, the end for which God created all things. Now, I am anxious to hear the other arguments."

Doctor.—"The other arguments are all founded on that truth to which you have now alluded, that God's object in creating the universe was to manifest in His works His unutterable and unfathomable greatness and infinite perfections. For instance, it is a truth and principle admitted by all Catholic theologians and philosophers, when they want to determine, more or less, the number of the different creatures which God has made, that such number must be inferred from the place which each creature holds in the scale of being; those holding a higher place in the scale having been created in larger number."

Adele.—"I don't catch the meaning of the principle."

Doctor.—"We have, as you remember, divided all the beings of the universe into five different kingdoms: the inorganic world, the living and organic world, the sensitive and animal kingdom, the intelligent world united to a body, and the purely intelligent world."

Adele.—"I remember that."

Doctor.—"Now, suppose we raise the question: Were purely inorganic species created in greater number than organic and living species, or were the latter created in greater number than sensitive species, or were sensitive species created in greater number than intellectual creatures united to a body, or were these in greater number than purely intellectual species? What is the principle which must guide us in solving the problem? St. Thomas, followed by all theologians and philosophers, answers that the principle which must guide us in determining the question, is the place which the species holds in the scale of being, those holding the lowest place having been created in the smallest number, and those holding the highest having been created in the greatest number. This is a cosmological law."

George.—"I cannot see the reason why."

Adele.—"Nor I."

Doctor.—"I will give you the beautiful reason of St. Thomas. What is the end or object for which God created the universe? That by and through every creature composing it He might manifest His own infinite perfections. We have said it so many times that it would seem useless to repeat it. Yet that truth is so fundamental and impregnated with so many truths, that we must fall back upon it even at the danger of being thought tiresome. Now mark the consequence, both of you. Which of the creatures of the universe belonging to the five different kingdoms do believe, can best express God's perfections, those which are lowest in the scale or those which stand at the summit?"

George.—"Evidently those which stand at the summit as being more comprehensive."

Adele.—"What do you mean by comprehensive?"

George.—"I mean that they contain more perfection. For instance, inorganic bodies do not exhibit any better idea than that of simple existence. Organic beings, besides the idea of existence, imply the idea of internal self movement, which apprehends, assimilates, and transforms external beings to itself for its own life and growth. Sensitive beings, besides existence and spontaneous self-movement, imply a certain kind of knowledge, and finally, intellectual beings, imply knowledge of the abstract universal and the infinite. Consequently, the higher we ascend in the scale of beings the more comprehensive we find their essences to be."

Adele.—"And what inference do you draw from that?"

Doctor.—Evidently that, as God's nature and perfections are an infinite abyss of being, they can be better imitated by creatures, the essence of which is more comprehensive, and composed of more elements than by creatures which are less so."

Adele.—"I perceive that perfectly now."

Doctor.—"Therefore we may conclude that the species of those creatures which could better express his infinite grandeur and attributes were created in much larger number than those which could express it less."

Adele.—"Granted; but I cannot see how that proves that in the starry worlds there must be intelligent substances incorporated in some sort of a body."

Doctor.—"It does perfectly. Because intellectual substances united to a body such as man, are highest in the scale of being next to the purely intellectual substances. Therefore they ought to be in much greater number than the species below them in the scale; they ought, according to the principle laid down, be more numerous than all the species of animals, than all the species of plants, than all the inorganic substances, each one of which at least may be considered a species, though some natural philosophers maintain that each of the innumerable atoms forming an inorganic body is a species by itself, as it has a nature and form of its own, constant and immutable. (See 'Encyclopædia Britannica,' art. Atom.) Now, as you are aware, there is one species of intellectual substances united to a body which we are acquainted with, that is, the human species; therefore either the principle is false, or there must be in the universe innumerable species of intellectual substances, incorporated into a body, to make true the cosmological law."

Adele.—"But are the principle and law so certain as all that?"

Doctor.—"It is absolutely certain, according to St. Thomas' philosophy, and the proof is capable of further development than we have hitherto given to it. Why, we may inquire, did God Almighty create a number of species at all, and was not content with creating one single species? What is the reason? The reason is to be found in the immense distance which must necessarily exist between an infinite, immense ideal type and pattern and the necessary finite nature of its copy, expression and imitation. God's infinite essence is the pattern and type of the universe. The latter must necessarily be limited and finite, because a created infinite is a contradiction in terms. How, then, can a finite being express and set forth an infinite model? The difficulty is somewhat obviated by creating an almost infinite number of species of creatures, each one endeavoring to reproduce a side—so to speak—of the infinite type. Imagine an infinite circle in which we could suppose an infinite number of concentric circles, beginning from the centre and gradually reaching the circumference. The circle being supposed infinite could not be reproduced or imitated by a corresponding finite circle. But we could imagine the existence of an almost infinite number of finite circles, each endeavoring to represent one of the concentric circle of the infinite figure. Thus, if we should not have an absolutely perfect imitation of that circle, we would at least have an imitation which somewhat expresses and reproduces it. God's essence is infinite perfection. No single created perfection can reproduce or imitate it. But a boundless almost infinite species of creatures could somewhat represent it by each species imitating a side, a moment, an element of that infinite perfection. And is it not evident that of the species created purposely to represent such elements, those intended to reproduce the higher and more comprehensive element would be greater in number, as the element to be represented would be more fecund. The principle, then, cannot be gainsaid. And see how beautifully in the hypothesis of the plurality of worlds, the exigency of the principle is satisfied and the law carried out to its utmost. First, inorganic species—they represent mere existence and form. Next, the organic species, in much greater number, as representing life and movement. Then sensitive species, the greater number yet, because approaching knowledge and consciousness. Then, intellectual substances united to a body in much greater and boundless number, as representing the true nature of the type, the spiritual substance and the intellect; and, finally, as we know from Revelation and can surmise from reason, the existence of myriads and tens of thousands of myriads of millions of angels, each one, according to St. Thomas, the angelic doctor, a species by himself. How beautifully and how charmingly is the principle carried out and the law kept in the hypothesis we are maintaining!"

Adele.—"It is beautiful, indeed, and I feel my mind and heart glowing with admiration and delight!"

Doctor.—"But there is another cosmological law which goes to prove the same thing. This is called the law of proportion and affinity, which is to be found governing the different creatures or species of the universe."

George.—" I partly guess what you mean, doctor, but I would like to hear it fully explained."

Doctor.—"We have to follow up the train of thought which has occupied us till now to understand that law. We have said that God's wisdom is obliged to create a variety of species in order to express the immensity and infinity of his nature and attributes. As a painter who has a vast design in his mind cannot reproduce it on canvas without a variety of objects and colors, likewise God cannot express the unutterable magnitude of His grandeur without a variety of creatures. Very well; but a variety of creatures or species or kingdoms, as we may call them, each one, so to speak, reproducing a side of that immense grandeur, must needs be reduced to unity; because the type and model which they must express is not a conglomeration or assortment of different aspects, but an infinite nature eminently one and simple. That variety must, then, be brought into unity. How can that be obtained? One of the laws which paves the way to that unity in the species of creation is that of affinity or proportion, that is to say, that, though the species are manifold and different, the extremes of each species must be softened down so as to gradually and insensibly diminish the variety and contrast between them and make way for the unity."

Adele.—"I think I catch the idea, but an example will make it clear to my mind."

Doctor.—"Take the species of the universe, such as they appear to us, and you will apprehend the law. The first kingdom which appears to us is the inorganic; the one above is the organic; the movement in the first originates in an external agent; in the latter, the movement is interior and spontaneous; the contrast is too great between those kingdoms or species. How to soften it down? By the creation of some species which acts like a link between them, or rather which serves as a shading down the extremes of each; this we find in the family of fungi or mushroom, the nature of which has not been ascertained, scientists being uncertain whether to classify it among the inorganic or the organic. Again: take the organic or living world and the sensible; there is certainly a hiatus, a gulf between them, too far apart to be crossed over, there being between pure internal movement and sensation an immense difference. The great and wise Creator has softened down the extremes of each by placing between them the species polypus, sponge, coral, which act as mediators between the purely organic kingdom and the sensitive. Scientists, again, cannot determine whether those families are plants or animals. Now, go a little further, between a sensitive being and a spiritual nature there is an immense difference. To soften down that contrast God has made man, who is the link between pure sensitive beings and a spiritual substance. That is, the law of affinity or proportion which obtains in the universe, and must also obtain in every work of art composed of different and varied elements. If a musician were to produce a composition made up of different parts, one succeeding the other, he would produce something jarring on, and distressing to, our ear, something disconnected, a number of parts having nothing at all to do with each other, in fact no parts at all; because a part to be such must be proportionate and subject to the whole."

George.—"Well, that law is certainly true and necessary, but I cannot see how it proves the existence of spiritual substances united to a body in the starry heavens?"

Doctor.—"One moment, yet, and you will see it. The world next to man's is the angelic. This we know for certain, from Revelation. But, as I have already intimated, reason surmises it. Now, a comparison between the intellect of the lowest angel and the highest human genius will solve the difficulty. Do you know, George, what is the real difference between these great men we call geniuses and common intellects?"

George.—"That is rather a difficult question to answer."

Adele.—"I think I can see the difference, but I have never explicitly accounted for it."

Doctor.—"The following qualities accompany the intellect of the genius: It is sublime, it is vast and comprehensive, it is penetrating and profound, but, above all, it is more or less intuitive with the rapidity of lightning. It is sublime. There are, in every science, truths and principles intrinsically high, such, for instance, as the infinitesimal Calculus in mathematics, the laws determining the different orbits of the planets in astromony, etc. The discovery of such truths is above the reach of common intellects, and such truths are, with difficulty, apprehended by such, after being discovered. But just such truths form the natural atmosphere of the genius; it lives, it breathes, it revels in them. They are its natural horizon. It is vast and comprehensive; it can perceive and apprehend a truth in all its magnitude and proportions. It is penetrating and profound. The glance of the genius searches, scrutinizes, digs, burrows, till it has seen the truth to its very depth, and sounded it to its very bottom. But, above all, it is intuitive. What men, endowed with fair parts, can see painfully and slowly, and, as it were, piecemeal, part after part, and after a long, difficult and hard reasoning, the genius sees at a glance and discovers its remotest consequences. Analogies, relations of things, very faint and imperceptible to other minds, are inspiration to him. It seems endowed with vision and divination. Finally, it is tenacious, it apprehends with a force, an energy, a grasp which nothing can surpass, and follows it up with a belief, a confidence, a trust, a resolution so strong, so firm, so unshaken as to cause miracles. Take an example—Napoleon the Great. It is on the field of battle—one of those pitched battles, in which tens of thousands are engaged on every side, is going on. The day seems to be going against the French. Napoleon, from an eminence, with an eye-glass, is surveying the whole field, remaining immovable and impassible. When all at once a thought flashes upon his mind. It electrifies him. He gives a few orders to his staff; they rush to communicate his commands; the orders are carried out, the battle is decided in favor of the great captain. In that thought, with the rapidity of lightning, he has seen all the movements of the enemy, guessed his intentions and his designs, has penetrated the whole plan of battle, has discovered its defects, has perceived the simplest and most energetic means to defeat that plan, and turn its defect in his favor—has given his orders with the clearness and energy; they are executed, the thing is done. There is the genius."

George.—"Excellently explained, doctor."

Doctor.—"Well, I want you to understand that one of these great geniuses, who must have had the consciousness of the immense loftiness and power of his intellect, has asserted, and his assertion may well be taken for granted, that between the intellect of the highest and loftiest human genius, and the intellect of the first angel next to us, there is an immense difference, as great and vast a difference as that which exists between the highest human intellect and that of a clownish, dull, uneducated peasant."

Adele.—"Who said that, uncle?"

Doctor.—St. Thomas. He hesitated not to assert that the difference between the highest human genius and the angel next to us is as great as that between the highest genius and a poor ignorant peasant. If we had time to study the nature and properties of angels, you would soon see that the statement is by no means exaggerated."

George.—"Well, doctor, what do you conclude from that statement?"

Doctor.—"I infer that there is too great a contrast between man and the angels, that the difference is too great, too deep, too vast, too discordant, so to speak; that it should, according to the law of affinity and proportion, be smoothed, softened down, that the extremes ought to be somewhat approached and brought together. And this can only be done by filling the starry heavens with spiritual substances attached to a body, the intellect of which substances, whilst surpassing that of the highest genius, may approach nearer and nearer that of the angel, and thus to keep the harmony of the creation and the unity of the universe."

Adele.—"I see now the whole drift of our argument, and I can perceive the whole universe, as it were, at a glance. It seems to rise up before my mind in the huge proportions of an immense pyramid, with the special circumstance that this, in opposition to all other pyramids, begins with a narrow base and enlarges as it rises up to the summit. I see at its base the immense world of inorganic matter, and next, the still vaster kingdom of organic matter, but between them some species which softens the two extremes. Higher up I see the whole animal world composed of numberless species, one more perfect than the other; then next, far up. I see a gleam of the spiritual substances, but between them I admire the existence of the mediator between the animal and the intelligent substance—man. Between man and the purely intellectual being, I perceive now an immense number and variety of intelligent substances scattered all over the starry heavens in the colossal worlds, floating in space in the far distant depths, substances united to a kind of material body, one species higher than another, and the next higher and much higher, till we almost grasp the summit occupied in boundless, immense, colossal proportions, by purely intellectual substance, one loftier, more exalted, more sublime, more soaring than the other, till we penetrate to the very highest and sublimest, which almost reaches the throne of the Infinite, but yet an infinite and insurmountable distance. Oh, how grand is God's work!"

THIRTY-FOURTH ARTICLE.

THE PLURALITY OF WORLDS IN HARMONY WITH CHRISTIAN REVELATION.

Adele.—"The opinion, the probability of which we have endeavored to demonstrate, has moved to the very depth all the instincts of my poetical nature. The harmonies of song and praises to the great Creator of all things, raised upon all the points of space from myriads of intellectual creatures, seem to linger on my ear and fill my heart with transport and enthusiasm. There is a philosophy of the heart as well as a philosophy of the mind, and the former fully convinces me that that opinion is true. I am only waiting for the proof how that opinion in no way contravenes any tenet of Catholic faith, and I will cling to it with all my heart."

George.—"I will follow you."

Doctor.—"Let us examine, then, the perfect accord of that opinion with the Christian Revelation. And, to be brief, I may as well say that the only dogma with which that opinion must be proved to accord is the mystery of the Incarnation and Redemption. George, do you know of anything which seems to be jarring against the mystery of the Incarnation in the plurality of worlds?"

George —"I do. In the first place, we have said that, supposing that opinion to be true, we may admit the existence of numberless intellectual substances, loftier and more sublime than man's intellect. Now, it seems to me that if the Son of God was to take up a soul and a body and unite both to His infinite Person, it would have been more befitting that He should take them from among the myriads of those noble productions existing in the starry heavens than to select a human soul and body."

Doctor.—"Why?'

George.—"I don't know exactly why; but, it appears to me, that He should choose among the best, and the noblest."

Adele.—"In that case He should have been united to the best angelic spirit."

Doctor.—"There is some truth about Adele's remark; but we will notice it by and by. Your remark, George, proceeds from a want of due consideration and reflection. Let us, for a moment, suppose it to be true; let us admit that the Son of God, willing to unite to Himself a created nature in the unity of this Divine Person, were obliged, by reason of fitness, to choose the very best that could be produced, we may inquire further is there such a thing as a creature, the very best which can be created? Is such a thing possible? On reflecting upon the question you will find that such a thing, as a creature the very best possible, is an impossibility."

Adele.—"Why, I cannot see the reason."

George.—"Nor I."

Doctor.—"It is easily explained. Allow, for a moment, the possibility of producing a creature, the very best; after all, it would only be a finite being."

George.—"Certainly; otherwise, how could it be a creature?"

Doctor.—"And can you put a limit to the perfecting of a finite being?"

George.—"By no means; though, the creature being finite, can never reach the infinite, yet it is capable of an indefinite, unceasing, interminable bettering and progress. The creature or the finite is like number. Though number can never reach the infinite, yet it is always capable of further addition, and there is no number to which we cannot add another unit and make it greater than the preceding one."

Doctor.—"Your reasoning is perfect, George; but it only proves you with mathematical evidence how the best creature possible is an impossibility and a contradiction. After we have imagined, in the highest flight of fancy, a creature gifted with the highest perfections and endowments, we could always imagine a better one."

Adele.—"Well, gentlemen, and what do you infer from this beautiful reasoning?"

Doctor.—"That George's assertion that it was befitting that the Son of God, wishing to unite to Himself a created nature, should choose the best and the noblest, proves too much, and therefore proves nothing at all. A creature, the best possible, is not supposible, as it cannot be produced. Therefore, the Son of God, in wishing to unite Himself to a created nature, was perfectly free to choose whatsoever nature He pleased."

George —"I perceive it now."

Doctor.—"The Son of God was not bound to choose the best, and could select any created nature He pleased. The only reasons of fitness which we can discover in the mystery of the Incarnation must be determined and drawn from the end which He freely proposed to Himself in wanting to assume a created nature to the dignity of a personal union with Him. If we investigate and find out what object God had in view, in assuming a created nature, we shall see the fitness of every detail and particular of that mystery."

Adele.—"I see perfectly. God being necessarily free to select any created nature to the unutterable dignity of a personal union with Him, it follows, as a necessary consequence, that the only way to know and to admire the nature, qualities, details, particulars of that mystery, is to inquire what was the object He had in view in assuming a created nature. It is only after having ascertained that object that we can study the fitness, seemliness and appropriateness of everything connected with it."

Doctor.—"Bravo, Adele. You have a very quick perception."

George.—"Let us, then, with all proper respect and reverence, investigate the end for which the Son of God determined to unite to Himself a created nature."

Doctor.—"The end is one, and yet manifold. First, it was to raise, to elevate, to exalt the whole universe in all its component species to a dignity actually infinite, and thus to solve the problem of creation. You need not start, Adele; I am going to explain. In our last conversation we said that God, to express His infinite nature and perfections was obliged to create a variety of species differing from each other, and yet all conspiring to exhibit a perfect whole by being moulded into unity by the laws of affinity and connection. The variety expressed the immense proportions and vastness of the type, the unity, the oneness, and simplicity of the same. The other laws fitted part into part, and made all conspire to exhibit a harmonious whole. But say what you will, the copy beautiful, magnificent, sublime, lofty, wondrous, as it may be of the infinite type, is only a finite sketch, faint picture, a distant reproduction, a shadowy portrait of that model. Still that copy could never be infinite in its nature and substance, otherwise it would no longer be a creature. What does the infinite wisdom of God devise, and His infinite condescension and goodness effect? The copy cannot be infinite in its essence and substance, said God's wisdom. Well, let it be infinite by a personal union with the type. Therefore was the union of the Son of God with a created nature decreed. But what created nature shall be chosen? What is the object to be attained? The divinization of the universe. Therefore a nature shall be chosen which recapitulates all the species of the universe; that is, a nature consisting of a spiritual substance united to a material body—the human nature which abridges in itself all created species, as it partakes of existence with inorganic beings, of life with the organic, of sensation with the animals, and is a spiritual substance like the angels. Hence, you see, Adele, why the Son of God could not have united to Himself the angelic nature. He would, by doing so, have excluded from the universal exaltation all creatures and species inferior to spiritual substances. We have seen, already, that He was not bound to assume the best and the noblest spiritual substance united to a body. Therefore, you see, that by assuming human nature, He has ennobled and divinized all the species of the universe, inorganic species, living species, sensitive species, spiritual substances of any degree, united to any kind of material body, and pure intellectual substances like the angels."

Adele.—"That is grand and sublime!"

Doctor.—"But mark wherein the best and loftiest of the aim in this universal divinization is to be found. I have already alluded to it, but it is well to put it in stronger and bolder relief. It was in order that God might be manifested, known, esteemed, honored, praised, glorified, loved by His creation with a knowledge, esteem, honor, love, fully and in every way adequate to His desert. An infinite intellect and an infinite will in the person of the Word of God are united by a personal bond to human nature the recapitulation of the universe. The whole universe, then, as it were, is illumined by an infinite intellect, governed and swayed by an infinite will; it throbs with the throbs of an infinite heart, and knows, and acknowledges, and esteems, and loves and praises, and worships its Creator with an infinite acknowledgment, love and subjection. That is the aim of the Incarnation. All that was realized by the Son of God becoming man. That is the whole Christian system and religion in a nutshell."

George.—"Dear me, I never knew my religion before this."

Adele.—"Nor I. Would to God that all men could understand it. Who could resist such grandeur, such loftiness and such wondrous beauty and loveliness!"

Doctor.—"Mark well, the union of the Son of God terminated in the human nature, not in any human personality. Hence, the universe in Christ has been elevated and divinized as to its species, inasmuch as they are represented by the human nature which was assumed. But how to raise the universe as to the personalities composing it? All individual persons, in order to partake in a certain degree of that sublimation and divinization are called upon to enter in personal communication and contact with Christ. This union, though real and most intimate, of course, is not the same as that existing between the human nature and the Word of God, because in the latter case the human nature subsists of the personality of the

Word and does not possess human personality; whereas, in the case of individual persons being united to Christ, this union must keep intact the personality of both terms united. Christ's personality and created personalities are to remain the same after the union. Hence the union we speak of between Him and created personalities is brought about by that great and supernatural force and agent called *grace*, which unites the created personalities to God in a most intimate manner, but leaves that personality whole and intact. Thus are created personalities enabled not only so as to exhibit one universe exalted and elevated in nature and persons, but shall attain also their own individual destiny and happiness. When Christ was on earth He associated to Himself certain persons whom He called Apostles, or messengers, and made them the living instruments for the realization of this union of created persons with Christ. This they have done and will do to the end of time by themselves and their successors. This grand and sublime living organism, which is to traverse centuries and generations to bring all created persons in union with Christ, is nothing less than Christ living in the Apostles, and through them bringing generation after generation into this grand union with Himself. Here we have, then, the whole universe in its species exalted in Christ and through Christ, raised to the summit of divinization; in its personalities called to come in contact with Christ, to personally partake of that sublimation. This was the plan of the Creator in order to make His works worthy of Him. Once this plan made and executed, no created personalites, be they angels, men, or inhabitants of the starry depths, can attain their end, except through this universe with Christ, the Sublimator of the universe."

George.—"Why?"

Doctor.—"Because the end of every individual personality must be subject to and moulded after the end of the universe. This is attained by a personal union with the Word of God, the second Person of the ever Blessed Trinity; therefore, every individual person must be joined to this union with Christ. Moreover, the nature of every personality of the universe, as represented in the human nature of Christ, is already in personal communication with Him. It would mar the whole plan; it would be incongruous if the personalities of those natures represented were not to be brought in contact with the Sublimator. We men are already, in a certain sense, connected with Christ; the tie of a common nature exists already between us. The same may be said of all other personalities of the universe. It is, therefore, befitting that we should not attain our own individual completion and destiny, except in and through that union."

Adele.—"Let me see if I understand the whole plan. God, in His infinite goodness, wanted to make the universe an infinite expression of Himself, at least by union. His divine Word, the infinite expression of his grandeur, came to reside in the universe by uniting to Himself the human nature in the bond of His own personality, and thus He divinized the whole universe, inasmuch as human nature represented all its existing species. The universe, then, was divinized, but only in its specific nature. Individual personalities were left out. These are called to come in contact and communication with Christ, and thus are enabled to partake of the universal sublimation. Without this union or contact with Christ, no sublimation for created personalities, no attaining of their ultimate destiny can be possible. The means of bringing all personalities into this union is Christ Himself, with all persons already associated with Him traversing centuries and generations; in other words, the Holy Catholic Church."

George.—"Excellent, Miss Adele. Then, doctor, if I understand you right, if they be inhabitants in the stars they cannot attain their destiny except by being united with Christ?"

Doctor.—"Certainly not. He has Himself said: 'None comes to the Father but by Me' (St. John). There is no exception made, none; neither angels nor men nor any other personality can attain their destiny except in and through Christ, the Mediator and Divinizer of the universe. As you know, in the case of us men, Christ not only raised us, but in consequence of the fall of our first parents, redeemed us from sin and all its consequence, reconciled us with God by paying with His blood and His life the ransom of our redemption. Of course we cannot tell how the case stands with other inhabitants of the heavens. Whatever may be their condition, the following truths must be held about them: First, they, like all other created personalities, must come in communion with Christ in order to partake of the sublimation of the whole universe, and in order to be able to reach their everlasting destiny. There is no exception for any one. Christ is the door; if any enters through it he shall be saved; if he does not, he cannot reach his destiny; he is a member out of joint, separate, astray, forsaken, and forming no part of the sublime harmony of the universe. Vae soli! Second, those inhabitants of the stars, one may easily surmise, were created by God and raised like our first parents to a personal union with Him, in view and for the sake of Christ, and their truth and fidelity put to a test and trial. Now, we may make a twofold supposition. They fell, or they stood the trial bravely and unscathed. If they stood, it was through the grace of Christ; if they fell, they needed redemption, like us, and when Christ died and paid the ransom of our redemption, He included them also in that ransom, the value of which was infinite and capable of redeeming innumerable worlds."

Adele.—"I understand all that very well. But when and how did those inhabitants of the heavens come to know Christ and to enter into union with Him ?"

Doctor.—'Of course, we cannot determine that. Christ, after His ascension, may Himself have brought the knowledge of Himself, and His Church to them, or He may have used any of the numberless means at His disposal to call them into union with Him and His Church. What is absolutely certain is, that if there be intelligent inhabitants in those worlds we are speaking of they were, like all things, made for Christ and after Christ and in view of Christ ; that they, in order to attain their ultimate destiny, must come in supernatural union with Christ; that if they enjoyed, like man, this union in anticipation before Christ actually appeared on this earth and were faithful to it they owe this constancy and fidelity to the grace of Christ. If they fell, they were included in our redemption, and were made partakers of this redemption and restored to the grace and friendship of God by Christ through any means which in His infinite wisdom He may have seen fit to adopt."

Adele.—"It is grand ; it is wondrously enchanting. The whole universe in everyone of its natures is united to Christ the Mediator, and thus it is raised to an infinite dignity and worth, and can fittingly and adequately represent its Creator. All created personalities, angels, men, inhabitants of the starry heavens are all called, to be united to the Mediator, and in Him and through Him, not only perfect the sublimation of the universe, but attain their own individual, eternal destiny. Truly through Christ and in Christ all created personalities from every point of heaven where angels dwell, from every spot of the infinite worlds stretching in space, from our own little insignificant speck, can sing to their Creator a canticle of praise, of adoration, of exultation, of delight, of complacency, of thanksgiving, of glory, fully and in every way adequate and befitting His infinite and immense grandeur, because they sing it in Christ, and through Christ their truth, way and life, and God cannot but be pleased with them. No words can fully express the sublimity and loftiness of such thoughts, we may as well be hushed and contemplate in unutterable silence such works. They brook no human utterance; but in the stillness of our soul we can feel the more keenly and more exquisitely their harmonies and divine music.

THIRTY FIFTH ARTICLE.
WHAT IS A MIRACLE ?

Doctor.—"We have hitherto compared the truths of Revelation with nearly all natural sciences, with geology, history, paleontology, biology, astronomy, and so forth, and we have invariably discovered that no conflict of any kind exists between those truths and the real facts and results of all those different sciences. We have to approach now another science, and compare its real results and laws with certain facts and statements of Revelation, with a view of studying whether any conflict exists between them. This science is physics, or natural philosophy."

Adele.—"And what are the statements and facts of Revelation which appear to conflict with natural philosophy?"

Doctor.—"Miracles, those supernatural facts which have been hunted down—by modern scientists especially—with an animus, a hatred, a rage, anything but honorable either to their intellect or indicative of that honesty, calmness, sincerity and impartiality, which one should naturally expect from a class who monopolize the good name of scientists."

George.—"I am glad we have come to this part of our discussion. I expect to have my notions and ideas set right and elucidated."

Doctor.—"I intend to discuss this question quite at some length in order to satisfy every possible objection which has been raised against miracles, and to put the subject in such clear, bold, unmistakable light as to leave no pretext or loophole against it."

Adele.—"What will be the first and principal questions connected with the subject?"

Doctor.—"In the first place we must inquire into the real idea of miracles; in other words, what does Revelation mean by a miracle? George, what do you understand by a miracle?'

George.—"I can easily give the general and etymological signification of the word miracle; but I am not quite sure that I can go much farther."

Adele.—"Let us hear."

George.—"The word miracle in its most general acceptation and meaning signifies something which surprises and astonishes, from the Latin *miraculum*, something to be startled at, which excites wonder and admiration. This wonder may be caused either by the grandeur and proportions of the phenomenon itself, or be produced by the rarity of its apparition."

Doctor.—"Very good, George; and in common language, anything which implies the presence of a great force or ability takes the name of magnificent and wonderful. Hence we hear of the miracles of genius, the miracles of industry, the miracles of arts, the miracles of eloquence, the miracles of poetry, etc. Also we speak of the miracles of nature, the miracles of germination, of fecundity, of light, of attraction; in fact, in this sense, as St. Augustine has remarked, the entire creation is a universal miracle."

Adele.—"But, I presume, you are not speaking now of the miracle in its strict and proper acceptation ?"

Doctor.—"No; we are taking the word miracle in its vague and common acceptation. To make you understand what is meant by a miracle in its strict and proper sense, I want you to observe that a phenomenon or a sensible effect may be supposed to be produced in two different ways; either by a force which God has created among the general forces of the universe expressly to produce it or by the immediate and direct action of God Himself. Take any natural fact as an instance of the theory; let us say a tree. We may suppose a tree to be able of being produced in two distinct ways either by the forces which God created, the seed, the earth, the light, the heat, and so forth ; or we may suppose it to be at once produced by the direct and immediate action of God Himself."

Adele.—"I understand that perfectly."

Doctor.—"Therefore, a sensible effect may be the result either of a permanent law, established by the Creator, when He made the universe, purposely to produce such effect; or it may be considered as the result of a free derogation of the law willed by the Lawgiver Himself. Mark well, both of you, we are not claiming now that such a distinction exists, and that these two classes and categories of facts are equally real; we are only affirming that we can at least perceive such a distinction, and we can represent to ourselves these two categories as being capable of forming the whole complexion of contingent facts. Once you understand and perceive that distinction you can easily understand what is meant by a miracle in its strict sense. We call miracles all the facts of the second category, that is, those facts which, having the Creator Himself as their immediate cause and agent, are beyond and above natural forces and the laws which govern them."

George.—"Then a miracle is a sensible phenomenon or fact, effected immediately and directly by God Himself, and for that reason, above and beyond all natural forces and the laws which govern these forces ?"

Doctor.—"Certainly."

Adele.—"Will you please to give me an example ?"

Doctor.—"We read of St. Vincent Ferrer, that on a certain occasion, passing by a building in the course of construction, he saw a poor workman fall from a high scaffold. The saint bade him, in the name of God, to stop from falling till he got permission from his superior to help him. The man was seen by a crowd of people stopping in midair till the saint returned. I see you smile, George."

George.—The saint might have helped him all at once, and make him fall without breaking any bones

Doctor.—"The saint, who was a great miracle worker, had been forbidden by his superior to perform any more miracles without permission. When he saw the man falling, his charity prompted him to rescue the poor man from death; but suddenly the command of his superior occurred to him, and therefore he instinctively bade the man to wait for him. When you are a little better acquainted with the lives of the saints, you will understand and appreciate that admirable union of the most heroic virtues, which enabled them to move mountains, coupled to a most childlike simplicity and unconsciousness of their worth, which made them obedient as children. But, at any rate, I am only mentioning the miracle as an instance to illustrate my theory. You see, Adele, the suspension of that man in mid-air, without any support whatever, is the result of an immediate and direct action of God; it is a phenomenon which cannot be accounted for by any law of nature; in fact it is beyond and above the laws of nature. According to the natural law of universal gravitation it should have fallen to the ground, subject to the laws of the fall of bodies—that is, with a speed advancing as the body comes near to the earth, instead of that body remained hanging without any support; no law of nature can do that."

Adele.—"I understand perfectly what a miracle is; that is, a sensible fact, immediately and directly produced by God above and beyond the forces which act in nature and the laws which govern them."

Doctor.—"Mark, then, every word of the definition. A miracle is a sensible phenomenon, that is, a fact which can be seen, handled by everyone possessed of the faculties of the senses of sight and of touch. We insist on that, not only to point out the sensible nature of the facts we are speaking of, but also in order to distinguish the miracle as a direct and immediate effect of God's action from other facts which are also the direct and immediate results of God's action, but may be spiritual in their nature, and therefore beyond the reach of the senses. For instance, when God illumines by His own immediate and direct action the intellect of man and inspires His will with strength and energy, this is also the direct result of God's action, and therefore beyond and above all the forces of nature, yet it is not, properly and strictly speaking, called a miracle, because it is an invisible and spiritual phenomenon. Then, in the second place, this phenomenon must be beyond the reach of the forces which act in nature and of the laws which govern them; in other words, it must be such a fact, which, considering its nature and all the circumstances which surround it, cannot be effected by any natural force or its laws. But observe, this may happen in two ways."

Adele.—"How?"

Doctor.—"A phenomenon may be above and beyond the energy of the natural forces in two ways: First, in itself, that is, considering its nature and substance; or, second, in the manner of its production, that is, considering how and in what manner it has been effected. The first is called a miracle of first order; the other a miracle of second order. A dead man is restored to life: it is a miracle of first order; because it is miraculous in its substance and in its own nature, since no force in nature can produce such a result. A man has a limb smashed; he is cured instantaneously and without any aid from medical art. This is a miracle of the second order, and as to its manner; because, though a fractured limb may naturally be cured, universal experience and physical certitude assure us that nature, left to itself, never repairs any injury in that manner, hence that effect is miraculous, not as to its nature and substance, but as to its mode of production."

George.—"The way you explained what a miracle is seems to be very easy and intelligible; and to smooth down difficulties which may arise in one's mind concerning miracles. That there may be a twofold class of facts or phenomena, the first the effect of the natural forces which God created, and the other the effect of His own immediate and direct action outside and beyond the natural order of things is certainly easy to be conceived and apprehended. I suppose that is the exact idea of a miracle according to the general doctrine of the Church ?"

Doctor.—"To be sure it is; and to remove all doubts or hesitation from you, I will quote the words of St. Thomas, preëminently *the* Doctor of the Church. In his 'Compendium' against the Gentiles he says: 'Only those facts should simply be called miracles, which are effected by God outside of the regular order of things.'—'Illa simpliciter miracula dicenda sunt quae *divinitus* praeter servatum ordinem in rebus fiunt' ('Contra Gentes,' 1, iii). Tell us now, George, everything which has been said against miracles."

George.—"In the first place, any number o. infidels, rationalists, and scientists ridicule and laugh at the very possibility of miracles. They maintain, that to suppose any fact or phenomenon to proceed from any but a natural cause is the height of folly and absurdity; so that some of them will not even condescend to argue the question and much less to bring forward any proofs for such alleged impossibility. They merely content themselves to affirm it, to take for granted that the thing is settled long ago in the mind of any reasonable man, and that any one believing otherwise must be a fool."

Adele.—"Many thanks for such liberal opinion."

George.—"Then many more go on to say: Granted for a moment that the miracle is possible, what have you gained by the admission ?

Why, a very sorry return for your credulity and your efforts. Because even admitting that possibility, it avails nothing for the end for which miracles have been invented."

Adele.—"Why?"

George.—"Because a miracle can never be ascertained; do what you will, there is no power on earth or in man to tell whether an effect or phenomenon is due to a Divine agency or to a natural cause."

Adele.—"I see, though, of course, I suspect there is a satisfactory answer to that."

Doctor.—"I rather think there is. Go on, George."

George.—"Our scientific friends go a step further in the case. Not only do they contend that a miracle cannot be really ascertained, that it is beyond man's power to do so, but they are sure that, as a matter of fact, no miracle has ever been ascertained. All the miracles spoken of in history or in the Scriptures, in the Old and New Testament, they consider as so many fables, legends that could not stand the least superficial examination and scrutiny of modern criticism. They must vanish under the blazing light of modern education and progress as the snow melts under the hot rays of the sun."

Doctor.—"You have condensed very accurately the errors of the enemies of miracles, and hence it appears evident how many questions we must discuss in order to thoroughly and completely sift the subject. The first problem, then, to be raised is—Are miracles possible? The next is—Can miracles be ascertained? The third question—As a matter of fact, has any miracle really been ascertained and acknowledged as such? We shall have to employ a whole conversation on each one of those questions and we may as well adjourn the present interview."

Adele.—'I beg your pardon, uncle, but I have a question which must be answered. George has said that scientists maintain that even if a miracle were admitted to be possible, it would not promote the object for which they have been invented Evidently, of course, God has an object in view when He performs a miracle. Now, I want to know what this object may be."

Doctor.—"I am glad you mentioned it, for it will give me an opportunity to point out the reason of the animus of scientists against the miracle. I will endeavor to explain that object as clearly as possible to facilitate your understanding of it. By that question you have raised the most important problem that can exist for man; the problem of the intercourse between him and his Maker. God has created the universe. He has also created man. He created the universe, its forces, and its laws, and the whole mundane order, to the end that, by all these things, He might speak to man of His infinite perfections and wondrous attributes. And man, by listening to this voice of the universe, comes to know somewhat of the inexhaustible grandeur of his Maker. The universe, then, is a means of communication between God and man; but it is a very unsatisfactory means, because it does not fill up the chasm between the Creator and man, nor does it bring the two terms of the communication really near each other, and much less in contact with each other. Now, suppose for a moment that the Creator does really wish to come in real, true, *bona fide* personal communication with man; and suppose, moreover, such a communication to be possible, how is God to make manifest His real descent and presence? Is there any clear, undoubted, infallible, unmistakable means whereby we may know that God is at hand? Remember that the usual and universal order of nature cannot officiate in such capacity, because, in that case, it would only be a question of the general, natural, usual communication between man and the Creator through the means of His work, and not a special sign of a real, true, personal contact. The sign, then, which would manifest God's real descent and presence, the infallible criterion that He would be at hand is the miracle, that is an effect or phenomenon above and beyond the created order of the universe, capable of being accounted for solely and exclusively by means of the Divine agency. This, then, is the end of the miracle. On the supposition that God wishes to enter with His intelligent creatures into personal relations and contact, He makes use of a miracle to signify His Divine Presence and action, so that when men see the sign they may exclaim instinctively and naturally, in the words of Pharaoh's magicians: 'The finger of God is here.'"

Adele.—"I understand, perfectly. The natural communication existing between God and man is not quite satisfactory, because it is only a communication by means of the works of the universe; it is like corresponding with one's friends by the means of some skillful work of their hands, neither more nor less. Now, suppose God wants to enter into real, immediate, true, personal relation and intercourse with His intelligent creatures, how will He manifest this propinquity and presence so that man may really say: I know with absolute certainty that God is here? The miracle, which can only be the direct, immediate effect of God, officiates in the capacity of this unerring, unmistakable means of exhibiting and manifesting God's presence."

Doctor.—"The end, then, of the miracle, is to manifest the propinquity, the advent, the presence of God, whenever He sees fit to descend into personal communication and contact with man."

George.—"But what need is there of a personal intercourse between God and man, and why should man not be content with that general, distant communication with his Maker by means of His works?"

Doctor.—"To give the reason why, would carry us too far; and such investigation does not properly and exactly enter within the limits of our interview. All I can tell you is, that mankind, at all times, in all places, in every age, has not been satisfied with the vague, meagre, distant intercourse which it can have with its Creator by means of His works. It has wanted more. It has wanted to have a true, real, immediate, personal relation with Him. This is proven by the general and constant fact that mankind, in every age, in all stages of civilization, has always prayed and offered up to God oblations and sacrifices, which demonstrates and puts in its most brilliant evidence that mankind craves after a personal, immediate intercourse with its Creator. Until your scientists have explained satisfactorily those two universal facts of prayer and sacrifices, we must take for granted the certainty not only of the possibility, but also of the reality of a supernatural, personal, immediate intercourse between God and man."

THIRTY-SIXTH ARTICLE.

IS THE MIRACLE POSSIBLE?

Adele.—"I suppose the subject of our conversation to day is the possibility of miracles?"

Doctor.—"To be sure, and as I want to thoroughly and completely discuss the subject, I will begin by saying that there are three distinct classes of opponents of the possibility of the miracle, Pantheists, Atheists and Deists. I presume you understand, Adele, what is meant by those three classes mentioned?"

Adele.—"Not at all."

Doctor.—"George, please to explain."

George.—"Pantheists are those who maintain that there does and can exist but one single substance, and that everything which has any existence at all is but the development and the unfolding and the modification of the same identical substance; in other words, that everything is but the necessary and indispensable modification of God; hence the name Pantheism, from *pan*, everything, and *theos*, God; everything is the necessary evolution of God. The upholders of such system explain it in a thousand ways, but the substance of all the systems may be declared as follows: there exists from all eternity something absolutely indefinite, indeterminate, vague, shadowy, in other words, infinite; that is to say, something neither really existing nor absolutely nothing, something neither substance nor accident, neither singular nor universal, neither matter nor spirit, because all those things imply some limit, boundary, determination, and this something is infinite. This something, infinitely vague, has an instinctive, necessary, irrepressible craving in its bosom to become something definite and determinate. After numberless successive evolutions and trials it becomes matter, as seen in the inorganic universe; then it assumes the form of life in the organic universe; afterwards, after many other efforts, it shoots into a sensitive life in the animal kingdom, and finally it rises up to intellectual life, to thought in man; but matter, organic life, sensitive life, intellectual life, are not something really and distinctly existing but the necessary development and forms which this Being-Nothing puts on in the struggles for development."

Adele.—"I see very well how the miracle in this system is impossible; because, as matter and the physical universe and the laws which govern it are the necessary, absolutely indispensable unfolding of this Being-Nothing, it is evident that everything must happen in constant, absolutely iron-bound manner, and no change, alteration, or exception is possible."

Doctor.—"Very good, Adele. And you see, also, that the miracle is impossible in the system of universal evolution, because that system is nothing better than Pantheism."

George.—"Atheism is the system of those who deny the existence of an infinite, intelligent free Being who has created the universe, but who hold that everything originates in one or more blind forces of that which they call nature."

Adele.—"Of course the miracle is impossible in that system as it holds that everything is done necessarily and blindly."

Doctor.—"In the beginning of these conversations we proved the existence of an infinite, supreme, intelligent, free Cause and Principle of the universe. Therefore we will pass by Pantheism and Atheism with that utter and supreme scorn which they deserve. Those two systems, though so tenderly and fondly caressed by the scientists of to-day and held in great veneration by the agnostics of the present time, imply nothing less than the utter annihilation of reason, the atrophy of all intellectual life, the actual extinction of all thought, and should be held up to ridicule and execration."

George.—"Remains the system of the Deists, that is, of those who acknowledge the existence of a supreme, intelligent, free Cause of the universe, who has created it and subjected it to certain fixed, immutable laws and order, but who after this can no longer interfere with His creation."

Doctor.—"These also maintain the impossibility of miracles, and condescend to give proofs for such alleged impossibility. But before we come to them I want to remark, that, in the eyes of an honest, conscientious, upright, dispassionate reason there is nothing more acceptable than the possibility of miracles. Because, once admit the existence of a supreme, infinite, intelligent free Cause who has created the universe, there is nothing more reasonable than that the same Cause should have the absolute and untrammelled control of the same universe and of the order He set upon it; and it seems to be the height of folly and absurdity to suppose that an Infinite Power, who was able to evoke that same universe from utter nothingness, should lose all control over it after creating it, nay, that it should be iron-bound, fastened hand and foot by the work which He has made and the laws He freely set upon them. This is so evident that even the most celebrated Deists have acknowledged it. Jean Jacques Rousseau wrote: 'Can God perform miracles? That question, if seriously treated, would be impious if it were not absurd. To punish one who should answer it negatively would be doing him too much honor. He should be sent to a madhouse.'"

Adele.—"The opinion of these gentlemen is truly laughable, if it were not profane. Why, it supposes the universe to say to God: 'It is true Thou hast created me from nothing, and many thanks for that; it is likewise true that if Thy Omnipotent hand did not uphold me every moment, I should return to that nothingness which presided at my birth; it is true that I cannot undergo the least possible movement or action without Thy own Omnipotent aid. All that is true; at the same time I must beg leave to remark that Thou hast no right whatever to interfere with the laws and order which it was Thy infinite pleasure to set over me. It is all good enough that I owe everything to Thee, but after all, too much interference is too much. Please to attend to other things and let me alone with the laws and order established over me. They are good enough for me.' Is this not the height of blasphemy, profanity and absurdity?"

George.—"Bravo, Miss Adele; an argument loses nothing by your handling."

Doctor.—"But they give reasons for their opinion, and we must examine and estimate them at their full value. The first reason they give is, according to them, out of respect to God's immutability and consistency. God, they urge, has established constant, immutable laws to preside over the physical order of the universe; He has chosen such order; He has willed it, and for you to come with the supposition that He can alter, change, disturb, upset, turn topsy-turvy that order and harmony, is to suppose that God can change this will and His purpose; it is to attribute to Him inconstancy and fickleness. Therefore your opinion and not ours is a profanity and absurdity."

Adele.—"We must then examine if it be true that a miracle argues a change in God's will and purpose?"

Doctor.—"That is our first inquiry. What do you think, George? does a miracle necessarily imply a change in the Creator?"

George.—"I am sure it does not."

Adele.—"How do you explain it?"

George.—"Because the miracle does not exhibit any of the elements of a change. When do we say that a man has changed his mind, his purpose, or his action? We will take as an example a legislator. Suppose a legislator, after all proper deliberation and examination, emanates a law. The law is carried into effect, and instead of procuring for the citizen and for the public utility and order that advantage which the legislator intended and expected, it produces the contrary effect. The legislator waits a sufficient time to test it thoroughly, and finally, convinced of the deleterious effects of the law, by another act revokes and abolishes it and substitutes another law. That is what I call a change; first, the will, the purpose, and the enactment of a certain act. Then the reconsidering of such an act, and the final determination to revoke such an act and the actual revocation. The legislator reconsiders his act, and takes it back and substitutes a different act. That is a change. Now, is that necessarily the case as to miracles? Certainly not. I see no necessity of any change; because the miracle, as I understand it now, is the exception to a general rule. Now the exception, instead of implying a change in the general rule, only confirms and strengthens the rule. Hence the working of a miracle is the right which God must necessarily reserve to Himself, of willing and of performing, exceptions by and in the same will with which He establishes the rule. Let us follow up the example of a legislator. He enacts a law, but at the same time and by the same will by which he establishes the law, he wills all the exceptions which he may see fit to make in future and in given cases. This power is implied in the very nature of a legislator or principle of the law, and it would be absurd to ask that the legislator should not contemplate it and have it in view when enacting law. Does it, then, follow that when the legislator does actually make an exception to the law in a given case he changes his mind and his purpose? Does it follow that his action is open to the charge of mutability and fickleness of purpose? By no manner of means."

Doctor.—"It is exactly the case as to miracles. God, in establishing the general laws of nature and the order of the universe, by the same act and at the same time willed all the exceptions which He saw fit to make for His own infinite, all-wise ends. Who can accuse Him of change and of fickleness of purpose?"

Adele.—"And this end was, as we said, to show His actual, true, immediate presence to His intelligent creatures whenever He saw fit. Hence, God enacted all the physical laws of nature, and made them constant and immutable; but at the same time and in the same will He ordained those occasional exceptions which should indicate unmistakably and infallibly His real and immediate presence to His intelligent creatures. The miracle, therefore, implies not even the shadow of change in the Creator."

Doctor.—"But our opponents allege a second reason why the miracle should be impossible. What is it, George?"

George.—"I suppose you allude to the argument which they draw from the constancy and immutability of the laws of nature?"

Doctor.—"Exactly."

George.—"Well, they say: You will acknowledge that the laws which govern the physical universe are constant and immutable. That very fact must exclude all possibility of a change, a break, an alteration or disturbance. Now, what is the miracle but a change and a disturbance, a break in the laws of nature? Granted, then, the constancy of the physical laws governing the universe, the miracle is an impossibility."

Doctor.—"This argument is the greatest arm in the hands of our opponents; it is believed to be unassailable and unanswerable, and yet it is one of the silliest arguments which can be brought forward."

George.—"How, d'tor? I believe it can be answered. At the same time I must own that I have always thought it to be one of the strongest against our subject."

Doctor.—"When we are through with it you will yourself acknowledge the truth of my statement. The whole difficulty depends on the question: What is meant by physical laws? What are they? What is their nature? When we have discussed that you will see the silliness of your strong objection. Your friends, the scientists, seem to regard all the physical agents of the universe as so many galley-slaves fastened, each one of them, hand and feet, to a strong iron chain. If one of them is to be liberated the chain must be broken or cut asunder. They imagine each body or natural agent to be so bound down to the production of its phenomenon by the law which governs it, that if it does not, the law is broken, altered, changed, disturbed, and sent to the four winds of heaven. Now, is such the fact? By no manner of means. Why? Because, according to all natural philosophers, to all physicists of every kind, the best and the *élite* amongst these being foremost, it has been demonstrated that, what are called laws of the physical universe, by no manner of means exist in the bodies or physical agents."

Adele.—"I do not apprehend very clearly."

Doctor.—"Let us take an example—the law of gravitation. This law implies that all bodies on this earth gravitate or are drawn by some hidden force to the centre of the earth. This law is universal and applies to the whole universe. As a stone, a pebble, an atom is drawn towards the centre of the earth, so do the planets in our solar system gravitate towards the sun, and so forth of the other systems in the heavens. Now, it is acknowledged by all physicists that though bodies act under, and are subject to this law, this rule or guide or force or whatever you may call it, does not exist either in each single body nor in the whole of them. It is outside and independent of those agents which are subject to it."

Adele.—"And what follows from that?"

Doctor.—"Various most important consequences. In the first place, if the law does not exist or proceed from the nature of the body which is subject to it, it follows that if in any given case it is not applied to it, it does not affect in the least its nature, nor does any violence to its properties. Secondly, this rule or mode of acting of the physical agents, called law, being really nothing else than the idea of it in the mind of the Creator and the will in Him to have it so carried out, remains in its generality and universality absolutely the same immutable, unchangeable constant, when in a given case it is not applied to a certain physical agent. Because, as it is evident, the law, as conceived in the Creator's mind and willed by Him remains just the same as it was notwithstanding, and in spite of its non-application in a given special case. If God does not apply, for instance, the law of gravitation to a certain body, does it follow that He has abolished or broken the general rule, that bodies should gravitate and be drawn to larger bodies?"

Adele.—"I conceive perfectly now. A natural law is not a chain to which a body is fastened in its action, so that if it does not act, or act in a contrary way, the chain must be broken. A natural law is that mode or rule of action, for bodies as it is in the mind of the Creator, and as it is ordained by His will. If an exception is made, that is, if a certain body in a given case fails to act, or acts in a sense contrary to the law, the latter is not broken nor suspended nor abolished; because that general mode or norm or rule of action for all physical agents remains the same unchangeable and inviolable in the mind and will of the Creator."

Doctor.—"Why, George, under man's actions and instruments all physical laws are contravened millions of times a day. Such is the force of the spirit over matter that it can analyze, divide the forces of nature, unite them in different combinations, and produce effects which could never be produced by the various forces employed, effects oftentimes contrary to those which they would naturally have brought forth. And does that suspend, alter, abolish, abrogate any law of nature?"

George.—"I am perfectly satisfied that the objection is a silly one. But there is another to which we must pay our respects now. It is alleged that physical certitude depends entirely on the constancy and permanence of the laws of the physical universe. To contravene such laws is to throw disorder among them, and consequently to cause the whole fabric of physical certitude to totter and to fall. Once we admit that a physical law may be suspended in a given case, a doubt is thrown over all cases; we can no longer be certain whether the law has been carried out or not in all other cases. Hence we are no longer certain about the existence and causes of physical phenomena."

Doctor.—"Does or does not man suspend the effects of some physical agents when he takes hold of those forces, combines them with others, and produces other and oftentimes contrary effects? And does that shake the foundation of physical certitude? Moreover, I will grant that if the miracles became too numerous and almost constant; if the exception became the rule, then the objection would hold; because in that case we could no longer be certain about the causes of physical phenomena. But an exception in a myriad of millions of cases can only confirm the rule. A lame man is made to walk, a blind man to see, a dead man to rise up, at the command of God. Will all these miracles prevent the sun from rising in the morning, or to laying down in the evening? Will they prevent all other natural causes from going on, and producing their natural result? Assuredly not."

Adele.—"The miracle, then, is possible because it does not imply as alleged, any change or mutation in God, since when God established the laws of nature He decreed at the same time the exceptions He should carry out, whenever He saw fit, to give evidence of His immediate presence and to connect the physical with the moral world. The miracle is possible because it does not imply any violence to physical forces or agents, as physical laws do not exist in bodies, but are the rule of their action as seen and willed by the Creator. Hence, no law is broken when a suspension of the action of a physical agent, in a given case, occurs to make room for God's immediate action. The miracle is possible because it does by no means disturb the general order of nature, since it is not so multiplied as to convert the exception into rule and the rule into an exception. God, then, can descend to establish personal communication and intercourse with His intelligent creatures; and the infallible sign is the miracle which bears on his forehead the inscription: 'Deus ecce Deus.'

THIRTY-SEVENTH ARTICLE.
CAN A MIRACLE BE ASCERTAINED?

George.—"You have demonstrated the possibility of a miracle, say our opponents; well, much good may it do to you. We are sure that a miracle can never be ascertained or found out to be such. Consequently you have thrown away your time in proving that which is of no avail in the present question. For, suppose we grant you that a miracle is possible, you are exactly where you were before for all practical purposes; because it is impossible to ascertain when a fact or phenomenon is really a miracle."

Adele.—"And why cannot the miracle be ascertained? I presume your great scientists have good reasons to be so highly confident."

George.—"To be sure they have."

Doctor.—"Before we enter upon the discussion in downright earnest, I want you to understand the real state of the question. The opponents of the miracle maintain that it is impossible to ascertain, to discover, to recognize a miracle. Well, let us at first inquire where this impossibility may be supposed to lie. Now, this impossibility may happen to be in the material fact and phenomenon itself, as being something so strange and different from other natural phenomena as not to be capable of being recognized."

Adele.—"I understand."

Doctor.—"Or this impossibility may be found, not in the real nature of the phenomenon, but in the disposition of our minds against it, which is perfectly natural to a certain extent."

Adele.—"I don't understand that."

Doctor.—"A miracle is a phenomenon which contravenes some law of nature. The general disposition and bias of our minds is to expect all natural agents to produce the effects which they are intended to bring about. There is in our minds, then, a general predisposition to assume for granted that natural causes will always produce their effects; hence, a bias in the same mind against anything strange, unusual, disturbing or contravening the action of natural agents."

Adele.—"I see; the general settled conviction of our minds that natural agents will go as they should, naturally creates a bias against anything seemingly contrary to that."

Doctor.—"Very good: finally this impossibility of ascertaining the miracle may fall on that which really causes the miracle. We have said that a miracle is an effect of the direct and immediate action of God. Now, we may suppose that the impossibility of ascertaining a miracle may fall exactly on that; in other words, it may be out of our power to really and truly ascertain that it is God Who acts and not some occult natural cause. Briefly, in order to come to a conclusion whether a miracle can be ascertained or not, we must examine the following questions: First. Is the real material make-up of the miraculous phenomenon in the way of our ascertaining its miraculous nature? Second question. Is the natural bias which the human mind has against any contravention of the regular usual course of nature such as not to be capable of being overcome, so that the mind may be truly convinced of a miraculous event? Third question. Is it really impossible to discover with certainty if a phenomenon proceed from the direct and immediate agency of the Almighty, so as not to be attributable to a hidden, unknown natural force or law? These three questions must be thoroughly discussed in order to make out our point that a miracle is really and truly capable of being ascertained. Let us begin from the first."

Adele.—"I don't see any difficulty about the first question."

George.—"Don't you?"

Adele.—"Certainly not. The question is: Is there anything about the material, sensible fact or its material surroundings which may be in the way of, or form an obstacle to, our recognizing it? I say no; for it seems to me that the material fact which forms the groundwork of the miracle is of the same nature as any other sensible phenomenon of the universe, and therefore to be easily ascertained by the same means by which we come to a knowledge of all natural phenomena."

Doctor.—"You are right, Adele, for a miraculous fact falls under the observation of our senses as every fact in the universe. Hence it may be seen, touched and handled, so to speak. An example will put the thing in its boldest light. Let us suppose the resurrection of a dead man: I have a friend; I have seen him a hundred times, a thousand times; I have conversed with him and pressed his hand. Surely none would dream of refusing me the power of being able to ascertain such fact and to be certain of it. On an evil day I have seen that same friend attacked by a dangerous sickness; I have seen him grow worse and worse, and finally I have seen him dead. I have been present at his last hour and received his last sigh; it was useless to indulge in any vain illusion; it was useless to keep him with me for three or four days in the forlorn hope that his death might be apparent, that he might be under an attack of lethargy; it was of no avail for me to put off the day of burial; for a horrible decomposition manifested itself, so as to preclude all possibility of doubt as to his real death. Could anyone be so unreasonable as to refuse me the capacity and power of ascertaining this fact? Under the plea that a lethargy may oftentimes cause one to appear dead, can anyone shake my conviction in the certainty of death before that body which is falling apart through putrefaction and decay? Here, then, are two facts: My friend, once glowing with life, and his certain death, which can be ascertained and verified like all other facts. Here is a third fact: A man comes, he offers prayers alongside of that corpse, and lifting up his eyes to heaven, cries out: 'Arise, in God's name.' I am present at the scene, and I behold my friend rising up full of life, of vigor, of strength and of force. 'It is he, it is he himself,' I exclaim, when I am recovered from my astonishment. 'I see his face, his lineaments, his carriage, his walk.' Can anyone deny the possibility of my ascertaining and recognizing my old friend, whom I have known ever so long, since our earliest childhood, and of speaking to him and by touching him ask him the question, "Is it you? is it you yourself?" Now I would beg to know, in these three different aspects of the same miraculous fact, what is there invisible, impalpable, problematic, mysterious? I have seen my friend in life, I have wept over him dead, I have to my great joy seen him alive again. Upon which of these three faces and sides of the same fact falls this pretended impossibility of my ascertaining it? Skepticism, usurping the name of science, may come and tell me time and again that I cannot have seen my friend alive; that, perhaps, I did not and could not see him dead; that with greater reason it is impossible that I can have seen him risen again. Skepticism, I say, may repeat all that, but it can never shake my conviction and my assurance. I know what I have seen. I affirm it, and if any one refuses to grant me the possibility of verifying that triple fact under the pretext of the critical science, I have every right to deny the possibility of the verification of any historical fact."

George.—"I see, a miracle considered as a sensible, visible, palpable fact may be ascertained and verified. But yet this will profit but little toward the conclusion that it is a miraculous fact. Because, whatever may be the proofs which we may appear to possess in favor of the existence of a miraculous fact, there is always another certainty stronger and mightier against them which annuls their force and cogency. It is absolutely certain that a human body in the full process of decay and putrefaction will never rise again; whatever proofs you may allege, they must necessarily pale and be weakened before that universal certitude and conviction."

Doctor.—"You have given, George, Hume's argument against the possibility of verifying a miracle in different words, 'The probability of a miracle, that is, of a derogation to the constant laws of nature is much less than the probability of a deception in the witnesses who affirm that derogation, or miracle.' Hence a miracle has in its favor not only the minimum degree of probability but no probability at all, as it has against it not only the probability, but the universal certainty of the laws of nature remaining constant and unaltered."

Adele.—"I think I see the argument. You say you have seen a miracle, that is, a derogation of the laws of nature. We will suppose that it is probable that such is the case. But, on the other hand, there is the constant universal conviction and certainty that the laws of nature are constant and unalterable. Hence, this latter certainty must necessarily defeat and dissipate whatever probability there may be in favor of the exception. The argument seems to be plausible enough."

Doctor.—"It is a pitiful and miserable sophism. If we said that the existence of an exception has only a probability in its favor, whereas the constancy of the order of nature and its law is certain, then the probability would have to yield to the certainty. But such is not the case. We require a miracle, and, if you will, a derogation of the laws of nature in a given case, to be attested and supported by such an array of witnesses, and these of such character as to fully counterbalance the previous and universal certainty of the constancy of the laws of nature, so that we may be as certain in the supposed case that the exception has taken place as we are certain of the general constancy and unalterableness of the laws of nature. Hence, whilst I am convinced of the general constancy of the order of nature, I remain also convinced that in the supposed case there has been an exception. Sir Charles Babbage, in his 'Ninth Bridgewater Treatise,' has handled this objection in a masterly way, and has triumphantly and forever disposed of it. He proves that, whatever may be the probability furnished by experience against the occurrence of a derogation to the laws of nature, that is, a miracle, we can always suppose a number of testimonies large enough to show the improbability of their being deceived to be greater than the improbability of the occurrence of a miracle. In other words, we can always conceive and assign such a number of competent and independent witnesses as to render the improbability of their united testimony being false much greater than the improbability of the occurrence of the miracle. He has gone further than this and has given figures which give the sophist a most solemn defeat."

Adele.—"I am glad of it. Why! Given that the certitude and conviction of the laws of nature remaining always constant and unalterable in themselves and in their action, so that we must always suppose in every case and under every circumstance they have had their cause and fulfillment, yet this antecedent and permanent conviction must not be carried so far as to claim that if God wants to produce any exception, a derogation, He cannot accumulate such a number of witnesses and proofs, as in spite of that previous permanent conviction, we may not acquire another, much stronger conviction, that in a certain case the exception has really taken place."

George.—"Well, there is no use in wasting much more time on this difficulty. Let us pass to the real objection which may be urged against miracles. You say, a miracle being contrary to the laws of nature or superior to them, must claim the immediate intervention of God for its cause. But how can you say that, without doubt or hesitation or with any kind of certainty? To affirm such a thing so positively and so confidently you should have a knowledge which it is impossible to attain."

Adele.—"And what is that?"

George.—"You should be acquainted neither more nor less with all the laws of nature; you should have a perfect, complete, full, adequate knowledge of all the laws of nature."

Adele.—"Why?"

George.—"Why! How can you possibly pronounce in a given case that the event is not and cannot be the effect of a natural cause, unless you know perfectly and distinctly, and almost numerically, each and every one of the laws of nature? Otherwise, in pronouncing that the given case is not and cannot be the effect of any natural cause, some one might say: How do you know but there may not be some occult natural cause fully adequate to account for the event—a cause which you know not of? This is the greatest objection against the possibility of ever verifying a miracle."

Doctor.—"The objection seems to be very strong and specious, but at the bottom it is no less flimsy than the other two, and can be broken as easily as the web of a spider. In the first place, those who allege it against miracles go much further than they suspect or wish. Because that same objection, if true, puts an end to all physical sciences."

George.—"I don't see how, doctor."

Doctor.—"Yes, sir, you had better look out. If that difficulty is good against us it is as good against you, for it leads directly and logically to the impossibility of verifying scientifically a single law of nature. How do you arrive at the knowledge of the laws of nature? By observing a number of phenomena and facts. Thus, by observing the tendency of all bodies to be attracted by larger bodies you infer the law of gravitation. Very good; but if your objection is good, that to be able to tell if such a thing is or is not the cause of this phenomenon, it is necessary to know all the laws of nature, we cannot, in any case, pronounce that such and such a thing is the cause of that phenomenon. For one could say: You assign such a cause for that phenomenon! How do you know that there is not some other cause with which you are unacquainted that may account for that fact? Do you know each and every law of nature to affirm so confidently that your cause is the real reason and no other?"

Adele.—"Ah! Mr. George, you are caught. I am glad to see you cornered so beautifully. Your grand objection amounts to this: you cannot tell when a natural law is not the cause of a fact, unless you are acquainted with each and every one of the laws of nature.

Very good. And we retort, you cannot tell when a natural law *is* the cause of a phenomenon, unless you are familiar with each and every one of the laws of nature. And if you cannot tell in a single case that such a law is the cause of such a phenomenon without knowing all natural laws, then, good-by to all knowledge of nature, good-day to all physical sciences."

George.—"I hope you will use your victory with generosity and compassion, Miss Adele."

Doctor.—"If your objection is true the consequence is perfectly just. It would render science impossible. Still, science exists and will exist and produce irresistible certainty; because your objection is false. Man knows that along with laws of nature there is harmony in nature; he knows that God, Who never contradicts Himself, has not and could not establish a certain law in nature and at the same time establish another in direct opposition to the former. Man knows that when nature, as God has created it, has said *yes* to-day, it will never say *no* to-morrow. Upon that base is founded science, and upon that base we establish the possibility of verifying a miracle. As in the mathematical world there cannot be a true formula in contradiction with another true formula, so in the physical world there cannot be a real law in contradiction with another real law of nature. If there is a law rendering it impossible for an organic body deprived of life and in complete decay and decomposition to return to life, there cannot be in the same nature another law rendering it possible, otherwise we could be certain of nothing. Hence, mark the consequence, George—in order to ascertain whether a fact is miraculous, that is, originates in the immediate action of God, all that is necessary to know is the particular law to which the phenomenon is naturally subject, and no more. If I know that particular law to which that phenomenon is subject, and find out that the law does not and cannot explain it, I have a perfect right to cry out, Miracle. Let us give some examples. It is demonstrated, as I have already remarked, that a body left to itself gravitates by its own weight towards the centre of the earth: this law is proclaimed absolute and sovereign, and we are sure that no future discovery shall ever exhibit or show forth another, in virtue of which a body left to itself on the surface of the earth will fly away from the centre of the earth instead of gravitating towards it."

George.—"Certainly, we are sure of that."

Doctor.—"Very well, if I see with my own eyes, in full daylight, an enormous mass of granite at once to lift itself up, apparently, by its own unaided movement and make its way towards the sky, can I not affirm with perfect certainty that that granite is lifted up by a force which is beyond the sphere of physical agents, that is, by God? And yet I do not know each and every one of the laws of nature. All I know is that that effort is contrary to the law of gravitation, and can only be produced by God. Again, it is proven by universal experience that an organism once broken is not readjusted instantaneously, or by itself, that a living body once dead cannot be exempted from the law of decay and decomposition, and can never appear again in life with the identity of its form and substance. Whatever wondrous transformations may take place in nature, we are absolutely certain of this law, that a body once a corpse cannot in a second reappear, living and radiant from the bosom of its putrefaction. If, then, a phenomenon of this nature occurs before my eye, before the eyes of a thousand, of ten thousand, if we have seen the dead body, if we have handled, so to speak, its very corruption, and if in three minutes we see at the prayer of a man that same dead body to rise again, blooming with fresh life, and full of vigor and manhood, have we not a right to exclaim loudly that here is a miracle of the greatest magnitude? And yet I am ignorant of all the laws of nature. I know only the one which is dominant in this case, the law of corruption and decay, and when I see the very contrary occurring, I triumphantly exclaim: the Omnipotence of God is here!"

Adele.—"Yes, the miracle can be ascertained and recognized, because it is a fact like all other facts, subject to the observation of our senses; it can be seen, handled, moved, like all sensible phenomena. It can be ascertained, because, though we may have a presumption always in favor of the constancy of the laws of nature, in spite of all strange occurrences, yet that presumption may be overcome by such an array of competent witnesses and proofs, testifying in favor of the strange event, as to render an error and a deception in those witnesses much more improbable than the occurrence of an exception in the laws of nature. Finally, a miracle may be ascertained because it appears clothed with God's glory and might, and because, to discover such a might, it is not necessary to know each and every one of the laws of nature, but only that law to which God, the Law-giver, says: 'Stand aside, I am the Master; it is I Who act;' and the law, feeling its Creator, retires; or, as I may express it in the words of Dryden, alluding to the miracle of Cana of Galilee:

"'The conscious water saw its Maker and blushed.'"

THIRTY-EIGHTH ARTICLE.

HAS A MIRACLE EVER BEEN ASCERTAINED?

Adele.—"Well, Mr. George, you ought to be perfectly satisfied with the demonstration we gave in our last interview?"

George.—"Certainly; we must own that a miracle may be ascertained; but that is not sufficient for the triumph of our cause. We must go further and attack the enemy of the miracle in his last stronghold."

Adele.—"And what is that?"

Doctor.—"They coolly tell you: No miracle, as a matter of fact, has ever been ascertained or verified, so that all your demonstration of the possibility of miracles, of the possibility of ascertaining them, is so much waste of time and trouble."

George.—"Certainly; they claim that we have no instance of any miracle ever having been examined under such conditions as to fully satisfy a scientist that a miracle has really taken place and ascertained as such."

Doctor.—"Very well, George. For the sake of clearness I wish to carry our discussion of this subject in dramatized form. We will suppose you to be a scientist, deputed by a congress of scientists, and in their name and by their authority to state the conditions to be observed in the verification of a miracle, in order that they may pronounce themselves satisfied. Adele will be the public and I the advocate."

Adele.—"I gladly accept my rolé."

George.—"And I agree to represent science, speaking through a congress, and authorizing me to name those conditions."

Doctor.—"Well, Mr. Scientist, will you be so kind as to state clearly and distinctly on what conditions you would consider a miracle as properly ascertained?"

George.—"State the case and I will name the conditions."

Doctor.—"Suppose the case of a man afflicted with an incurable disease, say the loss of an organ, and imagine that same man to have his organ suddenly restored to him, on what conditions would you consider that miracle as ascertained and proved beyond a doubt?"

George.—"I should, in the first place, require the most unimpeachable evidence proving that the man was really without the organ. I should want to put that fact beyond all possible doubt by exacting a clear, full accurate, a detailed history of his whole life, from his birth to the present moment, by investigating most scrupulously whether he was born without that organ, or whether he lost it gradually by sickness, or suddenly by some accident. I would not be satisfied with any hearsay, but should peremptorily demand the united testimony of competent witnesses. By competent witnesses, of course, I mean such as are perfectly acquainted with the facts, as having being placed in the best possible opportunity to acquire them, and such as would not and could not deceive even if they would."

Adele.—"You are very exacting."

Doctor.—"He is not. I fully agree to the conditions, Mr. Scientist. What else would you require?"

George.—"If I were told that the missing organ had suddenly been restored to him, I should exact an investigation before a most solemn tribunal of the *élite* of scientific men whose duty it should be, first, to ascertain again the fact of the missing organ by competent witnesses and to put that beyond all doubt; second, to acertain how and by whom and in what manner the organ had been restored to him. This should be proven by an overwhelming weight of competent testimony; third, the commission should thoroughly and exhaustively inquire whether any natural means had been used to effect that restoration, and if it were possible that the organ could have been restored by natural means; fourth, they should examine into the identity of the man and prove, by unimpeachable testimony, that the man is the same as the one who had the missing organ, and that no impostor had been substituted in his stead."

Doctor.—"I consent again in all these conditions. Would you exact anything more?"

George.—"Yes, I should require another instance, or a similar case; the same investigation gone over again, the same or stronger evidence, and the same verdict. Then I should say that a miracle has really been ascertained and verified. But when or where has a miracle been so investigated or examined and its evidence sifted as I have described?"

Doctor.—"In countless cases and in innumerable instances. I will take from among the mass of miracles of our holy religion one at random. And I am confident to prove that, in that instance, all your conditions were verified to the letter—the miracle of the blind man. One day as Jesus was passing by He saw a man blind from his birth, and taking pity on him, spat on the ground and made clay of the spittle and spread the clay upon his eyes; then said to him, g) and wash in the pool of Siloe, and the man obeyed, and washed. and came back seeing. Here is the fact; let us see if your conditions are fulfilled. What is it?"

Adele.—"The investigation into the reality of his blindness."

Doctor.—"There was a two fold strict, accurate, exact investigation into that fact. The first was made by the people. The blind man was a public character—a beggar, asking alms every day in the public places, and was perfectly known to everybody. When they saw him restored to sight and walking straight and erect without help, they naturally wondered, and began to make inquiries. The neighbors, says the Gospel, and those who had seen him before that he was a beggar said—is this not he that sat and begged? Some said—this is he, and others said—no, but he is like him. But the blind man said—I am he. They said—how were thy eyes opened? He answered, that Man, Who is called Jesus, made clay and anointed my eyes, and said to me: Go to the pool and wash, and I went, and ¡I washed, and I see. Here is the first investigation made by the people and the facts proved by competent witnesses."

Adele.—"But this would not satisfy our scientists. They must have a tribunal or commission of scientific men."

Doctor.—"They had one in the miracle we are examining. The people brought him that had been blind to the Pharisees, who were doctors of the law and the highest scientific tribunal of the nation. The investigation went on as follows: The first question they asked the man was—How did you receive the sight? He answered—He put clay on my eyes and I washed and I see. Upon this answer of the man a question arose among the judges. Our Lord had healed the man on the Sabbath day. The Pharisees, as it is well known, interpreted the observance of that day so strictly as to allow no one to do the least work on that day. Hence they pretended to be scandalized at the case of the poor blind man. Some of them, therefore, cried out; this man is not of God Who keepeth not the Sabbath, but others demurred and said—how can a man that is a sinner do such miracle? They agreed to hear the opinion of the man himself. What sayest thou of Him that hath opened thy eyes? He promptly answered—He is a prophet. But the doctors would not be satisfied with the alleged facts being attested by the people and by the man who was blind. They ordered the parents to appear before them, and inquired—Is this your son who you say was born blind? How, then, doth he see? They replied: we know that this is our son, and that he was born blind. Here is a confirmation by the most competent witnesses of the identity of the man, 'we know that this is our son,' and, of his blindness from his birth, 'and that he was born blind.' To the question of the commission, how, then, doth he see? they answer, 'we know not, nor who hath opened his eyes.' Of course, they had heard that Our Lord had healed their son, but would not mention it; first, because they were afraid of the Jews, who had threatened to put any one who sided with Our Lord out of the synagogue; secondly, because they had not been eye-witnesses of the miracle. They referred the judges to the man himself, saying, ask our son; he is of age, he ought to be able to tell. The judges ordered the man before them again, and put him under oath, saying: Give glory to God; we know that this man is a sinner. The man was very much astonished at such a statement, but contented himself with the answer: 'If He be a sinner, I know not; one thing I know that, whereas, I was blind, I now see.' They commanded him to tell his story over again. What did He do to thee? How did He open thy eyes? He replied: I have told you, and you have heard it, why would you hear it again? Will you also become His disciples? They waxed angry and began to revile him, saying, be thou His disciple. We know that God spoke to Moses; but, as to this Man, we know not from whence He is. The simple minded, honest man was astonished at such poor reasoning of the scientists of those days."

Adele.—"Like that of the modern one's, according to the many specimens we have had."

Doctor.—"And he cried out aloud before all the bystanders, saying: why, herein is a wonderful thing: You who ought to know better, you who are appointed to teach me, you who claim to be doctors, know not whence He is, and yet He has opened my eyes. We know that God does not hear sinners; but if a man is a server of God, and doth His will, him He hears. From the beginning of the world it has not been heard that any man has opened the eyes of one born blind."

Adele.—"Here, Mr. George, we have a miracle which fulfills all the conditions exacted by your scientists; investigation by the people; investigation before the tribunal of doctors, dead set against Our Lord; examination of competent witnesses as to the fact of the missing organ; examination and proof of his identity; full examination as to how, when, under what circumstances he was restored to sight. What will you have more? If a fact, the event of which scrutinized so strictly, so closely, so abundantly, is not proven and ascertained, why, nothing can be ascertained in this world, and we may as well turn skeptics outright?"

George.—"But there was no verdict by the tribunal?"

Adele.—"Let me see. Was there no verdict? I don't remember to have seen a verdict when I read the Gospel of St. John."

Doctor.—"Yes, there was a verdict, but one anything but creditable to the tribunal which examined the miracle."

George.—"And what was it, doctor?"

Doctor.—"Why, affirmative of course; they admitted that they had nothing to say against the miracle."

George.—"Why, like Miss Adele, I don't remember that St. John records any verdict?"

Doctor.—"I beg your pardon, but he does. He narrates that the Pharisees, seeing themselves in the impossibility of denying the fact of the miracle, and of the consequences which the blind man drew in support of the divine mission of Christ, became mad and had recourse to violence, the argument of those who have no good reason for their action. 'They answered,' says St. John, 'and said to him, Thou wast wholly born in sin, and dost thou teach us? And they cast him out.' If that is not a verdict much more eloquent than any sentence they could have formulated in favor of the miracle, I leave it to all fair-minded, honest judges."

Adele.—"Here the French saying comes apropos: *Tu te fâches et bien tu à tort.* You become angry, then you must be wrong."

Doctor.—"We have quoted the miracle of the blind man taken at ransom, but there are other miracles in which those conditions, exacted by scientists, are much better and much more manifestly fulfilled. Take the example of the resurrection of Lazarus, related in chapter xi. The first question is: Was Lazarus truly and really dead? How is that proven? First: When Lazarus falls sick his sisters sent word to Our Lord: Lord, behold he whom Thou lovest is sick. Our Lord for His own divine plan heeds not the summons and remains two days in the same place. Then He declares His intention to His disciples to go and see Lazarus in those words: Lazarus, our friend, sleepeth, but I go that I may awake him out of sleep. Some disciples misunderstood the meaning and said: Lord, if he sleep he shall do well. Then Jesus said to them plainly. Lazarus is dead, and I am glad for your sakes that I was not there that you may believe, but let us go to him. When Our Lord arrived in Bethania Lazarus had been dead four days and had been already buried. Our Lord stopped at some distance from the house outside the town and sent a messenger to the sisters that He had come. The messenger found them surrounded by many of the Jews who had come to comfort them concerning their brother. Martha ran to Our Lord and cried out to Him: Lord, if thou hadst been here my brother had not died. But now also I know that whatsoever Thou shalt ask of God, God will give it Thee. Jesus said to her: Thy brother shall rise again. Martha understood Him to mean of the general resurrection. Then she left and called her sister Mary secretly, and said the Master has come and calls for thee. As soon as she heard this she rose up to go to Our Lord Who was yet out of the town. When the Jews who were with her saw her rising up, they followed her, saying she goes to the grave to weep there. When Mary reached the place where Jesus stood she fell at His feet saying, like Martha, Lord, if Thou hadst been here my brother had not died. Can the fact of Lazarus' death be proven by stronger evidence? He falls sick, and the news is sent around; he dies, and, after a few days, is buried; large numbers of friends continue, according to the Jewish custom, to visit the bereaved sisters to comfort them. The assertion of Martha and Mary to Our Lord, that if He had been present, their brother would not have died, puts the seal to the evidence."

Adele.—"Everything seems to be prearranged to give the fact the utmost publicity."

Doctor.—"Our Lord said to Martha: Where have you laid him?

They said: come and see, and all proceeded towards the grave. Jesus was weeping on the way; and the Jews said—see how He loved him; but others remarked—could not He Who opened the eyes of the man born blind have caused that this man should not die? The company arrived at the grave. It was a cave, and a stone was laid over the opening. Our Lord ordered the stone to be removed, but to reach the climax of the evidence of Lazarus' death, Martha remarks, Lord, by this time he stinketh, for he is now of four days. Jesus replied, did I not say to thee, that if thou believe, thou shalt see the glory of God? And after a short prayer He cried out with a loud voice, Lazarus, come forth. And presently he that had been dead came forth, bound hands and feet with winding bands, and his face was bound about with a napkin. Jesus commanded him to be loosened, in order that he might go free. Can there be anything better proven than this miracle of the raising up of Lazarus from the dead? anything better ascertained than his death? anything better ascertained than his restoration to life in public, in daylight, in the presence of hundreds of people, some of whom surrendered all prejudices and believed in Christ? Can there be anything better attested than his resurrection, when we are told that some time after, when the sisters of Lazarus made a supper for Our Lord, a great multitude of Jews visited them, not for Jesus' sake only, but that they might see Lazarus, whom He had raised from the dead."

George.—"Was the thing examined by the doctors of the law?"

Adele.—"Fie with your doctors and your examination!"

Doctor.—"Be still, Adele. Don't you remember he represents our friends, the scientists? Yes, George, there was an examination and a verdict with a vengeance. Some, who had been present at the miracle, went to the Pharisees and told them the things that Jesus had done. The chief priests, therefore, and the Pharisees gathered a council, and in the impossibility of doing anything else, what verdict do you think they agreed upon?"

George.—"I am sure I cannot remember."

Doctor.—"Here are the words: 'What do we, for this man does many miracles?'"

Adele.—"Here is a verdict with a vengeance, not only admitting the miracle in question but other miracles."

Doctor.—"But what puts the climax on the whole examination, what gives the verdict in favor of the miracle of the resurrection of Lazarus its highest significance, is the determination and resolution they came to of common accord."

Adele.—"And what was that?"

Doctor.—"Nothing less than to remove the subject of the miracle itself. 'The chief priests,' says St. John, 'thought to kill Lazarus, because many of Jews, by reason of him, went away and believed in Jesus.' (St. John, Ch. 12, v. x-xi.)"

Adele.—"Lazarus was a standing, permanent proof and evidence of the miracle, and no wonder they wanted to do away with him."

Doctor.—"I have proved that miracles have been ascertained under such conditions as are exacted by scientists. I have done more than Christianity or common sense are bound to do, George. For, I maintain, that to ascertain a miracle, there is no special need of any scientific commission. It is amply sufficient that it be proven according to all conditions prescribed by human reason and common sense, which are the common patrimony of mankind, and not a monopoly belonging exclusively to a set of self-appointed judges and scientists. It is the height of insolence, of profanity and of blasphemy for scientists to set limits to God, and to prescribe Him conditions, whenever He condescends to speak to His creatures and to proclaim His divine presence by a miracle. The pride of Satan was humility and modesty when compared to that of the scientists of our day. The fallen angel was satisfied to reign in hell rather than to serve in heaven. Our modern scientists want to reign everywhere, and to cite to their tribunal every action of the Almighty under pain of excluding Him from His creation, of cutting Him off and of separating Him from those whom He has made. This is the very climax of insane pride."

Adele.—"Their pretensions amounts to this. They say to the Omnipotent: You want to perform a miracle to announce Your presence. If You took our advice You would let Your creation alone and allow the laws you have appointed to remain undisturbed. But You insist on performing a miracle? Very well, let it pass. However, You must distinctly understand that we will not consider a miracle as ascertained unless we examine it under such conditions as it shall please us to exact. You must, therefore, leave the whole matter in our hands, and be prepared, not only to afford proofs of Your action, but be ready, at any moment, when we shall consider it proper to repeat the experiment under similar or different circumstances as science may require. If You are not willing to submit to our conditions, why we forbid Your Omnipotence from performing and demonstrating a miracle. This is assuredly the very pinnacle of conceit and folly, and there are no words in human language to qualify or to rightly and adequately brand their impious character."

Doctor.—"Let us have done, Adele. Human science to day, in a great number of its would-be representatives, has lost all faith in the Infinite Creator of all things. It believes itself the supreme existence and judge of all things. No wonder that its followers proclaim an antagonism with Revelation. The latter loudly proclaims from the house top that there is a duality of truths, natural and supernatural, but both of which blend together and harmonize as they proceed from one supreme Principle and Cause of all things, God Almighty, the Omnipotent and All wise Origin of all. Science rejects any such first principle. It substitutes pure, naked nature, as interpreted by itself, as the origin, the cause, the end of all things. Consequently, it ignores anything above or beyond it, and must reject all supernatural truths, principle, existence, as contradictory, as absurd, as nonsense, as having no place whatever in its system. In all our conversations we have endeavored to establish that duality of truths and orders, and have pointed out its harmonious blending, and hence have concluded that true science is not contradicted by Catholic Truth. We have succeeded, and defy any scientist to prove the contrary. Meanwhile it behooves us as true Christians to offer up fervent prayers to the Father of Light, that He may enlighten, humble, destroy that fearful pride of the so-called scientists, that they may see and acknowledge the one true God and Him Whom He sent, Jesus Christ, Our Blessed Lord, and they shall find out that His divine action results in a most magnificent panorama, made of an immense number of degrees of creatures and orders, one rising upon the other, different from each other, yet blending together, so as to form one harmonious whole, and thus raising a sublime harmony to the honor and glory of their Creator. With these remarks we close our long, but, I trust, not uninteresting conversations on the Harmony between Science and Religion."

THE END.

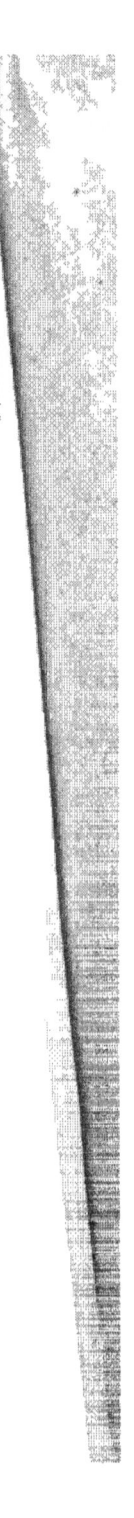

RETURN TO →	CIRCULATION DEPARTMENT 202 Main Library	
LOAN PERIOD 1 **HOME USE**	2	3
4	5	6

ALL BOOKS MAY BE RECALLED AFTER 7 DAYS
RENEWALS AND RECHARGES MAY BE MADE 4 DAYS PRIOR TO DUE DATE.
LOAN PERIODS ARE 1-MONTH, 3-MONTHS, AND 1-YEAR.
RENEWALS: CALL (415) 642-3405

DUE AS STAMPED BELOW

NOV 29 1987		
REC. MOFFITT NOV 16 1987		
AUTO DISC NOV 17 1987		
MAR 28 1988 AUTO MAR 25 1988		

UNIVERSITY OF CALIFORNIA, BERKELEY
FORM NO. DD6; 60m, 1/83   BERKELEY, CA 94720

www.ingramcontent.com/pod-product-compliance
Lightning Source LLC
Chambersburg PA
CBHW032140230426
43672CB00011B/2401